Chemical Weapon Destruction in Russia: Political, Legal and Technical Aspects

GW00686180

Chemical Weapon Destruction in Russia: Political, Legal and Technical Aspects

Edited by
John Hart and Cynthia D. Miller

sipri

Stockholm International Peace Research Institute

BONN INTERNATIONAL CENTER FOR CONVERSION
B·I·C·C

OXFORD UNIVERSITY PRESS
1998

Oxford University Press, Great Clarendon Street, Oxford OX2 6DP
Oxford New York
Athens Auckland Bangkok Bogotá Bombay
Buenos Aires Calcutta Cape Town Dar es Salaam
Delhi Florence Hong Kong Istanbul Karachi
Kuala Lumpur Madras Madrid Melbourne
Mexico City Nairobi Paris Saõ Paulo Singapore
Taipei Tokyo Toronto Warsaw
and associated companies in
Berlin Ibadan

Oxford is a registered trade mark of Oxford University Press
Published in the United States
by Oxford University Press Inc., New York

British Library Cataloguing in Publication Data
Data available

Library of Congress Cataloging in Publication Data
Data available
ISBN 0–19–829569–3

Typeset and originated by Stockholm International Peace Research Institute
Printed and bound in Great Britain on acid-free paper by
Biddles Ltd, Guildford and King's Lynn

Abstract

Hart, J. and Miller, C. D. (eds), *Chemical Weapon Destruction in Russia: Political, Legal and Technical Aspects*, SIPRI Chemical & Biological Warfare Studies, no. 17 (Oxford University Press: Oxford, 1998), xiv + 161 pp. (Stockholm International Peace Research Institute). ISBN 0–19–829569-3.

On 29 April 1997 the Chemical Weapons Convention (CWC) entered into force. Only the Russian Federation and the USA have acknowledged possessing chemical weapon (CW) stockpiles (approximately 30 000 and 40 000 agent tonnes, respectively). Russia signed the CWC on 13 January 1993, when it entered into force, but did not ratify it until 5 November 1997. This volume, supported by the Volkswagen Foundation and produced in cooperation with the Bonn International Center for Conversion (BICC), reviews Russian CW destruction efforts, factors which have hindered them and reasons why Russian CWC ratification was postponed. Information is provided on CWC destruction requirements; CW destruction; past destruction efforts; the Russian destruction legislation, technologies and programme; foreign assistance; and choice of destruction technologies. The contributors have been directly involved with these issues. 31 tables and 14 figures.

Contents

7. Risks posed by the chemical weapon stockpile in the Udmurt Republic   94

Vladimir Kolodkin

8. The Russian–US joint evaluation of the Russian two-stage process for the destruction of nerve agents   103

Irina P. Beletskaya

Preface

Russia and the USA possess the largest declared stockpiles of chemical weapons (CW). On 13 January 1993, the Convention on the Prohibition of the Development, Production, Stockpiling and Use of Chemical Weapons and on their Destruction (CWC) was opened for signature. It entered into force on 29 April 1997. Russia and the United States are both parties to it.

The parties to the CWC are obliged to destroy their chemical weapon stockpiles within 10–15 years. Russia is committed to on-site destruction of its CW stockpile, which is stored at seven locations. In the spring of 1998 the Organisation for the Prohibition of Chemical Weapons (OPCW), the international organization that is responsible for monitoring compliance with the CWC, successfully completed its initial inspections of Russia's CW facilities and established a verification regime to monitor Russia's CW stockpile.

One of the important factors hindering CW destruction in Russia is the lack of funding. Foreign destruction assistance has been provided by Finland, Germany, the Netherlands, Sweden and the USA. A special conference on CW destruction assistance for Russia was held in May 1998 in The Hague to which approximately 20 nations sent representatives. Italy, Japan and the UK, as well as the European Union, appear committed to providing destruction assistance. The Swiss Parliament has also considered how it might provide assistance. The greatest amount of financial assistance is the US funding—estimated to eventually total $600–800 million—for the construction of a pilot destruction facility at Shchuchye. Nonetheless, the major cost of CW destruction will be borne by Russia.

This volume is the final result of the conference Chemical Weapon Destruction in Russia, which was held in Bonn, Germany, on 8–10 November 1996. The conference, organized by the Bonn International Center for Conversion (BICC) and the Stockholm International Peace Research Institute (SIPRI), was attended by representatives of the Russian Government and by technical specialists and experts from non-governmental organizations in Europe, Russia and the United States. Representatives from the countries that currently provide assistance for Russian CW destruction also attended.

The project was developed from an idea conceived by Dr Thomas Stock, then Head of the SIPRI Chemical and Biological Warfare Project, and Dr Herbert Wulf, the Director of BICC. Ms Maria Haug (SIPRI), who was part of the project in its early stage, played an instrumental role in initiating contacts with key individuals involved with Russian CW destruction. Her tasks were taken over by Ms Cynthia D. Miller (BICC) and Mr John Hart (SIPRI), who organized the conference in Bonn in November 1996 and subsequently edited the contributions collected in this volume. We are grateful to Joseph Di Chiaro III and Dr Michael Brzoska, Research Director at BICC, for the support given to Ms Miller during the project. Preparation of a Russian manuscript and its publication in September 1997 was carried out by the Institute of World Economy and International Relations (IMEMO) in Russia, largely thanks to the efforts of Professor Vladlen Martynov (Director of IMEMO), Professor Oleg Bykov (Deputy Director of IMEMO) and Professor Alexander Kaliadine (IMEMO). Dr Benjamin Garrett kindly shared his insight and unique expertise on Russian CW-related matters with the project. Professor Joseph Bunnett also provided useful and much appreciated comments. Mr James Toppin graciously offered to translate one of the chapters. Realization of this project would not have been possible without the planning and support of Dr Thomas Stock and Dr Jean Pascal Zanders, current Head of the SIPRI Chemical and Biological Warfare Project and Series Editor of the SIPRI Chemical & Biological Warfare Studies. Jetta Gilligan Borg edited and prepared the camera-ready copy for this volume. Her efforts are very much appreciated. Finally, we would like to express our gratitude to the Volkswagen Foundation for providing the funds that made this project possible.

Dr Herbert Wulf
Director, BICC

Dr Adam Daniel Rotfeld
Director, SIPRI
August 1998

Contributors

Professor Irina P. Beletskaya
Department of Organic Chemistry
Moscow State University
Moscow 119899
Russian Federation

Professor Alexander Chimiskyan
Head of Organic Synthesis Technology
Russian Mendeleev Chemical
   Technology University
Miusskaya, pl., 9
Moscow 125047
Russian Federation

Mr Mark Felipe
Defense Analyst
Strategic Concepts and Systems
   Division
Science Applications International
   Corporation
1710 Goodridge Drive
McLean, Virginia   22102
USA

Mr John A. Gilbert
Director, International Chemical and
   Biological Compliance Program
Science Applications International
   Corporation
1710 Goodridge Drive
McLean, Virginia   22102
USA

Mr John Hart
Research Associate, Chemical and
Biological Weapons Project
Center for Nonproliferation Studies
Monterey Institute of International
   Studies
425 Van Buren Street
Monterey, California   93940
USA

Mr Harvey W. Hubbard
Manager of Industry Compliance
   Programs, International Chemical and
   Biological Compliance Program
Science Applications International
   Corporation
1710 Goodridge Drive
McLean, Virginia   22102
USA

Professor Natalya Kalinina
Federal Assembly of the Parliament
   of the Russian Federation
Duma Defence Committee
Okhotny ryad, d. 1
Moscow 103265
Russian Federation

Dr Igor Khripunov
Associate Director for NIS Programs
Center for International Trade and
   Security
204 Baldwin Hall
University of Georgia
Athens, Georgia   30602-1615
USA

Dr Vladimir Kolodkin
Director
Institute of Nature and Technogenic
   Disasters
Udmurt State University
Krasnogeroiskaya ul., d. 71
Izhevsk 426034
Russian Federation

Ms Cynthia D. Miller
SARD-ZC
Deputy Assistant Secretary of the Army
   (Chemical Demilitarization)
Room 11300
2511 Jefferson Davis Highway
Arlington, VA   22202
USA

Mr Robert F. Pruszkowski
Deputy Director and Operations
  Manager, International Chemical and
  Biological Compliance Program
Science Applications International
  Corporation
1710 Goodridge Drive
McLean, Virginia   22102
USA

Dr Vladislav Sheluchenko
Deputy Director of CW Destruction
  Problems
State Scientific Research Institute of
  Organic Chemistry and Technology
  (GosNIIOKhT)
Shosse Entuziastov, d. 23
Moscow 111024
Russian Federation

Dr Amy E. Smithson
Senior Associate
Chemical and Biological Weapons
  Nonproliferation Project
The Henry L. Stimson Center
11 Dupont Circle, NW, 9th floor
Washington, DC   20036
USA

Dr Thomas Stock
Mannesmann Demag
Energy and Environmental Technology
Theodorstrasse 90
D – 40472 Dusseldorf
Germany

Dr Anton Utkin
State Scientific Research Institute of
  Organic Chemistry and Technology
  (GosNIIOKhT)
Shosse Entuziastov, d. 23
Moscow 111024
Russian Federation

Acronyms and abbreviations

Acronyms not defined in this list are defined in the chapters of this volume.

BDA	Bilateral Destruction Agreement
BTWC	Biological and Toxin Weapons Convention
BW	Biological weapon
CASARM	Chemical agent standard analytical reference materials
CBDCOM	Chemical–Biological Defense Command
CIS	Commonwealth of Independent States
CSP	Conference of States Parties
CTR	Cooperative Threat Reduction
CW	Chemical weapon/warfare
CWC	Chemical Weapons Convention
CWDF	Chemical weapon destruction facility
CWPF	Chemical weapon production facility
DOD	Department of Defense
DRES	Defence Research Establishment Suffield
EU	European Union
FY	Fiscal year
GB	Sarin
GD	Soman
GosNIIOKhT	State Scientific Research Institute for Organic Chemistry and Technology
HD	Yperite
IMEMO	Institute of World Economy and International Relations
IMF	International Monetary Fund
JACADS	Johnston Atoll Chemical Agent Disposal System
MAL	Maximum allowable limit
MEA	Monoethanolamine
MOD	Ministry of Defence
MOU	Memorandum of Understanding
NATO	North Atlantic Treaty Organization
NGO	Non-governmental organization
NMR	Nuclear magnetic resonance
OPCW	Organisation for the Prohibition of Chemical Weapons
PrepCom	Preparatory Commission
R&D	Research and development
RMA	Rocky Mountain Arsenal
SARM	Standard analytical reference materials

Tacis	Technical Assistance for the Commonwealth of Independent States
TNT	Trinitrotoluene
TOCDF	Tooele Chemical Agent Disposal Facility
TS	Technical Secretariat
UNSCOM	United Nations Special Commission on Iraq

Conventions in tables

..	Data not available or not applicable.
–	Nil or a negligible figure.
b.	Billion (thousand million)
$	US dollars, unless otherwise indicated

1. The problems of Russian chemical weapon destruction

NATALYA KALININA

I. Introduction

Russia is committed to destroying its chemical weapon (CW)[1] stockpile, which totals approximately 40 000 agent tonnes.[2] On 25 April 1997 the State Duma passed comprehensive destruction legislation, the federal law On the Destruction of Chemical Weapons, which entered into force on 6 May 1997.[3] It serves as the legal basis for Russian CW destruction. Russia ratified the CWC[4] on 5 November 1997.[5] The problems of chemical disarmament facing Russia are extremely complex, and destruction of the CW stockpile requires not only political will but also active sustained effort by the legislative and executive branches of the Government of the Russian Federation.

Although Russia has an interest in eliminating its CW stockpile, it would be short-sighted not to consider the combined influence of certain political, economic and social factors on implementation of the CWC. This chapter examines some of the problems that have hindered CW disarmament in Russia.

II. Analysis of Russia's preparations for CW destruction

Background

Russia began producing and stockpiling chemical weapons before it began producing and stockpiling nuclear weapons. It is only recently, however, that a significant amount of CW-related information has become available in open sources. The *Russian Chemistry Journal*, for example, regularly published a series of articles analysing CW disarmament-related problems in 1993–95.[6] The first Russian international conferences on CW disarmament, Moscon 93[7] and

---

[1] CW is used throughout this volume as the acronym for chemical weapons/warfare.

[2] 'Federalnaya tselevaya programma' [Special federal programme], Federal government edict no. 305, 21 Mar. 1996, *Rossiyskaya Gazeta*, 2 Apr. 1996, pp. 5–6; and Russian Federation, Special federal programme, destruction of chemical weapons stockpiles in the Russian Federation, Preparatory Commission document PC-XIV/B/WP.7, 25 June 1996, pp. 19–20.

[3] 'Ob unichtozhenii khimicheskogo oruzhiya' [On the destruction of chemical weapons], Federal law no. 76-FZ, 25 Apr. 1997, *Krasnaya Zvezda*, 17 May 1997, pp. 3, 7.

[4] CWC is used throughout this volume as the acronym for the Chemical Weapons Convention. The Convention on the Prohibition of the Development, Production, Stockpiling and Use of Chemical Weapons and on their Destruction (corrected version), 8 Aug. 1994, is reproduced on the SIPRI Chemical and Biological Warfare Project Internet site at URL <http://www.sipri.se/cbw/docs/cw-cwc-texts.html>.

[5] 'O ratifikatsii Konventsii o zapreshenii rarabotki, proizvodstva, nakopleniya i primeneniya khimicheskogo oruzhiya i o ego unichtozhenii' [On the ratification of the Convention on the Prohibition of the Development, Production, Stockpiling and Use of Chemical Weapons and on Their Destruction], Russian Federation law no. 138-FZ, 5 Nov. 1997. An unofficial translation is published in *CBW Conventions Bulletin,* no. 38 (Dec. 1997), pp. 6–8.

[6] *Rossisskii Khimicheskii Zhurnal*, vol. 37, no. 3 (1993); vol. 38, no. 2 (1994); and vol. 39, no. 4 (1995).

[7] Moscon 93, First Conference on Chemical and Biological Disarmament, Demilitarization and Conversion, Moscow, 19–21 May 1993.

Moscon 94,[8] examined problems of chemical disarmament. The Center for Policy Studies in Russia (the PIR Center), in Moscow, has published four issues of a new series on chemical weapons.[9] As of January 1998 Green Cross Russia continued to co-sponsor on-site hearings on CW destruction.[10] The problems related to chemical weapons in Russia were discussed in over 200 popular publications in 1995–96, some of which are cited in this paper.

The Russian CW stockpile includes not only aerial, rocket and artillery munitions, and devices equipped with CW agents, but also CW agents stored in bulk containers.[11] Data on the distribution of the Russian chemical weapon stockpile by location and storage method have been published in several open sources[12] and in the Special Federal Programme for Chemical Weapons Destruction.[13]

Some of the Russian arsenals with large stocks of chemical weapons do not meet modern safety standards and need to be upgraded to improve the reliability and safety of CW storage. Of particular concern regarding the safety and condition of storage facilities are the facilities at Gorny in the Saratov oblast and Kambarka in the Udmurt Republic, where the vesicants lewisite, mustard and mustard–lewisite mixtures have been stored in bulk containers for over 40 years.

Every year Russia's CW stockpile becomes more obsolete and decrepit. An increasing proportion of the artillery and aerial chemical munitions is beyond or almost beyond the date at which it can be safely stored. Recognition of these conditions has occurred at all levels of government and the military. It is generally realized that continued storage of chemical weapons is unwise for military, economic and environmental reasons. Awareness of this situation has made CW destruction a national priority, which requires prompt attention within or ahead of the deadlines set by international agreements.

Russia is not the only country facing such problems. The need to eliminate deteriorating chemical munitions was the original stimulus for the development of CW destruction technologies in both Russia and the USA. Russian research

[8] Moscow Symposium on Chemical Weapons, Second Conference on Chemical and Biological Disarmament, Demilitarization and Conversion, Moscow, 20–21 Apr. 1994.

[9] *Khimicheskoe Oruzhiye i Problemi Ego Unichtozheniya*, no. 1 (PIR Center: Moscow, spring 1996); *Khimicheskoe Oruzhiye i Problemi Ego Unichtozheniya*, no. 2 (PIR Center: Moscow, autumn 1996); *Khimicheskoe Oruzhiye i Problemi Ego Unichtozheniya*, no. 3 (PIR Center: Moscow, winter 1997); and *Khimicheskoe Oruzhiye i Problemi Ego Unichtozheniya*, no. 4 (PIR Center: Moscow, summer/autumn 1997).

[10] *Treti Publichniye Slushaiya po Probleme Unichtozheniya Khimicheskogo Oruzhiya* [Third public hearings on the problem of chemical weapon destruction], Kurgan, Russia, 8–10 June 1997 (Regional branch of the National Organization of International Green Cross: Kurgan, Russia, 1997); Government of Udmurtia Republic and the National Organization of International Green Cross Russia, *Vtoriye Publichniye Slushaniya po Probleme Unichtozheniya Khimicheskogo Oruzhiya* [Second public hearings on the problem of chemical weapon destruction], Izhevsk, Russia, 14–16 May 1996 (Udmurt State University: Izhevsk, Russia, 1996): and Green Cross Russia, Final Statement: first public hearings on the problem of the destruction of chemical weapons in the Saratov Region, Saratov, 17–19 Oct. 1995. Green Cross Russia will hold at least 1 on-site hearing at each of Russia's 7 storage sites. As of June 1998, 4 on-site hearings had taken place: Kambarka (17–19 Oct. 1995), Izhevsk (14–16 May 1996), Kurgan (8–10 June 1997) and Kizner (May 1998).

[11] 'Federalnaya tselevaya programma' (note 2); and Russian Federation (note 2).

[12] *Yezhegodnik SIPRI 1995: Vooruzheniya, Razoruzheniye y Mezhdunarodnaya Bezopasnost* [Russian edn of the SIPRI Yearbook 1995] (IMEMO: Moscow, 1995); Trofimov, V., 'Khimicheskoe oruzhiya: proshloye bez budushchego?' [Chemical weapons: a past without a future?], *Nezavisimaya Gazeta*, 8 June 1995.; and Fedorov, L., *Khimicheskoe Oruzhiya v Rossii: Istoriya, Ekologiya, Politika* [Chemical weapons in Russia: history, ecology, and politics] (Russian Center for Environmental Policies and Union for Chemical Safety: Moscow, 1994).

[13] 'Federalnaya tselevaya programma' (note 2); Russian Federation (note 2); and chapters 2 and 6 in this volume.

in this area produced a mobile system for CW destruction, which was demonstrated to international negotiators at a military facility in Shikhany in 1987.[14]

Chronology of preparatory measures

The political leadership of the former Soviet Union decided to destroy its CW stockpile long before production stopped completely (i.e., while the multilateral negotiations on the Chemical Weapons Convention were still in progress). A decision was made in 1985 to build the first Soviet CW destruction facility, in Chapaevsk, Samara oblast. Construction of the facility was completed at the end of 1988.[15] It was never put into operation, however, owing to economic, political and social changes occurring in Russia and the public protests concerning the safety and environmental impact of the installation. The project was halted and the facility was later turned into a training centre for CW destruction specialists, including those training to be inspectors for the international Organisation for the Prohibition of Chemical Weapons (OPCW).[16]

The imperative for a change in the conceptual approach to chemical disarmament led to the first proposal for a state programme, which was submitted by the Ministry of Defence to the Soviet Supreme Council for consideration in 1990. These deliberations did not take into account the major political and economic transformations in the country. As a result, many key provisions of the destruction concept had to be revised including those on the number and location of facilities, and the establishment of a ban on the transport of chemical weapons on Russian territory. New requirements for the safety and environmental impact of destruction technologies also had to be drafted. The Ministry of Defence and the Committee on Problems of Chemical and Biological Conventions, which was established in 1992, then developed a second version of the state programme. It proposed the construction of two destruction facilities for vesicant agents in Gorny and Kambarka, the two regions where these compounds are stored. It also envisaged converting a former production facility near Novocheboksarsk in the Chuvash Republic into a destruction facility for organophosphorus CW agents. The Russian Supreme Council considered this version of the state programme in January 1993, but again did not approve it because of sharp criticism by representatives from the regions of the proposed facility sites. A major objection was that the interests of the citizens of the Russian Federation were not taken into account. A third version of the programme in the form of a 'concept' was submitted in early 1994 to Russia's new highest legislative body, the State Duma of the Federal Assembly of the

---

[14] Letter dated 16 December 1987 from the representative of the Union of Soviet Socialist Republics addressed to the President of the Conference on Disarmament transmitting a working paper entitled 'Information on the presentation at the Shikhany military facility of standard chemical munitions and of technology for the destruction of chemical weapons at a mobile unit', Conference on Disarmament document CD/789, 16 Dec. 1987; and *An Important Confidence-Building Step: Foreign Observers Visit the Shikhany Military Area in the Soviet Union* (Novosti Press Agency Publishing House: Moscow, 1988). It is noteworthy that, in the same year, the USSR ceased production of chemical weapons and closed its last production facility.

[15] Solovyev, V., 'History of the establishment of the facility for destruction of chemical weapons in Chapaevsk', Oral report presented to the International Conference on the Banning and Destruction of Chemical Weapons, Moscow, 9–11 Apr. 1991.

[16] OPCW is used throughout this volume as the acronym for the Organisation for the Prohibition of Chemical Weapons.

Russian Federation. In March 1994 the Duma committees on international affairs, defence, security, environment, industry and budget conducted hearings on the concept. Once again, after a critical analysis by deputies and outside experts, the Duma was unable to approve an overall concept for CW destruction because the interests of the regions and population were not adequately reflected.

In October 1994, the State Duma Committee on Defence, in an expanded meeting, conducted a thorough analysis of the chemical disarmament situation in Russia and then directed the highest agencies of the executive branch of government to accelerate the process of preparing Russia for the destruction of its CW stockpile. By this time, most members of the Committee on Defence already had their own clear priorities in CW destruction, chief among which were the establishment of a national legislative base for CW destruction, the development of a target federal programme and the ratification of the CWC.

As the various levels of the legislative and executive branches of government, as well as political, scientific and public interest groups, developed their conceptual positions on CW destruction, the legislative and regulatory base for this programme rapidly took shape.

Principal legal and regulatory documents

The principal legal and regulatory documents are: (*a*) the Special Federal Programme for Chemical Weapons Destruction, actually the fourth version of it;[17] (*b*) new articles (355 and 356) of the Russian Federation Criminal Code on punishment for illegal activities involving weapons of mass destruction, including chemical weapons;[18] and (*c*) a package of bills on problems relating to CW destruction. These bills include the fundamental law On the Destruction of Chemical Weapons, which entered into force in the spring of 1997;[19] the bill On the Social Protection of Citizens Working with Chemical Weapons; and the bill On Additional Compensatory Payments for Damage Caused by Toxic Chemicals to the Public Health and to the Property Interests of Natural and Legal Persons as a Result of Extraordinary Situations Arising During the Storage, Shipment, and Destruction of Chemical Weapons. Finally, there is the Russian CWC ratification act.[20]

This brief review of documents is indicative of the scope of Russia's preparatory measures for CW destruction and demonstrates the seriousness of Russia's intentions to destroy its chemical weapons.

Owing to the continuing financial crisis in Russia, however, the budget allocations for CW disarmament have fallen steadily. The appropriation to maintain

---

[17] 'Federalnaya tselevaya programma' (note 2); and Russian Federation (note 2).

[18] Articles 355 and 356, *Ugolovny Kodeks Rossisskoi Federatsii* [Criminal code of the Russian Federation], were approved by the Duma on 24 May 1996 and by the Federal Council on 5 June 1996. They entered into effect on 13 June 1996 when Russian President Boris Yeltsin signed Federalny Zakon o vvedenii v destvie ugolovnogo kodeksa Rossisskoi Federatsii [Federal law on entry into force of the criminal code of the Russian Federation], Federal law no. 64-FZ, 13 June 1996. The articles are published in *Sbornik Kodeksov Rossisskoi Federatsii* [Collection of Russian Federation laws] (Prospekt: Moscow, 1996), p. 844. The production or distribution of weapons of mass destruction is punishable by 5–10 years' imprisonment (Article 355). The use of weapons of mass destruction is punishable by 10–20 years' imprisonment (Article 356).

[19] 'Ob unichtozhenii khimicheskogo oruzhiya' (note 3).

[20] 'O ratifikatsii Konventsii o zapreshenii razrabotki, proizvodstva, nakopleniya i primeniya khimicheskogo oruzhiya i o ego unichtozhenii' (note 5).

CW storage facilities in a safe condition and prepare for CW destruction in 1994 was thus less than 50 per cent of the amount planned in the federal budget law and less than 30 per cent of the actual need. In 1995 the appropriation was approximately 30 per cent of the budgeted amount and less than 10 per cent of the amount required. In 1996 about 5 per cent of the needed funds were actually allocated.

The Interdepartmental Commission on Chemical Disarmament concluded on 7 August 1996 (Protocol no. 4)[21] that the minimum federal budget allocation for CW disarmament in 1997 should be 3.633 trillion roubles. However, the draft federal budget for 1997 allocated only 156 billion roubles—slightly more than 4 per cent of the necessary funding.

The exceptional crisis situation in the funding of chemical disarmament work in recent years has hindered completion of the work on the choice of environmentally friendly destruction of organophosphorus chemical agents to be completed. Nor has it allowed for: (a) completion of the groundwork for public health standards and other safety standards; (b) implementation of Russian Government decrees on faster regional infrastructure development in the vicinity of the proposed destruction facilities; (c) full and consistent assurance of the safe condition of CW stocks; and (d) provision of back pay for military personnel at CW storage bases. In addition, the other 1997 priorities that were identified by the Interdepartmental Commission on Chemical Disarmament in Protocol no. 4 are unlikely to be achieved because the scope of this work is based on a budget allocation of over 3 trillion roubles.

The Russian programme for chemical weapon destruction

Russia's scientific and legal/regulatory preparedness to fulfil its international obligations is clearly reflected in the federal CW destruction programme.[22] The main goals of the programme are to destroy the CW stockpile in Russia in accordance with the CWC, improve the environmental situation in the regions where chemical weapons are stored and are to be destroyed, and relieve public concern about long-term CW storage in these regions. The programme's first priority is to destroy the stockpile of bulk vesicants, which comprise 18.8 per cent of the total quantity of chemical weapons possessed by Russia. The second priority is to destroy the chemical munitions containing organophosphorus CW agents, lewisite, mustard–lewisite mixtures and phosgene.

After the chemical weapons have been destroyed, there will be a four-year period in which to decommission the destruction facilities, decontaminate the process equipment, clean up the sites and operate the solid-waste disposal areas. The total length of the programme is 15 years. This includes the preparatory work, 10 years of destruction operations (counting from the day of entry into force of the CWC, not from the date of Russian ratification), and 4 years of clean-up. The programme was to have been completed in 1995–2009 at a total cost of 16.6 trillion roubles (in January 1995 prices) plus $500 million for purposes related to international inspections. However, it is now clear that the programme deadlines are threatened because of the virtual absence of funding. As

---

[21] The protocol is not published.
[22] 'Federalnaya tselevaya programma' (note 2); and Russian Federation (note 2).

a result of the delay in implementing the full scope of the programme within the planned deadlines the cost will rise, less because of continuing inflation than because of the steadily increasing cost of maintaining the arsenals and the chemical weapons stored there in a safe condition. Therefore the true cost of the Russian CW destruction programme is unknown. The only certainty is that the actual cost will be much higher than envisaged in the programme.

The estimated cost of destroying the US CW stockpile has also increased substantially in recent years, from $8.6 billion in 1993 to approximately $10 billion in 1995 and to approximately $12.4 billion by the beginning of 1997.[23] The Russian costs will be much lower, although Russia has more chemical weapons than the USA. According to various experts, the cost of the Russian programme will not exceed $5–8 billion, even including the increases mentioned above. Analysts have various opinions on the difference between the costs of the Russian and US CW destruction programmes. Some attribute it to cheaper labour in Russia, lower construction costs for the facilities, cheaper land, and the fact that the destruction facilities will be built and possibly operated by military personnel, who work for virtually no pay. Others believe that the difference is because of the unwillingness of the country's leaders to ensure safety, protect the environment, and properly compensate the population and the employees for their risks (savings at the expense of public health). Still others maintain that the calculations were simply outdated by the time the programme was finally approved.[24]

The Russian law On the Destruction of Chemical Weapons

The Russian law On the Destruction of Chemical Weapons delimits the authority of the federal and constituent executive bodies of the Russian Federation during the process of CW destruction and prioritizes public health and environmental protection.[25]

The earlier drafts of the bill had serious shortcomings, and progress through the Duma was difficult. For example, even on the first reading, the bill was approved only on the third attempt.[26] The contentiousness regarding this bill stems from the desire of every ministry, department and governmental body of the regions where chemical weapons are stored or where destruction facilities are proposed to be located to protect their respective interests. After the first reading there were over 250 amendments to the bill. They were of such a varied nature that the Committee on Defence, which is responsible for advancing a bill in the Duma, decided to appoint a special working group of deputies and

---

[23] US General Accounting Office, *Chemical Weapons and Materiel: Key Factors Affecting Disposal Costs and Schedule*, GAO/NSIAD9718 (US General Accounting Office: Washington, DC, Feb. 1997), p. 4.

[24] Zanders, J. P. and Hart, J., 'Chemical and biological weapon developments and arms control', *SIPRI Yearbook 1998: Armaments, Disarmament and International Security* (Oxford University Press: Oxford, 1998), p. 463.

[25] 'Ob unichtozhenii khimicheskogo oruzhiya' (note 3). The bill entered into force on 6 May 1997.

[26] For a bill to be passed it must be approved by a majority of the members of the Duma. The bill is then sent to the Federal Council for review. The bill is considered passed if a majority of the Federal Council members vote in favour or if the bill is not considered within 14 days. If the Federal Assembly votes against the bill, then the legislation may be considered by a joint committee. Alternatively, the bill could be passed by a 2/3 majority of the Duma in a second vote. Article 105 of the Constitution of the Russian Federation.

experts in various fields to analyse these comments and make recommendations to the deputies on which amendments to incorporate into the revised bill.

A systematic analysis of these amendments shows that they pertain mainly to provisions concerning the distribution of authority among federal and regional governmental bodies, safety issues, and the expansion of the rights of citizens and public organizations. For example, many of the amendments proposed by the administration of the Bryansk oblast—where chemical weapons are stored, at Pochep, and which suffered the effects of the Chernobyl nuclear power plant accident—would have expanded the authority of local governmental bodies as regards the locating of CW destruction facilities on their territory and would have stipulated that all actions by bodies of the federal government conform to local laws and safety requirements. Their principle of 'maximum environmental safety and minimum damage to the environment' is actively supported by other regions, as well as by major Russian environmental organizations and movements, including the Social–Ecological Union and the Union for Chemical Safety.

Similar demands for expanded authority and greater safety were made by the government of the Udmurt Republic, which has two storage facilities, one of which (Kambarka) is a top priority for CW agent destruction under the Russian CW destruction programme.

The uneasiness of the regions is understandable and requires that maximum consideration be given to their demands, because they will bear the consequences of critical situations involving CW storage and destruction. At the same time, given the general problems in the country, there is apprehension about the desire of local authorities to apply 'certain pressures' on the federal authorities and to solve various regional economic and social development problems by means of the CW disarmament programme. These pressures can be exerted in various forms. For example, Bryansk oblast has issued a law declaring a moratorium on the construction of CW destruction facilities in the oblast for 15 years. In exchange for permission to locate CW destruction facilities on their territories, some regions are demanding guarantees from the government for the accelerated development of the technical and social infrastructure in and around the sites. Some local authorities are stipulating various social measures in their decisions to cede land and choose sites for these facilities. For example, while the administrations of Kirov and Kurgan oblasts and of Kizner rayon in the Udmurt Republic have given approval for technical and economic feasibility studies on the siting of destruction facilities on their territories, Penza oblast has not taken a stand on many issues concerning the locating of a CW destruction facility there. In general, all of the administrations of the oblasts with CW arsenals are very cautious in considering documents pertaining in any way to CW disarmament, so there are often delays in the development of the necessary documentation.

A substantial number of amendments to the bill are aimed at providing legal rights to obtain reliable information about the organization of the CW destruction process and about the measures for monitoring the safe operation of facilities, including the right of public organizations to directly participate in all stages of decision making and action by executive bodies of the government.

By September 1996, the Duma Working Group had completed a preliminary analysis of the amendments and presented the Committee on Defence with a new draft of the bill that reflected 'provisionally accepted and provisionally rejected' amendments. The revised version of the bill was reviewed in committee session and was generally approved.[27] The Committee on Defence voted to send the revised version to the President and the Government of the Russian Federation for review. In accordance with Duma procedures, the next step was to submit the revised bill to the State Duma Council, which scheduled a second reading at a plenary session of the full State Duma in the spring of 1997. In general, if a bill is approved on the second reading, all work on it must be completed within seven days, because only editorial changes that do not affect the substance of the law are allowed after a second reading. If the bill is not approved on the second reading and is sent back for further work, the procedure does not provide a deadline for reconsideration. That date depends only on how substantial the required changes are and how much time it takes to get them approved by the subject of the legislative initiative. In this particular case, that 'subject' is the President of the Russian Federation.

III. Problems associated with Russia's ratification of the CWC

General problems of ratification

Russia's preparations for ratification took place during an exceptionally severe economic and political crisis owing in large measure to major transformations in the industrial system and property rights. For this reason, Russia's political declaration in January 1993 of its intention to destroy its CW stockpile and sign the Chemical Weapons Convention was accompanied by a call to accommodate Russia's position on the two problems it considered most important: the fate of former CW production facilities and the potential high cost to Russia for international monitoring of Russian facilities. At the time the CWC was signed, most of the international community expressed understanding of Russia's problems. The governments of France, Germany, Italy, the UK and the USA pledged to help Russia achieve acceptable solutions to these problems.[28]

Former chemical weapon production facilities

The Russian Federation delegation to the OPCW Preparatory Commission (PrepCom)[29] worked to gain support for the position that CW production facilities which are destroyed or converted to peaceful purposes and which no longer contain any 'specialized equipment' for the production of chemical weapons at the time the convention enters into force for the party should not be required to declare such facilities as CW production facilities. Such facilities should be declared as destroyed CW production facilities. This approach does not contravene the principles or purposes of the convention and would substantially lower the overall cost to the party by virtue of the fact that production buildings and standard, non-specialized equipment could be retained.

---

[27] Not all amendments proposed by the Committee on the Environment were taken into consideration.
[28] Zanders, J. P., Eckstein, S. and Hart, J., 'Chemical and biological weapon developments and arms control', *SIPRI Yearbook 1997: Armaments, Disarmament and International Security* (Oxford University Press: Oxford, 1997), p. 447, fn 75.
[29] PrepCom is used as the acronym for Preparatory Commission throughout the volume.

A classic example of this approach is the conversion of the former CW production facility at Volgograd. This site was visited on different occasions by representatives of the USA, the Provisional Technical Secretariat for the OPCW and US companies interested in establishing new commercial production, including a Russian–US joint venture.[30] None of the visitors expressed doubts about the absence of CW production there. Nevertheless, Russia's position is not supported by the delegations from a number of countries, including the USA. Moreover, the USA is attempting to distort the Russian position, suggesting that Russia might be trying to exempt some Russian facilities from international monitoring.

Apart from the destruction of specialized equipment, Russia cannot accept the demands that the buildings and standard industrial equipment of former CW production facilities be destroyed when these are situated in large chemical complexes and are an integral part of the engineering infrastructure (general utilities, energy system, communications, water system, and so on). The destruction of buildings and general-purpose equipment would result in the complete shutdown of some nationally important, multi-product chemical complexes at great expense. According to some experts, the conversion of former production facilities is a minimum of an order of magnitude less costly than total destruction (e.g., based on 1994 prices, the entire conversion programme was estimated to cost 305 billion roubles, while the cost of physically destroying one Novocheboksarsk facility was estimated as 250 billion roubles). Given the number of facilities that must be destroyed (which ranges from 7 to 22, depending on the defining criteria), it is easy to calculate not only the total cost of destroying former facilities, but also the proportion of these unproductive costs in relation to the total cost of CW destruction.

From the above analysis, it is obvious that for the Duma the question of an economically acceptable approach to eliminating former CW production facilities was one of the main issues for discussion and became a major obstacle to ratification of the Chemical Weapons Convention.

Cost of international monitoring

Another problem is paying for the international monitoring of CW storage, production and destruction facilities. Under the CWC the cost is borne by the host party. Attempts are continuing to have the convention interpreted so that Russia must pay the cost not only of the actual inspections, but also the transport of equipment and inspectors from the OPCW headquarters to the site and back. Russian experts estimate that the direct cost to Russia of inspection activities alone will be $5 million annually. If the decision is made that the indirect cost of inspections must be paid as well, Russian costs will be severalfold higher, which is completely unrealistic for Russia's current meagre budget.

---

[30] On 12 Sep. 1997 DuPont and Khimprom announced a joint venture to produce pesticides at Khimprom's Novocheboksarsk facility. DuPont said that it would make an initial investment of $10 million. Prior to the agreement DuPont had asked Science Applications International Corporation (SAIC) to conduct an assessment to ensure that no part of the facility which will be involved in the joint venture had been previously used for the production of chemical weapons. DuPont, 'DuPont and A. O. Khimprom to form JV for crop protection products in Russia', Press Release, 12 Sep. 1997, URL <http://biz.yahoo.com/prnews/97/09/12/dd_y0006_1.html>, version current on 12 Sep. 1997; and Ember, L., 'Converting chemical arms plants to peaceful uses', *Chemical & Engineering News*, vol. 75, no. 38 (22 Sep. 1997), p. 10.

The view of Russia is that a more substantial portion of the inspection cost should be borne by all parties to the convention in accordance with the current UN scale of assessment.[31] The prospects for Russia to be able to comply with the provisions of the CWC will depend largely on how the above-mentioned issues are resolved.

International assistance

In addition to these two major issues which must be taken into consideration by the Chamber of Deputies, there is the problem of the implementation deadline for convention provisions. Given Russia's current economic difficulties, 10 years is too little time for Russia to destroy its CW stockpile. There is also a need for more international assistance for the destruction of Russia's CW stockpile, again because of the economic situation.

With the exception of US assistance for the construction of a pilot CW destruction facility at Shchuchye totalling approximately $600 million, the overall amount of international assistance has been insignificant and amounts to less than 1 per cent of Russia's total expenses. This is despite the fact that several countries, including Finland, Germany, the Netherlands, Sweden and the USA, have pursued international cooperation on CW demilitarization for several years. The issue of increased international aid to Russia for CW disarmament was raised at an international forum on the destruction and dismantling of chemical, nuclear and conventional weapons, which was held in Bonn, on 19–21 May 1996, under NATO sponsorship. Only the Netherlands delegation expressed open support, pledging $16 million of assistance to Russia.[32]

One reason for the low level of destruction assistance may be that the international community has thus far made relatively little use of mechanisms and forms of financial aid other than outright grants, in which many countries have no interest whatsoever. There is practically no indication in the open literature of any effort to find extra-budgetary means or methods of funding the Russian CW destruction programme, even though many countries might be highly motivated by proposals for target investments or by aid packages with compensation or other terms acceptable to them. There seems to be no investigation or analysis of the possibilities of partially funding some elements of the Russian CW destruction programme through world funds and organizations that already participate in general aid programmes to Russia. This aid could go to improving the environmental situation, medical services or the social infrastructure of the regions where chemical weapons are stockpiled. For example, the International Monetary Fund (IMF) is financing a road-improvement programme in Russia, but the regions with CW stocks are not included. Nor does the list of environmental projects funded by the IMF include any for general environmental improvement in regions with CW arsenals.

These examples are not the only possibilities for extra-budgetary funding sources, but merely serve to demonstrate the need for a broader view of this issue. Russia is committed to upholding its international obligations on chemi-

---

[31] The Russian Federation's base rate of assessment for 1997 according to the UN scale of assessment is 4.27%. The US base rate of assessment for 1997 according to the same scale assessment is 25%. 'Scale of assessment of members' contributions for 1998', International Atomic Energy Agency document GC(41)/15, 8 Aug. 1997, p. 15.

[32] Zanders, Eckstein and Hart (note 28), p. 447; and Zanders and Hart (note 24), p. 465.

cal weapons, and ratification of the CWC has been directly linked to the world community's willingness and pledges to provide financial support for the Russian programme of CW destruction.

Interpretations of CWC provisions and their influence on ratification

In the process of negotiating and signing the convention, the parties agreed that the articles would not be subject to reservations, nor would the annexes to the CWC be subject to reservations incompatible with the object and purpose of the convention. In order to ensure the conclusion of the negotiations in 1992 it was agreed that the remaining disagreements concerning the meaning of certain terms and definitions and verification procedures would be resolved by the PrepCom, in which the signatory states met, before entry into force of the CWC. Workable solutions and procedures were achieved in many instances, while in other cases only the practice of implementing the CWC can resolve the outstanding issues.

A serious obstacle to the ratification process was the procedure for chemical industry declarations. This procedure could threaten the national security of a country if excessive detail were required or result in the loss of state or commercial secrets if access to sensitive information were too open. On the other hand, if too little detail were required, there would be the possibility that the production of chemical weapons or components could be concealed.

No agreement acceptable to Russia was reached in the PrepCom on an interpretation of the term 'dual-use' chemicals or on the declaration regime for facilities that produce these chemicals, which are not only precursors for CW production but also components of mixtures made in Russia for peaceful purposes. Progress was especially difficult towards an agreement on a 'challenge inspection' procedure. The problem here was to safeguard against abuses of the right of inspection because, according to the convention, no inspection can be refused by any facility anywhere under the jurisdiction or control of any party, including facilities outside the national boundaries of the state. In other words, under this provision, challenge inspections may be performed on any strategic military facility even, in principle, one which is only remotely related to chemical weapons. The provision also applies to research and industrial facilities in advanced fields of science and engineering unrelated to chemistry, so that some degree of access to these facilities must be provided.

A sensitive point for Russia was finalizing the procedure for determining the national ownership of 'abandoned chemical weapons' because the destruction cost must be borne by the state which abandoned them on the territory of another state.

There are contentions about other vague provisions in the CWC where the absence of technical means to monitor full compliance with it might allow violators to conceal not only militarily significant quantities of chemical weapons but also the production facilities for them. Another danger in this regard was the view that ratification of the convention might convey a false sense of security or protection from the threat of chemical warfare, resulting in less attention being given to CW protection for troops and the civilian population. Unfortunately, these threats cannot be completely ruled out, because although the convention entered into force on 29 April 1997, chemical weapons will remain in the possessor member states for the 10–15 year destruction period provided by the convention. Furthermore, some states that possess chemical weapons have not signed or ratified the convention, others have the advanced technologies to make chemical weapons, and still others have unstable political regimes capable of unpredictable actions. Most importantly, these situations and other latent threats are present not far from Russia's borders. Such concerns complicated Russia's preparation for ratification of the CWC.

Ratification and implementation of the convention

Russian governmental officials and politicians felt that if Russia rushed to ratify the convention without first establishing adequate financial and organizational capabilities to meet its conditions this would result in major political damage, a substantial limitation of Russia's rights in the OPCW and other unfavourable political and economic consequences. Russia nonetheless ratified the CWC on 5 November 1997. Further delays long after the CWC had entered into force would have cost Russia the chance to participate in setting up the system and the agencies for monitoring compliance with the convention. Russia also would have experienced a deterioration in relations with many countries that were parties to the convention. The most immediate consequence of worsening relations would have been mandatory CWC trade restrictions affecting not only the export and import of chemical products, dual-use goods and advanced technologies, but also the availability of credits from international organizations. According to some experts, these losses could have totalled hundreds of millions of dollars per year, which is comparable to the cost of the Russian CW destruction programme.[33] The long-term consequences of a lengthy delay in ratification would have included: (a) a more expensive CW destruction programme because of the higher cost of maintaining arsenals in a safe condition, (b) delays in implementation of measures to ensure public safety and protect the environment, (c) higher costs for regional infrastructure development, (d) a diminishing of Russia's authority and role in other programmes for the non-proliferation of weapons of mass destruction and (d) less consideration of Russia's position in other international agreements on reducing military threats and strengthening collective security measures.

Even before ratification Russia's commitment to carry out CW destruction was demonstrated by a number of concrete actions. The legal and regulatory foundation for implementing the convention was completed in accordance with the requirements of the CWC. Russia also signalled its willingness to implement the convention by the following initiatives:

(a) the finalization of a mechanism for verification inspections in accordance with Phase II of the 1989 Wyoming Memorandum of Understanding;[34]

---

[33] Gorbovsky, A., 'Khimicheskoye oruzhiye pod zapret na rubezhe dvadtsat pervogo veka' [Chemical weapons prohibited at the turn of the 21st century], *Khimicheskoye Oruzhiye i Problemy Ego Unichtozheniya*, no. 1 (note 9), pp. 8–10.

[34] The Agreement Between the United States of America and the Union of Soviet Socialist Republics on Destruction and Non-production of Chemical Weapons and on Measures to Facilitate the Multilateral Convention on Banning Chemical Weapons is reproduced in Chemical Weapons Convention Bulletin, no. 8 (June 1990), pp. 19–22.

(*b*) the conclusion and successful implementation of executive agreements with the USA for verifying the effectiveness of Russia's technology for destroying organophosphorus chemical warfare agents;

(*c*) substantial progress on the issue of building a CW destruction facility at Shchuchye in the Kurgan oblast, financed by grants from the USA;

(*d*) the preparation and enactment of the 1994 draft destruction plan[35] and the 1995 statute Procedures For Controlling the Export of Chemical Substances, Equipment and Technologies Which are Intended for Peaceful Purposes but Can Be Used for Developing Chemical Weapons;[36]

(*e*) a special seminar, held in August 1995, to prepare the chemical industry for the declaration procedures and to adapt for local conditions the Declaration Handbook for the Convention on the Prohibition of the Development, Production, Stockpiling, and Use of Chemical Weapons and on Their Destruction, which was developed by the OPCW PrepCom with Russia's participation; and

(*f*) the approval by the Russian State Committee for Statistics of chemical industry declaration forms meeting the requirements of the convention, and the development of instructions for filling out these forms.

Moreover, the Russian Federation Committee on Problems of Chemical and Biological Conventions had worked purposefully to prepare Russia to fulfil its convention obligations. It will assume the functions, required by the CWC, of the National Authority for monitoring the implementation of the convention.

IV. Conclusions

Russia's desire to begin destroying its CW stockpile as soon as possible does not contradict its national security interests and confirms its willingness to fulfil the requirements of the CWC. Progress was especially substantial in 1993–97 on establishing a national legal base for CW disarmament. The main obstacle to ratification of the convention, Russia's exceptionally severe economic situation, was caused by the change of the state structure. A stimulus to accelerate the CW destruction process in Russia would be for the world community to more actively support democratic reform in Russia. Support is needed not just in the form of political declarations but also in specific financial measures, including those targeted at CW disarmament. If other countries recognize this historic opportunity, they can make a crucial contribution to Russia's success in fulfilling its political obligations to implement CW disarmament and the CWC, and to help ensure the effectiveness of the convention as an international document.

[35] The 'concept of destruction of toxic chemical agents' plan is discussed in Stock, T. and De Geer, A., 'Chemical and biological weapons: developments and destruction', *SIPRI Yearbook 1995: Armaments, Disarmament and International Security* (Oxford University Press: Oxford, 1995), p. 349.

[36] It is reproduced in Bertsch, G. and Khripunov, I. (eds), *Russia's Nonproliferation and Conventional Weapons Export Controls: 1995 Annual Report* (Center for International Trade and Security, University of Georgia: Atlanta, Ga., 1995).

2. Russia on the path towards chemical demilitarization

ALEXANDER CHIMISKYAN

I. Introduction

The history of human use of poisons and toxins, including for settling dispute with enemies, goes back for more than 1000 years.[1] The perfection of the first substances for the impregnation of arrows and spears led, little by little, to the establishment of the production of synthetic poisons in industrially developed countries. Mankind experienced the horrors and consequences of the use of this weapon of mass destruction in World War I. The world community has been undertaking efforts aimed at outlawing the use of toxic substances for military purposes ever since.[2] The signing of the Protocol for the Prohibition of the Use in War of Asphyxiating, Poisonous or Other Gases, and of Bacteriological Methods of Warfare (Geneva Protocol) in 1925,[3] a 1932 League of Nations resolution 'On the prohibition of chemical, bacteriological and incendiary warfare',[4] a decision of the United Nations Committee on Disarmament in 1954 to create a Subcommittee on Chemical Weapon Destruction,[5] and a 1961 statement by the Soviet Union and the United States on the need to examine the problem of CW disposal within the framework of complete and comprehensive disarmament are evidence of this.[6]

In recent years it has been recognized that not only the use of chemical weapons for military purposes, but also their transfer and storage pose a threat to the environment and human health. Chemical weapons have lost much of their military utility as a consequence of the development of modern methods of warfare and weapons with great destructive power. The existence of a range of defences against chemical weapons sharply reduces their ability to produce mass casualties. Moreover, the mobility of modern military operations makes the suitability of CW use for tactical operations questionable. As a result of the

---

[1] Lohs, Kh., *Sinteticheskie Yadi* [Man-made poisons] (Foreign Literature Publishers: Moscow, 1963).

[2] Agadzhanov, G.A. *et al.*, 'Mezhdunarodnie saglasheniya v oblasti khimicheskoro razoruzheniya i problemy obespecheniya bezopasnoro unitchtozheniya khimicheskoro oruzhiya' [International chemical weapon disarmament agreements and problems of ensuring the safe destruction of chemical weapons], *Rossiiskii Khimicheskii Zhurnal*, vol. 37, no. 3 (1993), pp. 8–10.

[3] *Sbornik deistvuyuschixkhdogovorov, soglashenii i konventsii, zaklyuchennikh SSSR s inostranni gosudarstvami,* [Collection of current treaties, agreements and conventions concluded by the USSR with foreign governments], 5th edn (Moscow, 1930); and Goldblat, J., SIPRI, *Agreements for Arms Control: A Critical Survey* (Taylor & Francis: London, 1982), pp. 135–36.

[4] Sokolov, G.A., 'Termoyadernoe, khimicheskoe i bakteriologicheskoe oruzhie: sredstva massovogo porazheniya' [Thermonuclear, chemical and bacteriological weapons: means of mass destruction], *Zhurnal vsesoyuznogo khimicheskogo obschestva umeni D. I. Mendeleeva*, vol. 13, no. 6 (1968), pp. 602–607; and *A Collection of Documents 1919–55*, Subcommittee on Disarmament, US Senate, 84th Congress (US Government Printing Office: Washington, DC, 1956).

[5] Kuntsevich, A.V., Nazarkin and Yu., K., *Khimicheskoe oruzhie: pod polny zapret* [Chemical weapons: to be completely banned] (Nauka: Moscow, 1987).

[6] 'Soobshenie praviteltsva SSSR o dvukhstoronikh sovetsko-amerikanskikh peregovorakh po voprosam razoruzheniya' [Communication of the Government of the USSR on bilateral Soviet–American negotiations on disarmament issues], *Vneshnyaya politika Sovetskogo Soyuza i mezhdunarodnye otnosheniya, sbornik dokumentov 1961 god* [Foreign policies of the Soviet Union and international relations, collection of documents of 1961] (IMO [Institute for International Relations]: Moscow, 1962), pp. 364–417.

end of the cold war it has become more difficult to justify stockpiling chemical weapons for military and strategic reasons. Moreover, maintaining CW stocks presents an environmental threat to one's own territory. In this regard, protests by those living in the regions where chemical weapons are stored will almost certainly increase over time.

The risks involved with long-term storage of chemical weapons depends on the age of the chemical fill, its degradation and the destructive action it has had on the interior surface of the munitions or storage containers. If the integrity of the munition has been breached by corrosion or internal pressure a crisis may result which must be dealt with immediately. Substantial cost is involved in the protection and maintenance of the CW stockpile. Criminal and terrorist organizations are known to be interested in obtaining CW agents, as demonstrated by the terrorist acts of the Aum Shinrikyo sect in Tokyo.[7] In addition, some countries continue to consider the possible use of chemical weapons as a way to further national aims.

The Chemical Weapons Convention was opened for signature in Paris on 13 January 1993 and entered into force on 29 April 1997.[8] Russia ratified the CWC on 5 November 1997, and it is currently implementing the appropriate legislative, scientific, technical, environmental, social and economic measures to guarantee fulfilment of the provisions of the convention.[9]

II. Plans for chemical weapon destruction

In accordance with a statement by Russian President Boris Yeltsin[10] and the Agreement between Members of the Commonwealth of Independent States, signed in Tashkent,[11] Russia accepted the obligations of the former Soviet Union with regard to CW destruction and earlier international agreements on chemical disarmament. Russia agreed to guarantee the destruction of its CW stockpile and confirmed its adherence to fulfilling the Soviet–US Bilateral Destruction Agreement (BDA).[12] In the summer of 1996 Russian Prime Minister Viktor Chernomyrdin informed US Vice-President Al Gore that the Russian Federation was abrogating the BDA. However, there is continuing interest in the USA to implement the BDA, and bilateral discussions on the

---

[7] Stock, T., Haug, M. and Radler, P., 'Chemical and biological weapon developments and arms control', *SIPRI Yearbook 1996: Armaments, Disarmament and International Security* (Oxford University Press: Oxford, 1996), pp. 701–704; and Zanders, J. P., Eckstein, S. and Hart, J., 'Chemical and biological weapon developments and arms control', *SIPRI Yearbook 1997: Armaments, Disarmament and International Security* (Oxford University Press: Oxford, 1997), p. 467.

[8] The CWC (corrected version), 8 Aug. 1994, is reproduced on the SIPRI Chemical and Biological Warfare Project Internet site at URL <http://www.sipri.se/cbw/docs/cw-cwc-texts.html>.

[9] Gorbovsky, A., 'Khimicheskoe oruzhiya pod zapret na rubezhe dvadtsat pervovo veka' [Chemical weapons to be banned at the beginning of the 21st century], *Khimicheskoe Oruzhiye i Problemi Ego Unichtozheniya*, no. 1 (spring 1996), pp. 8–10.

[10] Speech given by Russian Federation President Boris Yeltsin on Central Television, 29 Jan. 1992; and Letter dated 29 January 1992 from the Permanent Representative of the Russian Federation to the United Nations addressed to the Secretary-General, UN document A/47/79, 29 Jan. 1992.

[11] Soglashenie mezhdu gosudarstvami-uchastnikami Sodruzhestva Nezavisimykh Gosudarstv v otnoshenii khimicheskogo oruzhiya [Agreement between members of the Commonwealth of Independent States on chemical weapons], Tashkent, 15 May 1992, *Izvestia*, 23 May 1992.

[12] Agreement between the United States of America and the Union of Soviet Socialist Republics on Destruction and Non-Production of Chemical Weapons and on Measures to Facilitate the Multilateral Convention on Banning Chemical Weapons. The text is reproduced in *SIPRI Yearbook 1991: World Armaments and Disarmament* (Oxford University Press: Oxford, 1991), pp. 536–39.

Table 2.1. Distribution of the Russian chemical weapon stockpile by storage site

Figures are percentages.

Storage site	%	VX	Sarin	Soman	Mustard	Lewisite	Mustard–lewisite mixture	Phosgene
Kambarka, Udmurt Republic	15.9	–	–	–	–	+	–	–
Gorny, Saratov oblast	2.9	–	–	–	+	+	+	–
Kizner, Udmurt Republic	14.2	+	+	+	–	+	–	–
Maradikovsky, Kirov oblast	17.4	+	+	+	–	–	+	–
Pochep, Bryansk oblast	18.8	+	+	+	–	–	–	–
Leonidovka, Penza oblast	17.2	+	+	+	–	–	–	–
Shchuchye, Kurgan oblast	13.6	+	+	+	–	–	–	+

– = not present at the site, + = present at the site.

Source: 'Federalnaya tselevaya programma' [Special federal programme], Federal government edict no. 305, 21 Mar. 1996, *Rossiyskaya Gazeta*, 2 Apr. 1996, pp. 5–6; and Russian Federation, Special federal programme, destruction of chemical weapons stockpiles in the Russian Federation, Preparatory Commission document PC-XIV/B/WP.7, 25 June 1996, pp. 19–20.

subject have continued. The obligations undertaken confirmed that the Russian Federation would inherit a total of 40 000 tonnes of chemical weapons from the Soviet Union and should take concrete steps towards their destruction.[13] Table 2.1 shows the locations of the CW storage sites and the percentage and type of chemical weapons at each facility.

The initial approach to destruction

Work in the Soviet Union on the scientific and technical aspects of CW destruction began in the 1970s. Initially, it focused on the establishment of a mobile destruction facility for munitions that were in poor condition. The result was publicly displayed to journalists and participants of the negotiations on CW disarmament in 1987 at the military base at Shikany. Approximately 4000 munitions containing more than 280 tonnes of chemical fill were destroyed by this facility in 1980–87.[14]

[13] Petrov, S. V., 'Osnovnie problemi unichtozheniya khimicheskoro oruzhiya v Rossiisskoi Federatsii' [Fundamental problems of chemical weapon destruction in the Russian Federation], *Rossiisskii Khimicheskii Zhurnal* (note 2), pp. 5–7.

[14] Nikitin, A. I. (ed.), 'Problemi zaprescheniya i unichtozheniya khimicheskoro oruzhiya' [Problems of the prohibition and destruction of chemical weapons] (Center for Political and International Studies: Moscow, 1994); Union of Soviet Socialist Republics, Complex for the destruction of faulty chemical munitions (KUASI), Conference on Disarmament document CD/CW/WP.369, 8 Oct. 1991; and Union of Soviet Socialist Republics, Letter dated 16 December 1987 from the representative of the Union of Soviet Socialist Republics addressed to the President of the Conference on Disarmament transmitting a working

On the basis of discussions at various levels of government the USSR decided in 1985 to establish a permanent CW destruction facility. Thus, two years before the 1987 unilateral Soviet ban on CW production,[15] the country had already begun laying the groundwork for disposal of its CW stockpile. The facility, which was established in 1989 near the town of Chapaevsk, was intended to be the first large-scale Soviet base for such activities. The experience of operating the facility would have permitted proposals to be developed for the establishment of one or two other similar facilities and thus resolve the problem of destruction of the CW stockpile in the Soviet Union. However, the Chapaevsk facility was not put into operation because of local protests against a potentially dangerous enterprise. These protests were also supported by neighbouring regions which banned the transport of chemical weapons through their territories. Thus despite a positive evaluation by a number of expert committees, the facility was never used to destroy chemical weapons but was instead modified for scientific and training purposes in accordance with a decision by the Soviet Government.[16] The experience with the Chapaevsk facility reflects the government's failure to take into account the important role of the public and the media. The excessive secrecy of the project together with the perceived inadequacy of the accompanying social programme and plans for development of the regional infrastructure resulted in opposition by the local population to the construction of the facility. This occurred despite that fact that there were provisions for protecting the environment and ensuring the safety of those living near the facility. The experience at Chapaevsk demonstrated that only by the adoption of a special government programme can the questions related to CW destruction be resolved.

Planning destruction

A draft of the first CW destruction programme was prepared in 1990 and submitted to the Supreme Soviet of the Soviet Union.[17] An examination by an expert panel under the aegis of the Soviet State Committee for Protection of the Environment and other discussions had previously taken place.[18] Alternative destruction technologies for various CW agents were presented to the expert panel.[19] The methods proposed were underground nuclear explosion, placing the CW agent in a layer of magma and various thermal processes (ranging from

paper entitled 'Information on the presentation at the Shikhany military facility of standard chemical munitions and of technology for the destruction of chemical weapons at a mobile unit', Conference on Disarmament document CD/789, 16 Dec. 1987.

[15] Lundin, S. J., Perry Robinson, J. P. and Trapp, R., 'Chemical and biological warfare: developments in 1987', *SIPRI Yearbook 1988: World Armaments and Disarmament* (Oxford University Press: Oxford, 1988), p. 108.

[16] Evstafev, I. B. and Kholstov, V.I., 'Predisloviie k tematicheskomu vypusku "Problemy unichtozheniya khimicheskogo oruzhiya"' [Preface to special edition on 'Problems of chemical weapon destruction'], *Rossiisskii Khimicheskii Zhurnal* (note 2), p. 3.

[17] Union of Soviet Socialist Republics, 'Programma po unichtozheniyu khimicheskogo oruzhiya (proekt)' [Programme on chemical weapon destruction (project)] (Ministry of Defence: Moscow, 1990).

[18] 'Ob obrazovanii ekspertnoi komissii dlya provedeniya gosudarstvennoi ekspertizy proekta "Programmy po unichtozheniyu khimicheskogo oruzhiya"' [On the establishment of an expert commission for carrying out a state review of the project 'Programmes for the destruction of chemical weapons'], Decision of the State Committee of the USSR on Environmental Protection, no. 44, 26 Nov. 1990.

[19] Kuntsevich, A. D., 'Khimicheskoe oruzhie: legko li ego likvidirovat?' [Chemical weapons: are they simple to destroy?], *Krasnaya Zvezda*, 22 Oct. 1993.

the use of plasma[20] to various types of furnaces, including liquid-fuel jet furnaces). The technologies presented to the expert panel for the destruction of munitions that did not require disassembly were the pyrolysis[21] and radiation processes. It was judged that a two-step process would be suitable: chemical detoxification, followed by treatment of the reaction product.[22]

For the detoxification of organophosphorus-based CW agents reagents that ensure their hydrolysis, solvation or ammonolysis were proposed.[23] The best detoxification agent for sarin and soman was determined to be monoethanolamine, and for VX a mixture of ethylene glycol and orthophosphoric acid was found to be most suitable.[24] Several alternative technologies were proposed for the destruction of lewisite including chlorination,[25] catalytic hydrochlorination and alkaline hydrolysis.[26]

Various modifications of the hydrolysis and ammonolysis (including mono-ethanolamine) methods were proposed for the treatment and detoxification of yperite.[27] It was shown that polycondensation[28] of yperite with polysulphide alkaline metals would result in the formation of high molecular weight compounds suitable for the production of thiokol rubber. Detoxification of yperite–lewisite mixtures with molten sulphur was viewed as promising and practical. For the second stage of destruction thermal treatment of the initial detoxification products or bituminization of the reaction mass was proposed. This approach created two barriers that together ensured the complete destruction of the CW agent and the safety of the process. It was also recognized that biological methods for CW destruction could be used for final purification of waste streams and supplementary treatment of associated products.

The draft legislation was submitted to the Cabinet of Ministers in 1991,[29] but because of the dissolution of the Soviet Union it was not enacted. In the spring of 1992 the Committee on Problems of Chemical and Biological Conventions was formed.[30] The committee was given the task of acting as the interdepart-

---

[20] Plasma is completely ionized gas that is composed of electrons and positive ions.

[21] Pyrolysis is chemical decomposition occurring as a result of high temperature.

[22] Tarasevich, Yu, 'Rossiya sevodnya podgotovlena k unichtozheniya khimicheskoro oruzhiya' [Today Russia is prepared to destroy its chemical weapons], *Khimicheskoe Oruzhiya i Problemi Ego Unichtozheniya* (note 9), pp. 2–5.

[23] Hydrolysis is the decomposition or alteration of a compound as a result of contact with water. Solvation is the process by which a substance is exposed to a solvent. In this case, ammonolysis is the breaking of bonds by the addition of ammonia.

[24] Zhadonov, V. A. *et al.*, 'Metodi unichtozheniya fosfororganicheskich otravleyauschick veschestv' [Methods for destroying phosphororganic chemical weapons], *Rossiisskii Khimicheskii Zhurnal* (note 2), pp. 22–25.

[25] Chlorination is a process by which chlorine is added to a compound.

[26] Fedorov, V. A. *et al.*, 'Problemi polucheniya mishyaka i ero soedinenii osoboi chistoti na osnove luizita' [Problems in the formation of highly pure arsenic and arsenic-based compounds from lewisite], *Rossiisskii Khimicheskii Zhurnal*, vol. 38, no. 2 (1994), pp. 25–33.

[27] Shantrocka, A. V. *et al.*, 'Khimiko-technologicheskie napravleniya v probleme unichtozheniya i utilizatsii kozhno-narivnich otravlyauschich veschestv' [Scientific directions on the question of destruction and utilization of blister agents], *Rossisskii Khimicheskii Zhurnal* (note 26), pp. 23–35. Thiokol is a polymer which is readily prepared by reacting dichloroethane and sodium sulphide or sodium polysulphide. In principle, the reaction of sulphur mustard with sodium sulphide or sodium polysulphide should produce a polymer similar to thiokol.

[28] In the polycondensation process a gas becomes liquid, resulting in the formation of a polymer.

[29] 'O gosudarstvennoi programme unichtozheniya khimicheskogo oruzhiya' [On the state programme for chemical weapon destruction], Presidential edict no. RP-1601, 10 Mar. 1991, *Vedomosti Sezda Narodnikh Deputatov SSSR i Verkhovnogo Soveta SSSR*, no. 11 (13 Mar. 1991), p. 372.

[30] 'O sozdanii Komiteta po konventsialnym problemam khimicheskogo i biologicheskogo oruzhiya pri Prezendente Rossijskoi Federatsii' [On the establishment of the presidential Committee on Problems of Chemical and Biological Weapon Conventions], Presidential decree no. 160, 19 Feb. 1992, *Vedomosti*

mental coordinator for guaranteeing the resolution of all problems related to CW destruction.

A comprehensive plan for a multi-stage CW destruction programme[31] was elaborated to fulfil a 1992 presidential decree[32] and ruling of the Supreme Soviet of the Russian Federation.[33] The plan proposed that the Novocheboksarsk CW production facility be converted into a facility for the destruction of organophosphorus CW agents and that CW destruction facilities should be built in Gorny in the Saratov oblast and Kambarka in the Udmurt Republic for destruction of the stocks of blister agents stored there. Unresolved problems arose during the process of agreement on plans with the local bodies of these regions. These problems were related to the location of facilities and the transport of chemical weapons which required the elaboration of new approaches to the resolution of problems related to CW destruction in Russia.[34]

In accordance with a 1993 government edict,[35] institutional government purchasers, the Ministry of Defence, and the Committee on Problems of Chemical and Biological Conventions were able to elaborate a new concept of on-site CW destruction.[36] The concept envisaged the use of specific technologies for a variety of stockpiled CW agents and provided information on the technological and technical aspects of such agents. The importance of the two-step technology was confirmed. The approximate cost for carrying out the programme was placed at 500 billion roubles (1993 prices).[37]

sezda narodykh deputatov Rossijskoi Federatsii i Verkhovnogo Soveta Rossijskoi Federatsii, no. 9 (27 Feb. 1992), p. 573; 'O dyatelnosti Komiteta po konventsialnym problemam khimicheskogo i biologicheskogo oruzhiya pri Prezendente Rossijskoi Federatsii' [On the activity of the Presidential Committee on Problems of Chemical and Biological Weapon Conventions], Presidential decree no. 523, 25 May 1992, *Vedomosti sezda narodykh deputatov Rossijskoi Federatsii i Verkhovnogo Soveta Rossijskoi Federatsii*, no. 22 (4 June 1992), p. 1557; and 'O nekotorykh operativnykh merakh po obespecheniyu deyatelnosti Komiteta po konventsialnym problemam khimicheskogo i biologicheskogo oruzhiya pri Prezendente Rossijskoi Federatsii' [On several implementing measures for ensuring the activities of the Russian Federation Presidential Committee on Problems of Chemical and Biological Weapon Conventions], Presidential decree no. 86-rp, 5 Mar. 1992, *Vedomosti sezda narodykh deputatov Rossijskoi Federatsii i Verkhovnogo Soveta Rossijskoi Federatsii*, no. 10 (5 Mar. 1992), p. 676.

[31] Russian Federation, Kompleksnaya programma poetapnogo unichtozheniya khimicheskogo oruzhiya v Rossijskoi Federatsii [Comprehensive programme for multi-stage destruction of chemical weapons in the Russian Federation], 1992.

[32] 'O pervoocherednykh merakh po podgotovke k vypolneniyu mezhdunarodnykh obyazatelstv Rossii v oblasti unichtozheniya zapasov khimicheskogo oruzhiya' [On preliminary measures for preparing for implementation of Russia's international obligations in the area of destruction of chemical weapon stockpiles], Article 1416, Presidential decree no. 304-rp, 12 June 1992, *Vedomosti sezda narodykh deputatov Rossijskoi Federatsii i Verkhovnogo Soveta Rossijskoi Federatsii*, no. 25 (25 June 1992), p. 1755.

[33] 'Ob obespechenii vypolneniya mezhdunarodnykh obyazatelstv Rossijskoi Federatsii v oblasti khimicheskogo i biologicheskogo oruzhiya' [In fulfilment of the international commitment of the Russian Federation in the area of chemical and biological weapons], Article 1727, Ruling of the Supreme Soviet, 8 July 1992, *Vedomosti sezda narodykh deputatov Rossijskoi Federatsii i Verkhovnogo Soveta Rossijskoi Federatsii*, no. 29 (23 July 1992), p. 2135.

[34] Makartsev, V., 'Khimicheskogo oruzhie srazu ne zadushish, ne ubesh' [Chemical weapons do not strangle, do not disappear immediately], *Rossiyskaya Gazeta*, 22 Oct. 1992.

[35] 'O pervoochednykh rabotakh do prinyatiya Kompleksnoi programmy unichtozheniya khimicheskogo oruzhiya v Rossijskoi Federatsii' [On preliminary tasks before implementation of the comprehensive chemical weapon destruction programme in the Russian Federation], Government edict no. 207-r, 12 Feb. 1993, Article 628, *Sobranie aktov Prezidenta i Pravitelstva Rossijskoi Federatsii*, no. 7 (15 Feb. 1993), p. 756.

[36] *Concept for Chemical Weapon Destruction in the Russian Federation* (Russian Federation Government: Moscow, 1994).

[37] Nikitin, A. I. (ed.), *Problemi Zaprescheniya i Unichtozheniya Khimicheskoro Oruzhiya* [Problems of the prohibition and destruction of chemical weapons] (Center for Political and International Studies: Moscow, 1994), p. 19.

Table 2.2. Proposed deadlines and amounts for destruction of chemical weapon stockpiles in the Russian Federation

Amounts are in thousand tonnes.

Year	Amount
1996	–
1997	–
1998	0.11
1999	0.31
2000	2.40
2001	6.09
2002	9.19
2003	10.20
2004	8.03
2005	3.67
Total	**40.00**

Source: [Special federal programme: destruction of the CW stockpile in the Russian Federation], Federal government edict no. 305, 21 Mar. 1996, *Rossiyskaya Gazeta*, 2 Apr. 1996, pp. 5–6 (in Russian).

Hearings conducted by committees of the Duma clarified some of the difficulties associated with establishing and implementing a CW destruction plan.[38] It was emphasized that it would be difficult to secure the agreement of the regions on whose territory CW destruction facilities would be located unless laws were passed to serve as a broader legal basis for destruction.[39]

The 1994 destruction concept was valuable because it reflected the accumulated experience of the preparatory work and outlined a model for its practical implementation.[40] A 1994 government edict confirmed that the plan would be used to prepare for ratification of the CWC.[41] The main provisions called for a competitive evaluation of the alternative technologies. To achieve this, the Ministry of Defence had an expert evaluation of the possible organophosphorus chemical agent destruction technology conducted.[42] A presidential decree served as the basis for the comprehensive CW destruction act that was passed by the Duma on 25 April 1997 and signed by President Yeltsin on 2 May 1997.[43] The multi-stage destruction of the CW stockpiles is to begin in 1998. The deadlines and amounts to be destroyed are shown in table 2.2.

[38] State Duma of the Federal Assembly of the Russian Federation, 'Ob uchasti Rossijskoi Federatsii v mezhdunarodnykh sorlasheniyakh o likvidatsii khimicheskogo oruzhiya' [On the participation of the Russian Federation in international agreements on the destruction of chemical weapons], Recommendations of parliamentary hearings, 24 Mar. 1994.

[39] Babievskij, K.K. *et al.*, *Problemy Zapresheniya Unichtozheniya Khimicheskogo Oruzhiya* [Problems of chemical weapon destruction] (Moscow, 1994).

[40] *Concept for Chemical Weapon Destruction in the Russian Federation* (note 36).

[41] 'Ob utverzhdenii plana pervoocherednykh meropriyatij po podgotovke Rossijskoi Federatsii k ratifikatsii Konventsii o zapreschenii razrobotka, proizvodstva, nakopleniya i primeneniya khimicheskogo oruzhiya i ego unichtozheniya' [On confirmation of priority measures in preparing the Russian Federation for ratification of the Convention on the Prohibition, Development, Production, Stockpiling and Use of Chemical Weapons and on Their Destruction], Government edict no. 764, 2 July 1994.

[42] Kholstov, V. I. *et al.*, 'Podkhodi k otsenki tekhnologii unichtozheniya khimicheskoro oruzhiya' [Approaches to evaluating chemical weapon destruction technologies], *Rossisskii Khimicheskii Zhurnal* (note 26), pp. 42–45.

[43] 'O podrotovke Rossijskoi Federatsii k vypolneniyu obyazatelstv v oblasti khimicheskogo razoruzheniya' [On the preparation of the Russian Federation for fulfilment of obligations with respect to chemi-

Composition of the stockpile

The Russian CW stockpile consists of chemical munitions, shells and CW agents stored in bulk (see table 2.3). CW destruction facilities for blister agents will be established first. These stocks will be destroyed at facilities at Kambarka and Gorny. The facility at Gorny is scheduled to begin operation in 1998, and the facility at Kambarka in 2000. Both facilities will be capable of destroying approximately 1800 tonnes of chemical weapons per year. The remaining organophosphorus CW agents are mostly filled shells that are under the control of the rocket forces and artillery. They will be destroyed starting in the second stage of CW destruction after 2000.

The technical activities related to CW destruction include: (a) scientific investigation and laboratory-scale work, (b) compilation and evaluation of the resulting data, (c) design of facilities, and (d) establishment of the full-scale facilities and the infrastructure necessary for their construction and operation. The safety of the local population and protection of the environment are addressed by the legislation on CW destruction in the section on the establishment of the technical base. The necessity of protecting people who live in the region where the facilities are to be established is heavily emphasized. The cost of CW destruction is now estimated at 16.6 trillion roubles.[44]

The major costs for implementing the programme are presented in table 2.4. One significant expense will be the labour force (estimated at 22 260) that will be needed to carry out the programme. There will be a need for trained specialists and employees who have had practical work experience related to CW destruction. The importance of specialist training and development of practical work experience on the part of CW specialists with chemical weapons is strongly emphasized in the programme.

III. Alternative CW destruction technologies and prospects of their implementation

In the past 10 years Russia has progressed significantly, accumulating experience of scientific investigations in the area of CW destruction with alternative technologies. Increasing emphasis is being given to the environmental aspects of various projects related to CW destruction. The methodological guidelines that were used in the competitive evaluation of alternative technologies played a significant role in this process.[45] The methodological guidelines continue to be refined.[46] The basis for forming expert commissions changed when the participation of independent experts and representatives of regions where the placing of CW destruction facilities was planned began to be widely sought.

---

cal weapon disarmament], *Sobranie Zakonodatelstva Rossijskoi Federatsii*, no. 3 (27 Mar. 1995), pp. 2095–99; and 'Ob unichtozhenii khimicheskogo oruzhiya', Federal law, 25 Apr. 1997, *Krasnaya Zvezda*, 17 May 1997, pp. 3, 7.

[44] Zanders, J. P. and Hart, J. 'Chemical and biological weapon developments and arms control', *SIPRI Yearbook 1998: Armaments, Disarmament and International Security* (Oxford University Press: Oxford, 1998), p. 463.

[45] Criteria for assessing destruction technologies continue to be developed and expanded.

[46] Petrov, S. I. *et al.*, 'Osnovi metodologii otsenki technologii unichtozheniya khimicheskoro oruzhiya' [Methodological foundations for assessing chemical weapon destruction technologies], *Rossisskii Khimicheskii Zhurnal*, vol. 39, no. 4 (1995), pp. 42–45.

Table 2.3. Distribution of Russian chemical agents by amount and type of storage[a]

Chemical agents	Amount (thousands of tonnes)	Weaponized[b] (%)	Bulk (%)
VX	15.20	*100*	–
Sarin	11.70	*100*	–
Soman	4.80	*100*	–
Yperite (mustard)	0.68	–	*100*
Lewisite	6.80	*2*	*98*
Yperite–mustard mixture	0.21	*40*	*60*
Phosgene	5.00	*100*	–

[a] Phosgene is not included in the Russian 40 000-tonne CW stockpile.

[b] Weaponized means prepared to be delivered as weapons.

Source: Petrov, S. V. *et al.*, 'Report: practical action of Russia on preparation of stockpiled lewisite and mustard destruction', Paper presented at the NATO Advanced Research Workshop Chemical Problems Associated with Old Arsenical and Mustard Munitions, Lodz, Poland, 17–19 Mar. 1996; and Beletskaya, I. and Novikov, S., 'Khimicheskoe oruzhie Rossii: perspektivy khraneniya i unichtozheniya' [Russian chemical weapons: views on storage and destruction], *Khimicheskoe Oruzhie i Problemy Ego Unichtozheniya*, no. 1 (spring 1996), pp. 15–17.

However, a number of assessments suggest that fundamental local concerns and problems are still being ignored.[47]

It is difficult to assess technologies before the results of full-scale experiments are available and without a comprehensive environmental assessment. Such an assessment is the determining factor in choosing a destruction technology. A technology assessment is carried out on the basis of many factors (chemical, technical, engineering, environmental, sanitary, risk, accident scenarios and methods of dealing with them, and relevant data from monitoring devices). The comparative evaluations, however, do allow for a preliminary assessment of alternative technologies.

Lewisite

In June 1994 a comparative analysis was conducted to evaluate destruction technologies for lewisite.[48] A working group of experts selected alkaline hydrolysis followed by electrolysis of the reaction mass as the best technology. Ammonolysis and liquid-phase alcoholysis were rated second and third. Alkaline hydrolysis followed by electrolysis of the reaction mass (the preferred technology) and ammonolysis are destruction technologies which allow for the formation of metallic arsenic during the destruction of lewisite. The use of this method minimizes the expense of this destruction method to a certain extent. The resulting arsenic and its further processing is the subject of special investi-

[47] Menshikov, V. and Fedorov, L., 'Ekologicheskaya bezopasnosti: tri godi chozhdeniya po krugy' [Environmental safety: three years of avoiding the real issues], *Khimicheskoe Oruzhiye i Problemi Ego Unichtozheniya* (note 9), pp. 20–22.

[48] Petrov, S. V., 'Expertnaya otsenka technologii unichtozheniya luizita' [Expert assessment of destruction technologies for lewisite stocks], *Rossisskii Khimicheskii Zhurnal* (note 46), p. 4.

Table 2.4. Expenditure items and financing for the destruction of chemical weapons

Items	Financing (years)	Amount (b. roubles)
Ensuring safety	15	300.4
Scientific R&D and pilot-plant work	6	480.9
Establishment of facilities	15	2 876.6
Operation of facilities	12	3 081.4
Implementation of legislation	13	3 300.0
Ensuring readiness for inspection	10	50.8
Other expenditures	15	655.9

Source: Compiled by the author.

gation since the quantities created during the destruction of arsenic-based chemical weapons significantly exceed the annual worldwide demand.[49]

Adamsite

The destruction of adamsite,[50] another arsenic-based CW agent, is also important for Russia. In the early 1960s approximately 3000 tonnes of adamsite that were stored in various types of containers were buried at the Shikany CW military facility in accordance with a decision by the Soviet Government. The likelihood of adamsite and its natural degradation products seeping into the soil and groundwater owing to deterioration of the containers has increased over time.[51]

Various detoxification methods for sites where adamsite is buried are currently being investigated in Russia. The work focuses on the extraction of adamsite, followed by further chemical detoxification. Methods for adamsite destruction that employ the substitution of chlorine for other atoms and functional groups significantly reduce the prospect of dioxin formation in the decomposition products, but other arsenic compounds are created that require special treatment if they are to be utilized.[52]

Various oxidation methods for adamsite deserve attention when considering the suitability of arsine oxides, salts and acids for long-term storage. Difficul-

[49] Beker, S., Derre, R. and Shtelt, E., 'Bezopasnoe unichtozheniya vysokotoksichnich veschestv' [Safe destruction of highly toxic substances], *Rossisskii Khimicheskii Zhurnal* (note 2), pp. 29–33. It has been estimated that *c.* 2300 tonnes of arsenic could be retrieved from the lewisite stored at Kambarka. If highly pure this amount of arsenic could be worth up to $230 million. Without purification it could be worth as little as $5 million. 'West to help in safe but costly disposal of Russia's CW stocks', *Jane's Defence Weekly*, vol. 26, no. 6 (7 Aug. 1996), p. 15.

[50] Adamsite was stocked for use as a lethal agent and for riot control. However, it is generally considered too dangerous for use in riot control and too ineffective for battlefield use. It is not considered a chemical weapon in the BDA (note 12) and need not be declared under the CWC since the adamsite in question was buried before 1 Jan. 1977. In general, stocks of lethal CW agents must be declared under the CWC. Chemical weapons which were dumped before 1 Jan. 1985 or which were buried on the territory of the state party before 1 Jan. 1977 and which remain buried need not be declared. CWC, Article III, para. 2.

[51] Gormai, V. V. *et al.*, 'Problema unichtozheniya i utilizatsii adamsita' [The problem of destruction and use of adamsite], *Rossisskii Khimicheskii Zhurnal* (note 26), pp. 39–42.

[52] Destroying arsenic-containing compounds is difficult since they tend to be highly toxic.

ties related to the recovery method and separation of highly dispersed arsine oxide aerosols from product mixtures of incineration are among the drawbacks of these methods. Moreover, there exists the possibility of producing dioxins with low-temperature methods.[53]

Adamsite destruction technologies that yield arsenic trichloride and diphenylamine are promising from a practical point of view. Such detoxification methods treat adamsite with chlorine or hydrogen chloride. The most important factor for the effectiveness of this technology is the extraction of arsenic trichloride from the reaction mass and its further treatment. Adamsite can also be detoxified with phosgene and vaporized paraffin.[54]

There are technical problems related to the full-scale use of destruction technologies that require the recovery of volatile detoxification products by, for example, direct application of thermal or plasma-arc methods to soil contaminated by adamsite.

Yperite

Yperite is one of the more studied CW agents for which there are well-elaborated chemical and physical detoxification methods. Nevertheless, various destruction technologies for yperite are being developed in Russia.[55]

High-temperature oxidation of yperite by direct incineration is notable for its effectiveness. By varying the parameters of the process a level of destruction as high as 99.9999 per cent can be achieved. However, possible dioxin and benzofuran emissions are a negative aspect of this technology. High-temperature pyrolysis methods, including the use of plasma, significantly reduce the prospects for dioxin formation in the decomposition products. The potential for implementing such methods will be determined by the ability to develop and maintain the necessary equipment and processes.

Traditionally, various modifications of hydrolysis methods have been proposed for the destruction of yperite (e.g., the use of alkalines and catalysts). One modification of these methods appears to solve the problem of the destruction of yperite–lewisite mixtures.

Oxidation methods such as oxidative chlorination in conjunction with hydrogen peroxide, calcium hypochlorite or solutions of calcium hypochlorite can also be used. However, these technologies require special solutions for the equipment owing to the corrosive nature of the reaction mass.

Methods for detoxifying yperite by transforming it into non-toxic polymers suitable for subsequent use have also been developed.[56] Such approaches are promising because they limit the cost of destruction, and the majority of the other technologies for the destruction of yperite are expensive. Polycondensation of yperite with alkaline metal polysulphides guarantees its detoxification.

[53] Dioxins are produced when the products of incineration cool and benzofurans are formed.

[54] Chimiskyan, A., 'Old chemical weapons mutual disposal method', Paper presented at the NATO Advanced Research Workshop Chemical Problems Associated with Old Arsenical and Mustard Munitions, Lodz, Poland, 17–19 Mar. 1996, p. 6.

[55] Umyarov, V. A. *et al.*, 'Metodi unichtozheniya i utilizatsii adamsita' [Methods for destruction and use of adamsite], *Rossiisskii Khimicheskii Zhurnal*, vol. 37, no. 3 (note 2), pp. 25–29.

[56] Examples include plasticizers and sorbent metals. Shantrocka, A. V. *et al.,* 'Khimiko-technologicheskie napravleniya v probleme unichtozheniya i utilizatsii kozhno-narivnich otravlyauschich veschestv' [Scientific directions on the question of destruction and utilization of blister agents], *Rossisskii Khimicheskii Zhurnal* (note 26).

In Russia 700 tonnes of yperite must be destroyed, and thiokol technologies are impractical since the annual amount of polysulphide rubber is thousands of tonnes.

Destruction of yperite by ammonolysis may create products that can be used by the chemical industry. The amounts are not large and there is therefore limited demand for them. This is significant in that yperite is a complex mixture of chlorinated alkylsulphides with a significant amount of various admixtures. The use of monoethanolamine as a detoxicant in ammonolysis of yperite may have practical value. This technology produces a promising class of organic compounds, including a range of N-(2-hydroxyethyl)-thiomorpholines,[57] and it is based on the method used for traditional military detoxification mixtures that contain monoethanolamine.

Organophosphorus agents

An expert evaluation of destruction technologies for organophosphorus chemical weapons that was conducted in September 1995 prioritized the processes related to such destruction. The most effective method was to react VX with RD-4[58] with subsequent bituminization of the reaction mass.[59] This technology will be used at the destruction facility at Shchuchye. Experimental testing of it is currently being conducted within the framework of a 1992 bilateral agreement between Russia and the USA.[60] The second most effective method was a pyrolysis technology for the destruction of organophosphorus CW agents by binding them into solid substances. This technology allows small munitions to be successfully destroyed without prior disassembly. The third most effective method was a novel destruction technology for organophosphorus chemical weapons which also does not require disassembly and is based on a hydrolysis process directly within the munition. This method is geared towards the destruction of Russian munitions that are stored without energetics.[61] The detoxicant is poured into the energetics cavity. Mixing of the detoxicant and chemical agent is ensured by lowering the temperature of the munition. The frozen detoxicant bursts the cavity and comes into contact with the CW agent.

The final step of this technology appears promising for use at the CW destruction facility at Chapaevsk. A reaction mass is formed within the munition during detoxification which corresponds to Level III on the Russian scale

---

[57] Luganskii, I. N. *et al.*, 'Osnovie technologicheskie i ekologicheskie aspekti problemi unichtozheniya iprita' [Fundamental technological and environmental aspects of destruction problems for yperite], *Rossisskii Khimicheskii Zhurnal* (note 26), pp. 34–36.

[58] RD-4 contains N-methyl pyrrolidinone, potassium isobutylate and isobutyl alcohol. Bechtel National, Inc. and US Army Program Manager for Cooperative Threat Reduction (PM-CTR), *Joint Evaluation of the Russian Two-Stage Chemical Agent Destruction Process, Final Technological Report: Phases 1 & 2* (Bechtel National, Inc. and US Army Program Manager for Cooperative Threat Reduction, July 1996 revision), p. 16.

[59] Petrunin, V., 'Technologicheskie podchodi k unichtozheniu khimicheskoro oruzhiya' [Technological approaches to the destruction of chemical weapons], *Khimicheskii Oruzhie i Problemi Ego Unichtozheniya* (note 9), pp. 18–19.

[60] Agreement Between the Department of Defense of the United States of America and the President's Committee on Conventional Problems of Chemical and Biological Weapons of the Russian Federation Concerning the Safe, Secure and Ecologically Sound Destruction of Chemical Weapons, signed by Under Secretary of Defense Donald Atwood and General Anatoly Kuntsevich, Pentagon, Washington, DC, 30 July 1992.

[61] Energetic compounds are explosives and propellants, including fuses, boosters, bursters and solid rocket propellants. The energetics and associated metal parts are often contaminated with CW agent.

of toxicity.[62] There are no transport restrictions on Level III chemical substances. After the delivery of such munitions to Chapaevsk their further detoxification could be accomplished using existing technological equipment. Given
properly organized efforts with the local population and administration and
with the support of the local population this plan's implementation will secure
significant resources which can be directed towards social programmes in the
region. Past expert evaluations of technology do not exclude the possibility of
elaborating effective and original processes to be presented for future competitive choice.

IV. Problems, the regions and ratification of the convention

Financial problems and foreign assistance for destruction activities

Undertaking the ratification of the CWC in Russia presented difficult political
and economic problems. The experience from discussions of the CW destruction programmes in the former Supreme Soviet and the current State Duma of
the Russian Federation is evidence of this. The hearings conducted by the Environmental Committee—together with the Committee on Labour and Social
Policies and the Committee on Safety and Defence—on 21 May 1996 entitled
'On environmental safety of chemical weapons destruction' were no exception.
The hearings were held as part of the discussions on the federal law On
Chemical Weapon Destruction and, to a significant degree, touched upon the
basic provisions of the Special Federal Programme for Chemical Weapons
Destruction in the Russian Federation.

In order to secure the legislative basis for CW destruction the hearings proposed that the preparatory work for enacting the law On Chemical Weapon
Destruction be accelerated and that its environmental aspects be strengthened.
The law guarantees government and civilian control over work related to chemical weapons.[63] The necessity of faster review and enactment of laws was
emphasized in various measures on environmental safety and on social protection of citizens exposed to the harmful effects of toxic substances during the
production, experimentation, storage, burial and destruction of chemical
weapons. Hearing participants requested the president to stop implementation
of government edict 305 and presidential decree 542.[64] The laws are related to
the Special Federal Programme for Chemical Weapons Destruction and
'environmental expert evaluation'. It was suggested that a comprehensive
expert evaluation be included as part of the programme.

---

[62] In the Russian scale of toxicity (Russian State Standard 12.1.007-76), there are 4 levels of LD_{50} toxicity for reaction products: Level I, extremely dangerous (2–15 mg/kg); Level II, highly dangerous
(15–150 mg/kg); Level III, moderately dangerous (150–5000 mg/kg); and Level IV, slightly dangerous
(> 5 000 mg/kg).

[63] State Duma, Committee on the Environment, Decisions and Recommendations of Parliamentary
Hearings, 'Ob ekologicheskii bezopasnosti unichtozheniya khimicheskoro oruzhiya' [On environmental
safety of chemical weapon destruction], 21 May 1996.

[64] Special federal programme: destruction of the CW stockpile in the Russian Federation, Federal government edict no. 305, 21 Mar. 1996, *Rossiyskaya Gazeta*, 2 Apr. 1996, pp. 5–6 (in Russian); and 'O
prisvoenii Federalnoi tselevoi programme "Unichtozhenie zapasov khimicheskogo oruzhiya v Rossijskoi
Federatsii statusa Prezedentskoi"' [On the award of presidential status to the Federal Special Programme
'Destruction of chemical weapon stockpiles in the Russian Federation'], Presidential decree no. 542,
13 Apr. 1996, *Sobranie zakonodatelstva Rossijskoi Federatsii*, no. 16 (15 Apr. 1996), p. 4024.

The reasons for these decisions are explained not just by the existing contradictions between the executive and legislative branches of the Russian Government. Various political groups in Russia disagreed on the prospects for ratification of the convention. The disagreement was partly because of the absence of a necessary legal base for CW destruction and disagreement over the nature of Russia's security requirements. Ratification of the CWC was viewed by some as unnecessarily weakening Russia's defence. Although the cold war had ended the prospect of NATO expansion (i.e., NATO's borders coming closer to Russia) was viewed as an action which required a response. Failure to ratify the CWC was considered as a possible part of such a response. Such considerations and concerns found a natural audience in the public in part because of a failure to clarify chemical weapon-related issues (e.g., the nature of chemical weapons, their limited military utility, and so on). It would also have been useful in this regard to formally and publicly drop chemical weapons from Russian military doctrine. The need for such clarification has traditionally been underappreciated both within the Russian Government and among foreign destruction assistance donors.

Finland, Germany, the Netherlands, Sweden and the USA continue to provide assistance to Russia for CW destruction. The United States provides financial support within the framework of the Cooperative Threat Reduction (CTR) programme.[65] Finland has reportedly offered 2 million Finnish marks in assistance, and Germany has pledged 7.7 million Deutschmarks for Russian CW destruction.[66] The Netherlands continues to provide funding within the framework of its Partnership for Peace programme. Sweden also continues to finance the work on assessing risk factors at the Kambarka facility. Despite the receipt of foreign financial assistance, the main weight of financial expenses must be borne by the Russian budget.[67]

The difficult economic situation in Russia complicates the allocation of necessary financial resources for carrying out preparatory work and fulfilment of the obligations of the CWC. Financial constraints restrict how those problems related to the regional positions on questions about the placing of CW destruction facilities on their territory can be dealt with. The time-frames for carrying out social programmes and measures to improve regional infrastructure are breaking down here because of an absence of significant financing. Environmental and sanitary–hygienic monitoring and special medical investigations at storage areas and the planned locations for CW destruction facilities are not being conducted. In other words, baseline information that is necessary for comparison with information obtained during the environmental monitoring of destruction operations is lacking.

Foreign assistance remains significant if Russia is to acquire the necessary computers and instruments for monitoring and gathering data on toxin CW agent concentration and the products of their destruction. These instruments and data-processing systems should ensure the provision of data at threshold

---

[65] The CW aspects of the CTR programme are discussed in Zanders, Eckstein and Hart (note 7), p. 448; and Zanders and Hart (note 44), p. 466. The CTR programme and the Shchuchye facility are also discussed in chapter 10 in this volume.

[66] Zanders and Hart (note 44), p. 465.

[67] Khripunov, I., 'Programma Nanna–Lugara i khimicheskoro razoruzheniya v Rossii' [The Nunn–Lugar programme and chemical disarmament in Russia], *Khimicheskogo Oruzhiya i Problemi Ego Unichtozheniya* (note 9), pp. 12–14.

concentrations in accordance with the requirements of Russian standards. Table 2.5 illustrates that in general the Russian indicators are an order of magnitude stricter than in other countries. Russia does possess monitoring equipment that is capable of detecting low concentrations of CW agents.

Chemical weapon destruction and the republics

The Udmurt Republic conducted data collection on information related to environmental assessments and the socio-economic situation. Mathematical models were established of the spread of arsine-containing compounds, taking into consideration the geology of the region and climatic conditions. The work demonstrated an understanding of the problem and a readiness to actively participate in further work on environmental and medical monitoring. The results were presented in the media in order to address questions about CW destruction and to increase openness about future such activities.[68] The involvement of the media is important for clarification of the problems related to chemical weapons.

Unfortunately, many environmental organizations consider themselves the only specialists and competent overseers of CW storage and destruction facilities.[69] Their current political ambitions cause them to exaggerate problems that may not be relevant and which often complicate the resolution of important problems related to CW destruction. The suggestion that areas where chemical weapons were formerly produced be remediated (detoxified) and that inhabitants of such areas and former production plant employees be compensated for possible health problems is legitimate.[70] However, these issues should not be allowed to hinder implementation of comprehensive CW destruction.

The local populations and administrations of the affected regions understand the necessity of establishing CW destruction facilities on their territories (despite the lack of funding) as well as the need to plan the establishment of such facilities and the regional social infrastructure. However, they have presented demands that their safety be ensured by adequate legislative measures, that a mechanism be instituted for civilian monitoring of CW destruction and that they be guaranteed compensation in the event of an accident. Pochep in the Bryansk oblast is the one region which has opposed the establishment of a CW destruction facility on its territory. The area which has been designated for the facility has been set aside by the regional administration for resettlement of the population from other areas in the oblast which have high radioactive contamination as a result of the Chernobyl nuclear reactor accident.

[68] Kolodkin, V. (ed.), *Prognoz Posledstvij Avarij na Obekte Khraneniya Boevykh Otravlyayuschikh Veschestv v Rajone g. Kambarka* [Prognosis of accident consequences at the Kambarka chemical weapon storage facility] (Udmurt State University: Izhevsk, 1995).

[69] Erotova, M., 'Ukorotit by tichoro ubiitsu' [If only to shorten the slow killing], *Pravda*, no. 77 (19 May 1996), p. 2.

[70] Fedorov, L. and Mirzoyanov, V., 'My beli khimicheskuyu boinu na sobstvennoi territorii' [We conducted chemical warfare on our own territory], *Nezavisimaya Gazeta*, 30 Oct. 1992; and Fedorov, L., 'Mify i legendy khimicheskogo razoruzheniya' [Myths and legends of chemical disarmament], *Izvestia*, 2 Dec. 1992.

Table 2.5. Russian and US safety standards for levels of CW agents in air

CW agent	Russia		United States	
	Air in working zone (mg/m^3)	Atmosphere (c. mg/m^3)	TWA workplace limit (mg/m^3)	TWA general population limit (mg/m^3)
Sarin (GB)	2×10^{-5}	2×10^{-7}	1×10^{-4}	3×10^{-6}
Soman (GD)	1×10^{-5}	1×10^{-7}	2×10^{-5}	3×10^{-6}
VX	5×10^{-6}	5×10^{-8}	1×10^{-5}	3×10^{-6}
Yperite (HD)	2×10^{-4}	2×10^{-6}	3×10^{-3}	1×10^{-4}
Lewisite (L)	2×10^{-4}	4×10^{-6}	3×10^{-3}	3×10^{-3}

TWA = time-weighted average.

Source: Kalinina, N., 'K voprosu o standardtach bezopastnosti pri unichtozhenii khimicheskoro oruzhiya' [Towards the question of safety standards during chemical weapon destruction], *Toksikologicheskii vestnik*, no. 3 (1994), pp. 6–9.

V. Conclusions

Major difficulties had to be overcome before Russian ratification of the Chemical Weapons Convention on 5 November 1997 and the start of the destruction of chemical weapons in Russia. Despite political, social and environmental difficulties the legislative basis for destruction has been established.

The evaluation of and preliminary work on the Special Federal Programme for Chemical Weapons Destruction created a plan for the realization of the provisions of the CWC in Russia. However, the economic situation in Russia and its effect on the prospects of financing CW destruction are a cause for concern. Without international assistance it will be difficult for Russia to fulfil its obligations and meet the schedule for chemical weapon destruction set by the convention.

3. Russia's legal basis for chemical demilitarization

IGOR KHRIPUNOV

I. Introduction

As the successor state to the Soviet Union the Russian Federation inherited the entire Soviet stockpile of chemical weapons and most of the former CW production facilities. Immediately after the disintegration of the Soviet Union in late 1991 and the emergence of Russia as a sovereign state, the Russian leadership committed itself to the destruction of its chemical weapons (i.e., chemical demilitarization). On 15 May 1992 all but three of the countries constituting the Commonwealth of Independent States (CIS) signed an agreement under which the Russian Federation assumed an obligation to destroy chemical weapons in accordance with international agreements.[1] Agreement was reached on cooperative efforts to destroy chemical weapons, including a joint funding scheme to be regulated by a later, separate agreement.[2]

On 30 July 1992, Russia's explicit responsibility for the destruction of the Soviet CW stockpile was delineated in the Agreement between the Department of Defense of the United States of America and the President's Committee on Conventional Problems of Chemical and Biological Weapons of the Russian Federation Concerning the Safe, Secure and Ecologically Sound Destruction of Chemical Weapons, which is known as the Bilateral Agreement.[3] Like other similar bilateral demilitarization agreements, the document was derived from the Agreement between the United States of America and the Russian Federation Concerning the Safe and Secure Transportation, Storage and Destruction of Weapons and Prevention of Weapons Proliferation, which was signed by the Russian and US presidents on 17 June 1992 (often referred to as the 'umbrella agreement').[4]

In January 1993 Russia signed the Chemical Weapons Convention, and it was submitted to the Duma on 17 March 1997 for ratification.[5] When the CWC entered into force on 29 April 1997 Russia had not yet ratified it. However, at the first Conference of the CWC States Parties in May 1997 President Boris

---

[1] The countries which signed were Armenia, Azerbaijan, Kazakhstan, Kyrgyzstan, Moldova, Russia, Tajikistan, Turkmenistan and Uzbekistan. [Agreement Between States Parties to the Commonwealth of Independent States Regarding Chemical Weapons of 15 May 1992], *Krasnaya Zvezda*, 23 May 1992 (in Russian); *Military News Bulletin*, vol. 1, no. 5 (1992), pp. 2–3; and Ferm, R., 'Chronology 1992', *SIPRI Yearbook 1993: World Armaments and Disarmament* (Oxford University Press: Oxford, 1993), annexe B, p. 796. Belarus, Georgia and Ukraine were not parties to the agreement.

[2] *Krasnaya Zvezda* (note 1). Like many other CIS arrangements, this separate agreement did not materialize and Russia assumed all responsibility for destroying the Soviet CW stockpile.

[3] Bechtel National, Inc. and US Army Program Manager for Chemical Demilitarization, Office of the Product Manager for Cooperative Threat Reduction (PM-CTR), *Joint Evaluation of the Russian Two-Stage Chemical Agent Destruction Process, Final Technical Report: Phases 1 & 2* (Bechtel National, Inc. and US Army PM-CTR, July 1996 revision), p. 1.

[4] Note 3.

[5] Under the 1993 Constitution the Russian parliament, the Federal Assembly, consists of a lower chamber, the Duma, and an upper chamber, the Council of the Federation.

Yeltsin committed Russia not to act in contravention of the objectives and principles of the CWC. On 5 November 1997 Russia ratified the convention.

II. The scope of chemical demilitarization

There are no exact or reliable data as to the total tonnage of chemical weapons or agents produced by the Soviet Union in the many decades of the CW arms race. While in his official capacity General Anatoly Kuntsevich (ret.), former chairman of the Committee on Problems of Chemical and Biological Weapon Conventions (also known as the Presidential Committee), admitted that not a single ministry or agency has complete information on the amounts of CW produced or the sites where they were sunk or buried.[6] Both the USSR and Russia have declared that the CW stockpile is 40 000 agent tonnes,[7] but independent estimates suggest that this is only a fraction of what was produced. Well-known environmentalist Alexey Yablokov and others claim that the actual amount is 100 000–200 000 agent tonnes. Yabokov has expressed concern that the balance dumped, buried or sunk is 'the underwater portion of the iceberg which poses a more serious environmental threat than civilized CW destruction'.[8] Dr Lev Fyodorov, chairman of the Union for Chemical Security, alleges that the aggregate tonnage produced is 500 000 tonnes.[9]

The range of the estimates indicates that significant amounts of toxic chemicals were disposed of in a manner similar to that used for industrial and household waste in complete disregard of environmental concerns and with little understanding of the effect of such actions on human health. The March 1996 Federal Programme for CW Destruction (also called the Federal Programme) was criticized for focusing on what is stored at the CW storage facilities while largely ignoring the immense task of cleaning up the sites of past dumping and burial of chemical weapons.[10] In addition, it was felt that inadequate attention was given to compensating individuals whose health had deteriorated as a result of past employment at CW production facilities or of residing in their vicinity. It has yet to be determined if current and future legislation regulating the CW demilitarization programme in Russia will focus only on the destruction of existing chemical weapons or if it will also deal with a wider range of issues such as site clean-up and worker compensation. The latter approach was supported by the Interdepartmental Commission for Environmental Security of Russia's Security Council which in 1995 urged the federal government to develop a comprehensive legislative programme covering not only the physical

---

[6] ['Chemical weapons: is it easy to destroy them?'], Interview with Anatoly Kuntsevich, *Krasnaya Zvezda*, 22 Oct. 1993 (in Russian).

[7] 'Agent tonne' refers to the weight of the CW agent alone. Munition weight is sometimes included in CW estimates.

[8] ['Alexey Yablokov: for many I am dangerous and no pressure should be put on me'], Interview with Alexey Yablokov, *Nezavisimaya Gazeta*, 24 Mar. 1995 (in Russian).

[9] Fyodorov, L., *Khimicheskoe Oruzhie v Rossii: Istoriya, Ekologiya, Politika* [Chemical weapons in Russia: history, ecology, politics] (Center for Ecological Policy of Russia: Moscow, 1994), pp. 91–93. This figure may include the weight of the munitions.

[10] [Special federal programme: destruction of the CW stockpile in the Russian Federation], Federal government edict no. 305, 21 Mar. 1996, *Rossiyskaya Gazeta*, 2 Apr. 1996, pp. 5–6 (in Russian).

destruction of CW, but also the consequences of past CW testing, production and burial.[11]

III. Chemical demilitarization legislation: its structure and evolution

The elements of the Russian legal system which apply to CW demilitarization can be described as a pyramid whose structure is derived from the 1993 Constitution. The May 1997 Law on CW Destruction is the top of the pyramid.[12] It is a comprehensive law which will be complemented by several other laws that will have a more narrow scope.[13] These laws will protect the individuals involved in the handling of chemical weapons and CW destruction and provide compensation for damage to health and the property of physical and legal entities as a result of emergency situations related to CW storage, transport and destruction. Presidential decrees and federal government edicts comprise the next two tiers of the pyramid. The base of the pyramid is formed by the locally developed legal documents which are consistent with the constitution and the specific power-sharing arrangements that enable the 'subjects of the federation' to contribute to national CW demilitarization.[14] The majority of this legislation will be enacted at a later stage as CW demilitarization is implemented.

This legal structure heavily emphasizes non-parliamentary acts and reflects the legacy of the past when the totalitarian Supreme Soviet of the USSR was a 'rubber stamp' legislature and the administrative command system operated largely on the basis of government edicts. Government edicts were routinely used to fill gaps in the amorphous body of Soviet legislatively enacted laws, and they were generally given a status equal to such laws. Russia has also inherited the unwritten Soviet practice of giving unpublished ministerial instructions precedence over published parliamentary legislation. Under the current constitution government edicts are intended to be used to implement parliamentary legislation or presidential decrees.

The underdeveloped legal system together with the tradition of dealing with most issues outside a legislative framework apparently prevented the federal government from realizing that the long-term, costly project of disposing of the CW stockpile inherited from the former Soviet Union would require a solid and credible legal foundation. The federal government failed to stress that the success of the CW destruction programme depended on developing and adopting appropriate legislation related to it. For example, President Yeltsin instructed the Presidential Committee to draft proposals for the construction of CW destruction facilities and a provision for related logistic, financial and personnel support together with the other ministries and agencies and in coordination with

---

[11] ['Only legislative support and funding can save Russia from an environmental disaster following the destruction of radioactive waste and chemical weapons'], *Udmurtskaya Pravda*, 31 Jan. 1995 (in Russian).

[12] [On the destruction of chemical weapons], Federal law no. 76-FZ, *Rossiyskaya Gazeta*, 6 May 1997 (in Russian).

[13] At the time of writing (Oct. 1997) most of these laws were still in the draft stage.

[14] According to the 1993 Constitution, the Russian Federation consist of 89 subjects of the federation: 32 ethno-national territories and 57 administrative entities (republics, krais, oblasts, 1 autonomous region and autonomous areas). The chemical demilitarization efforts involve 6 of these entities: 1 republic (Udmurtia) and 5 oblasts (Bryansk, Kirov, Kurgan, Penza and Saratov). The entities have their own legislative bodies, some of which are still officially called Supreme Soviets.

local bodies.[15] The resulting document recommended measures for developing the social infrastructure and improving the standards of living in the areas where CW will be destroyed, but no reference was made to the legal framework under which these proposals would be developed and approved.

The Presidential Committee formulated a chemical demilitarization programme in 1992 which called for the destruction of 43 per cent of the CW stockpile—more than 17 000 agent tonnes—in the first phase of destruction. Mustard gas, lewisite and mixtures of mustard gas and lewisite that were stored in bulk were to be disposed of at storage sites at Kambarka in Udmurtia and Gorny in the Saratov oblast. Organophosphorus munitions were to be transported from Kizner in Udmurtia and Shchuchye in the Kurgan oblast to a former CW production facility in Chuvashia to be converted for destruction.

The draft programme was submitted to Russia's Supreme Soviet in the autumn of 1992 for discussion and approval. However, before Chuvashia reached consensus the Supreme Soviet of the neighbouring republic, Tatarstan, declared itself a zone free of production, storage and transport of weapons of mass destruction. That decision inspired the Chuvash Supreme Soviet on 25 December 1992, to issue its own resolution banning CW disposal or the construction of destruction facilities on its territory. In the absence of a comprehensive federal law on CW destruction, Tatarstan and Chuvashia tested and challenged Moscow's authority by taking advantage of the largely unclarified power-sharing arrangement which existed at that time between the Moscow-based federal government and the regions.

The Russian Supreme Soviet was also unfocused in its efforts to create a comprehensive law on CW destruction. For example, although the Supreme Soviet recommended that President Yeltsin submit proposals for such legislation a June 1992 resolution emphasized a draft programme for CW destruction rather than a comprehensive law.[16]

In January 1993 the draft CW destruction programme proposed by the Presidential Committee was rejected by the Russian Supreme Soviet. Legislative action was needed to break the deadlock, but the government continued to ignore the need for such action. On 20 April 1993, Yeltsin responded to 'concerns by the public of several regions with the problem of CW destruction' by promising that CW destruction would be carried out in a safe manner and that improvements would be made to the infrastructure and social conditions of the areas near the destruction sites.[17] In the absence of an appropriate legislative basis these assurances were met with scepticism by those to whom they were addressed.

IV. Parliamentary approval of chemical demilitarization legislation

Ultimately, the federal government took steps to promote a law on CW destruction that would regulate the destruction process on a more sophisticated and

---

[15] Rasporyazhenie [Presidential instruction], N. 304-rp, 12 June 1992.

[16] [On ensuring the implementation of international obligations of the Russian Federation in the area of chemical, bacteriological (biological) and toxin weapons], Resolution of the Supreme Soviet no. 3244-1, 8 July 1992 (in Russian).

[17] *Beregina*, no. 4 (1993), p. 2.

comprehensive level than a technical implementation programme. Most of the Russian subjects of the federation recognized that such a law was needed to fill the legislative void regarding CW destruction and to serve as a guarantee of their rights and prerogatives. For example, a resolution adopted on 30 March 1995 by the Udmurt Conference on Environmental Protection urged the government of the republic to delay CW destruction in Kambarka and Kizner (the two CW storage facilities in Udmurtia) until 'an appropriate federal law is enacted'.[18] In future the role of parliamentary approved legislation will probably increase and assume central importance not only as regards chemical demilitarization, but also in other areas.

In 1994 the first draft Law on CW Destruction was circulated for comment to the relevant ministries and agencies and to the leadership of the subjects of the federation which would be affected by it. Before it was formally submitted to the Duma on 15 September 1995, the text was modified drastically. Comparison of the 1994 draft with the 1995 draft provides insight into the thinking of the federal government at that time.

The original draft was watered down to provide more decision-making leverage for the federal government at the expense of the Federal Assembly and the subjects of the federation. For example, the new Article 2 no longer identified the Federal Assembly as the primary source of guidance and funding authorization for the CW demilitarization programme. In addition, only the president was authorized to determine the procedures and timeframe for the CW demilitarization programme.

There are indications that the text of Article 2 was amended to enable implementation of the Federal Programme for CW Destruction without the need to submit it to the Federal Assembly. The revised text of the article was limited to a provision requiring CW destruction at specially built facilities in a given subject of the federation, but it did not reaffirm the previously declared principle of destruction at the CW storage sites (i.e., on-site destruction). This formulation gave the federal government greater latitude to shape the chemical demilitarization programme and determine the location of existing storage and future CW destruction facilities. In addition, the new provisions contained references to the transport of CW, which was barely mentioned in the first draft. In the second draft the transport of chemical weapons was presented as a component of the CW destruction programme and was given equal importance with CW storage and destruction. As a result, the original approach of severely limiting the transport of chemical weapons was considerably weakened.[19]

The 1994 draft of the Law on CW Destruction focused on four areas of jurisdiction: (a) federal; (b) joint—involving federal bodies and the subjects of the federation; (c) the subjects of the federation; and (d) local government. The

---

[18] [Resolution of the Republican Conference on Environmental Protection adopted in Izhevsk on 30 March 1995], *Udmurtskaya Pravda*, 21 Apr. 1995 (in Russian). In addition to the adoption of a federal law and other terms and conditions, the recommendations of the conference to the Udmurt Government included: (a) approval of the Federal Programme, (b) competitive selection of safe destruction technologies, (c) assurances to be provided by the federal government and the state procuring agency (Ministry of Defence) to the effect that the CW destruction efforts will be fully funded on a continuous basis. The main text of the resolution identifies 'the relevant legislative basis' as the major prerequisite for step-by-step destruction of chemical weapons in Udmurtia.

[19] In practice, this approach was meant to enable the federal government, if faced with stiff opposition from local authorities, to select sites at a greater distance from storage sites rather than continue time-consuming negotiations with the representatives of the local authorities.

1995 version of the law abolished joint jurisdiction and the jurisdiction of local government but strengthened the federal government. Joint jurisdiction was incorporated into federal jurisdiction. There were serious gaps in the jurisdiction assigned to the subjects of the federation, and their new role was inconsistent with the trend towards a greater voice for the regions in developing and implementing the federal programmes affecting them.

The 1995 draft ignored local government, which created the potential for problems. In the 1994 draft local governmental bodies had been eligible to participate in decision making on various aspects of CW destruction, including the location of CW destruction facilities on their territory, supervision of activities of the executive branch related to safety and environmental protection, and the like. The 1995 draft did not address the issue of participation by local government in these issues.

The draft Law on CW Destruction was submitted to the Duma on 15 September 1995. In October 1995 the Duma Council gave the Defence Committee primary responsibility to coordinate preparation of the text for the first reading.[20] The construction, energy, environment, security and transport committees were also involved in preparation of the text.[21] Some committees supported the draft, while others agreed with the concept but suggested amendments. Only the Committee on Environment completely opposed adoption of the draft law. This committee urged drastic revision of the text to strengthen it and to define the authority of the state bodies and public organizations responsible for supervising CW destruction and ensuring that it was conducted safely. It was proposed that the title of the draft law be changed to reflect its expanded scope and that a Duma committee other than the Defence Committee coordinate efforts in the Duma leading to adoption of the law.[22]

After two voting sessions, during which the Duma failed to achieve the majority required to approve the text in the first reading, approval was given to the draft law on 5 December 1995. Successful conclusion of the first reading made it possible to take the next step: soliciting comments, suggestions and amendments to the text from the presidential administration, federal government and the subjects of the federation. Thirty of the subjects of the federation submitted responses that basically supported the draft, and 16 of them suggested approximately 170 amendments.

The amendments focused on delineating jurisdiction, the safety of CW destruction and the rights of individuals and public organizations. All six of the subjects of the federation where CW storage facilities are located insisted that their participation in decision making be strengthened as regards CW destruction. Bryansk oblast, which was heavily affected by the 1986 Chernobyl

[20] In Russia's legislative process most bills pass through at least 3 readings with the bulk of amendments and modifications usually introduced between the 1st and 2nd readings.

[21] For more information on the Duma's consideration of the draft law see Kalinina, N. [On the deliberation in the State Duma of the law on CW destruction], *Khimicheskoe Oruzhie I Problemy Ego Unichtozheniya* [Chemical weapons and problems of their destruction], no. 1 (spring 1996), pp. 10–12 (in Russian).

[22] Tamara Zlotnikova, chairperson of the Duma Committee on Environment, stated: [this committee] 'must become an obstacle in the way of politicians who want to hastily start CW destruction and disparagingly treat the imperatives of environmental security which is ensured for Russia's citizens by the Constitution as their right to favourable environment'. Zlotnikova, T. [None of environmentalists are opposed to CW destruction because the population must not become hostage to the situation], *Khimichekoe Oruzhiye I Problemy Ego Unichtozheniya* [Chemical weapons and problems of their destruction], no. 2 (autumn 1996), p. 13 (in Russian).

nuclear reactor accident and whose legislative assembly enacted a ban on CW destruction, was particularly active in developing these ideas. Other amendments concerned the establishment of monitoring and supervising bodies, possible compensation for the personnel at the CW destruction facilities and the people living near the facilities, dissemination of reliable information and the rights of public organizations to be involved in relevant decision making and implementation. The Defence Committee set up a working group to evaluate the proposed amendments and comments with a view to holding the second reading. As a result the draft law was substantially revised.

The result was that the decades-old grip of the Ministry of Defence (MOD) on storage facilities and the flow of information was loosened. Article 7 of the revised law gave state administrative bodies, including non-military actors, the opportunity to establish safety criteria and standards not only for CW transport and destruction, but also for CW storage. Article 10 permitted the departments of the executive branch which had supervisory and control functions to be involved in the development of requirements for enhancing operational reliability and safety at both CW destruction and storage facilities.

Other changes made the controversial provisions of the law more general, thereby providing greater opportunity for interpretation and compromise on unresolved issues such as the availability of information. The law was changed so as to make information on CW storage, transport and destruction more widely available. In the revised text information could be requested by individuals and public organizations and not just by physical and legal entities as had been stipulated in the earlier text. On the other hand, the Russian state administrative bodies were empowered by Article 7 to 'classify information regarding CW storage, transportation, and destruction as constituting state secrets' without clear guidelines as to how such determinations were to be made. In Article 20 on the right of individuals and legal entities to obtain information an ambivalent phrase was retained which may be key to the regulation of information: 'Information to be made available about the conduct of work related to CW storage, transport, and destruction must be unclassified and public unless treated otherwise in Russian Federation legislation'.

In recognition of their expanded role Article 9 restored the jurisdiction of the local governmental bodies. It did not specify the exact nature of their jurisdiction but stated that these bodies could be given some state powers if material and financial resources were made available for implementation of the provisions of the law related to CW storage, transport and destruction.

The revised text was improved by its identification of three categories of people involved in the implementation of the law. They were ranked by the potential threat posed to them by activities such as handling or being exposed to chemical weapons. The categories were: (a) 'facility personnel': the personnel at CW storage and destruction facilities; (b) 'participating employees': personnel involved in relevant R&D, industrial-technological and other work for ensuring safety; and (c) 'persons residing and working in the zones within which protective arrangements are applied': permanent or semi-permanent residents of zones within which protective measures are taken and employees of organizations located in such zones regardless of their organizational or legal form (i.e., both state-owned and private organizations). Each category was treated differently in terms of benefits and compensation.

Unlike its predecessor, the revised text accommodated the need to provide equal treatment to foreign nationals involved in Russia's CW demilitarization programme. In Articles 16–21 reference to 'Russian Federation citizens' was replaced by 'persons' or 'individuals', making these provisions applicable to foreign nationals participating in work related to CW storage, transport and destruction.[23] In addition, the scope of international cooperation as a federal administrative function was expanded and the previous text ('organization of international cooperation in CW destruction while ensuring safety during CW destruction') was replaced with new text ('organize international cooperation in CW destruction and in ensuring the safety of the population and environmental protection during the conduct of work related to CW storage, transport and destruction'). Greater flexibility was built into Article 26 on international cooperation, and a reference to Russian international agreements on chemical disarmament was replaced by one to international agreements in general. The revised text gave the provisions of Russia's international agreements precedence over federal law, even if federal law previously had stipulated otherwise.

The revised draft law was clearly improved, and it successfully passed its third and final reading in the Duma on 27 December 1996. However, the Council of the Federation failed to approve the text. Environmental concerns were the main obstacle to its final adoption. The Duma overrode the veto of the upper chamber by a new vote on 25 April 1997 and sent the draft law to President Yeltsin, who signed it into law on 2 May 1997.[24]

V. Presidential decrees

Despite the growing importance of legislatively approved laws presidential decrees have acquired increased significance under the 1993 Constitution. Article 11 stipulates that the Russian President occupies a special and separate position from the other branches of government: 'State power in the Russian Federation shall be exercised by the Russian Federation President, the Federal Assembly, the Russian Federation government and Russian Federation courts'. The constitution assigns to the president the fundamentally important task not only of coordinating the functions of state bodies, but also of ensuring that the functions performed by the legislative, executive and judicial branches conform to legal requirements.

Article 115 of the constitution assigns presidential decrees, which may be of 'normative' nature, a status comparable to federal laws. Article 80 lists the issues on which the president may exercise his prerogative, but the wording is so general that it is open to wide interpretation and, consequently, controversy. However, with the adoption of new laws, such as the Law on Defence, the president's purview is becoming better defined and more focused.[25]

---

[23] Articles 16, 17, 18, 19, 20 and 21 deal with the right to safe living conditions and employment; the right to receive social benefits and compensation; the right to health care; the right to compensation as a result of emergency situations; the right to obtain information; and the right to access to CW storage and destruction facilities, respectively.

[24] Interfax (Moscow), 3 May 1997 (in English), in 'Russia: law details how chemical weapons to be destroyed', Foreign Broadcast Information Service, *Daily Report–Central Eurasia (FBIS-SOV)*, FBIS-SOV-97-123, 6 May 1997.

[25] [Law on Defence], Federal law no. 61-FZ, 31 May 1996, *Rossiyskaya Gazeta*, 6 June 1996 (in Russian).

The major presidential decrees that constitute part of the legal basis for chemical demilitarization range from those that introduce substantive guidelines to those which regulate the organizational side of CW destruction, including interdepartmental decision making. One of the first was Yeltsin's decree 'On the activity of the Presidential Committee on Problems of Chemical and Biological Weapon Conventions'.[26]

It was a surprise to most observers that a separate committee with a staff of up to 150 persons, rather than established governmental structures, was given the task of dealing exclusively with chemical and biological weapon matters. There are at least three possible explanations. First, as negotiations on the CWC were being finalized it was understood that a massive national effort would be needed to cope with its implementation and that unprecedented interdepartmental coordination would be required. Second, the previous controversy over Soviet non-compliance with the 1972 Biological and Toxin Weapons Convention (BTWC) culminated in early 1992 in the admission by President Yeltsin that the Soviet Union had violated the BTWC by continuing to maintain an offensive BW capability.[27] In order to address that situation a mechanism was needed that would operate outside the ministries and agencies which existed prior to Russia's independence. Third, Anatoly Kuntsevich, a leading authority on CW, took advantage of the direct access which he had to Yeltsin's presidential advisers and to Yeltsin himself in order to make a strong case for the committee over the objections of the other ministries and agencies involved.

Another important presidential decree was 'On preparing the Russian Federation for the implementation of its international obligations in chemical disarmament'.[28] It included a provision that abandoned the option of regional CW destruction (following failure to persuade Chuvashia to accept such a facility on its territory) and accepted the principle of on-site destruction. The decree strengthened interdepartmental coordination by setting up a high-level commission on chemical disarmament to be chaired by the president's national security adviser, Yuri Baturin. Attached to the decree was a detailed breakdown of the roles and functions assigned to the individual ministries and agencies involved in the chemical demilitarization process. An additional presidential decree, 'On the Interdepartmental Commission for Chemical Disarmament', established *inter alia* the statutes of the commission.[29]

The Interdepartmental Commission was set up to prevent a continued tug of war between the Ministry of Defence and the Presidential Committee, which was the unchallenged leader in the interdepartmental process when it was headed by Kuntsevich. However, in the spring of 1994 Kuntsevich was replaced by Pavel Siutkin, a person of less influence. Simultaneously, the MOD attempted to obtain more power over CW destruction, which had the effect of calling into question the accomplishments of the Presidential Committee. It was

---

[26] [On the activity of the Presidential Committee on Problems of Chemical and Biological Weapon Conventions], Presidential decree no. 523 (25 May 1992) (in Russian).

[27] [On complying with the international obligations with regard to biological weapons], Presidential decree no. 390, 11 Apr. 1992, *Rossiyskaya Gazeta*, 27 Apr. 1992 (in Russian).

[28] [On preparing the Russian Federation for the implementation of its international obligations in chemical disarmament], Presidential decree no. 314, 24 Mar. 1995, *Yaderny Kontrol,* no. 8 (Aug. 1995) (in Russian).

[29] [On the Interdepartmental Commission for Chemical Disarmament], Presidential decree no. 1079, 6 Nov. 1995, *Rossiyskaya Gazeta*, 15 Nov. 1995 (in Russian).

suggested that the head of the Presidential Committee serve as the only deputy chairman of the Interdepartmental Commission and be given a wide range of functions, but the proposal was not accepted by the MOD, which insisted that it be represented by another deputy in order to counterbalance the Presidential Committee. Ultimately, the approach of having two deputies was chosen. One deputy was the chairman of the Presidential Committee, and the other was a first deputy of the Chief of the General Staff. However, the statutes of the Interdepartmental Commission permitted only the chairman to convene its sessions, and no deputy was allowed to substitute for the chairman in his absence.

VI. The role of the executive branch

Upon entry into force of the 1993 Constitution the President of the Russian Federation ceased to be the head of the executive branch. It became important not only to find a clear and reasonable delineation to preserve and strengthen the federal laws, but also to prevent presidential decrees from encroaching on the legal domain of the government. That legal domain is defined very generally in the Russian Constitution: 'On the basis of and pursuant to the Constitution of the Russian Federation, federal laws and normative decrees of the President of the Russian Federation, the government of the Russian Federation shall issue edicts and orders and ensure their implementation'.[30]

The Law on Defence provides an example of how the jurisdictional division can function. In describing the powers of the government the law states that the government 'organizes the development of plans for deploying on the territory of the Russian Federation of facilities with nuclear weapons as well as facilities for destroying weapons of mass destruction and nuclear waste'.[31] It also stipulates that the president has the authority to approve such plans.[32]

The 'Destruction of the stockpiles of chemical weapons in the Russian Federation' is a fundamental document which outlines the Russian CW destruction programme.[33] Its comprehensive nature is reflected in the objectives set for the programme which include: destruction of chemical weapons in accordance with the CWC; improvement of the ecological situation at CW storage and destruction sites; easing the psychosocial tension of people living near a CW storage facility for a prolonged period; and preparation of draft federal laws and other legislative acts on CW destruction. The programme is based on the presidential decree 'On preparing the Russian Federation for the implementation of its international obligations in chemical disarmament'[34] and other government edicts. Immediately after the programme entered into force it was given the status of a presidential programme, an upgrade which ought to give it higher priority in terms of budgetary allocations.

There was, however, a notable inconsistency concerning the programme. Apparently, in order to ensure speedy approval the draft programme was not

[30] Constitution of the Russian Federation, Article 115, para. 1.

[31] [Law on Defence] (note 25), Article 6, para. 16.

[32] [Law on Defence] (note 25), Article 4, para. 16. Article 4 includes 20 paragraphs that list the powers of the president related to national defence.

[33] Note 10; and Russian Federation, Special federal programme: destruction of chemical weapons stockpiles in the Russian Federation, Preparatory Commission document PC-XIV/B/WP.7, 25 June 1996, pp. 19–20.

[34] Note 28.

submitted to the Duma, as had been done with a 1992 draft. Instead, the draft was formulated and agreed upon in the interdepartmental process and presented to Prime Minister Viktor Chernomyrdin for his signature. This course of action of first obtaining approval from the executive branch was apparently chosen because of the way the constitutionally mandated division of labour is structured: the Duma engaged in work on the text of the Law on CW Destruction while the government focused on formulating an appropriate plan of action. It seems incongruous, however, that the programme to provide guidance for practical implementation was approved before the draft law was finalized by the legislature.

The government also has a regulatory function related to foreign assistance to the Russian CW destruction programme. A December 1996 government edict provides guidelines for accepting US assistance to build a central analytical laboratory.[35] It also outlines the US pledge of financial and technical support for necessary laboratory and analytical equipment and refurbishment of one of the laboratories at the State Scientific Research Institute for Organic Chemistry and Technology (GosNIIOKhT).

A separate category of special government edicts was planned for the CW storage sites where destruction facilities will be built. Edicts were approved for Gorny in the Saratov oblast and Kambarka in Udmurtia.[36] The edicts assigned tasks to the ministries and agencies involved, set time schedules for construction projects and specified long-term government commitments to local communities to improve the social infrastructure and living conditions. However, inadequate funding of Russia's chemical demilitarization efforts prevented the edicts from being implemented as planned. They joined hundreds of other edicts which exist only on paper and were never carried out, thereby seriously damaging the credibility of the federal government.

VII. Other legislation related to chemical demilitarization

The chemical demilitarization legislation described above as a multi-tiered pyramid is a limited set of legal acts dedicated to the CW problem which, given the complexity and long-term nature of the CW destruction process, must be complemented, supported and clarified by other legislation. In addition to those described above, there are at least three major types of legislation which affect the planning and implementation of CW demilitarization. They address *inter alia*: *(a)* power sharing between the federal government and the subjects of the federation; *(b)* health and environmental protection; and *(c)* the role of public organizations and local government. Ideally, the pyramid of chemical demilitarization legislation described above should interact closely with this legislation. However, there may be inconsistencies between the two bodies of legislation,

---

[35] [On the establishment of a central chemical analytical laboratory for monitoring work in the area of chemical disarmament], Federal government edict no. 1447, 7 Dec. 1996, *Rossiyskaya Gazeta,* 19 Dec. 1996 (in Russian).

[36] [On the organization of work for building a facility to destroy the stockpiles of poisonous agents stored on the territory of the Saratov oblast], Federal government edict no. 1470, 30 Dec. 1994 (in Russian); and [On the organization of work for destroying the stockpiles of lewisite stored on the territory of the Kambarka Rayon of the Udmurt Republic], Federal government edict no. 289, 22 Mar. 1995, *Udmurtskaya Pravda*, 14 Apr. 1995 (in Russian).

and some of the legislation described here may not be fully developed or well coordinated.

Power sharing between the federal government and the subjects of the federation

Chemical demilitarization in the Russian Federation may be influenced by power-sharing arrangements or the lack of them. In contrast to previous constitutions and the 1992 Federation Treaty,[37] the 1993 Constitution treats all of the subjects of the federation equally in terms of sharing power with the federal government. There is one difference, but it does not significantly affect the legal status of the subjects of the federation. Under Article 5 the republics are referred to as states and are given the right to adopt their own constitutions and elect their own legislative bodies. The other subjects of the federation are entitled to their own charters and legislative bodies.

There are three basic types of jurisdiction under the 1993 Constitution. First, Article 71 lists the powers of the federal government which are to be exercised for the benefit of all of Russia (in certain instances these may be inconsistent with the interests of some of the subjects of the federation). Second, Article 72 enumerates the joint jurisdiction, shared by the federal government and the subjects of the federation, which makes it possible to accommodate the interests of some regions to the fullest extent possible. Third, unspecified by the constitution and outside the authority of the first and second types of jurisdiction, is the power that the subjects of the federation can exercise independently. The constitution also provides a degree of flexibility by allowing the federal government and the subjects of the federation to delegate to each other a portion of their constitutionally mandated jurisdiction by mutual consent and without prejudicing their jurisdictional status.

Under the Federation Treaty and the 1993 Constitution the relationship between the federal government and each of the subjects of the federation is regulated by 'custom-made', power-sharing arrangements—a process which was originally initiated with the republics because they were legally and organizationally more advanced. Later, other types of subjects of the federation became involved. The inclusion of such arrangements in formal treaties is regulated in part by a presidential decree issued by Yeltsin.[38]

Udmurtia possesses one-third of Russia's CW stockpile, and its relationship with the federal government can be used to illustrate the evolving pattern of such relations and their implications for chemical demilitarization. The 1995 so-called Power Sharing Treaty—signed by President Yeltsin, Prime Minister Chernomyrdin and the Udmurt leadership—specifies that 'the matters of destruction of chemical weapons, poisonous substances and other weapons of

[37] The 1992 treaty consists of 3 agreements. One of them, the Agreement on the Prerogatives and Powers between the Federal Authorities of the Russian Federation and Those of the Republics Within the Russian Federation of 31 Mar. 1992, was not signed by Chechnya and Tatarstan. The 1992 treaty was the formal mechanism by which the Russian Federation Government established legal jurisdiction over its subjects (i.e., the constituent republics and local and regional bodies). Salmin, A. M., 'Russia's emerging statehood in the national security context', ed. V. Baranovsky, *Russia and Europe: The Emerging Security Agenda* (Oxford University Press: Oxford, 1997), pp. 112–13,

[38] [On the approval of the procedures for drafting power sharing arrangements between the federal authorities and Russian Federation subjects and for mutual transfer of parts of their jurisdiction], Presidential decree no. 370, 12 Mar. 1996, *Rossiyskaya Gazeta*, 14 Mar. 1996 (in Russian).

mass destruction' present in Udmurtia fall under 'the joint jurisdiction of the Russian Federation and the Udmurt Republic'.[39] Article 3 of the treaty states that 'before a federal law on the specific area of joint jurisdiction is enacted, the Udmurt Republic can exercise the right to legally regulate this particular area of jurisdiction on its own'.

At the local level there is concern about the threat chemical demilitarization could pose to people and the environment, and this has led to increased involvement, both directly and indirectly, by the relevant local institutions. In 1996 the Udmurt Government formed the Ministry for Natural Resources and Environmental Protection, a new ministry whose major function is to coordinate nature preservation activities and monitor the environment. The Law of the Udmurt Republic on Administrative Liability for Ecological Violations entered into force on 29 June 1996.[40] It gives the new ministry the power to investigate violations and punish those responsible for them in cases of non-compliance with the conclusions of environmental assessments (ekologicheskaya ekspertiza), providing delayed or distorted information, preventing state bodies or public organizations from conducting environmental monitoring and committing of other offences. Such matters are clearly relevant to chemical demilitarization. However, there is a potential for conflict with the federal government and the measures which it intends to implement.

An additional complication is that in some of the subjects of the federation the local legislation is at odds with federal law. Udmurtia has generally experienced close cooperation and coordination with the federal government, but other subjects of the federation have had difficulties. For example, the Constitution of the Republic of Tuva outlawed private land ownership, even though the 1993 Constitution explicitly permits such ownership. The Constitution of the Republic of Chuvashia contravened federal law by stating that conscripts from Chuvashia could do military service only in Chuvashia. President Yeltsin has set up a presidential commission to bring the constitutions and the charters of the subjects of the federation into line with Russia's Constitution. Unless the trend is reversed and the varying legislation properly coordinated the Russian Federation is in danger of evolving into a loose confederation. Naturally, this would have implications for demilitarization efforts.

Russian CW destruction faces serious challenges from the resistance of some subjects of the federation to conduct destruction on their territories. The Bryansk oblast, for instance, is strongly opposed to such activities, and its legislative body has enacted a ban on CW destruction. This opposition is not surprising, however, because the Bryansk oblast was severely affected by the Chernobyl disaster: 39 000 hectares of land could no longer be used for farming; a large amount of timber could not be used because it was radioactive; and 28 communities were forced to move from the area most affected. It remains to be seen whether or not the federal government will be able, by a combination of 'sticks and carrots', to convince the Bryansk oblast and other similarly minded oblasts to change their positions. If the oblasts persist in maintaining their cur-

---

[39] [Treaty on the Delineation of Jurisdiction and Powers Between the Bodies of State Administration of the Russian Federation and the Bodies of State Administration of the Udmurt Republic of 17 October 1995], *Udmurtskaya Pravda,* 24 Oct. 1995 (in Russian).

[40] [The Law of the Udmurt Republic on Administrative Liability for Ecological Violations], *Udmurtskaya Pravda*, 19 June 1996 (in Russian).

rent point of view, it may not be possible to conduct destruction at the CW storage sites—the approach that the Russian Federation has declared it prefers.

Protection of health and the environment

The Russian Soviet Federal Socialist Republic (RSFSR) Law on Environmental Protection of 19 December 1991 was the first law to address environmental issues.[41] It remains valid despite its adoption prior to the emergence of Russia as an independent state. Article 40 states that environmental safety and the protection of health are the underlying principles which must guide feasibility studies and the design, construction and operation of industrial and other facilities. If these principles are not complied with the environmental protection and Sanitary and Epidemiological Oversight officials can stop such projects.

The Law on Security, adopted on 5 March 1992, defined environmental security as an important component of Russia's security.[42] The Interdepartmental Commission for Environmental Security of Russia's Security Council was established, and a presidential decree gave it responsibility for *inter alia* providing adequate protection to the population during the chemical, nuclear and other weapon destruction required by Russia's international obligations.[43]

The environmental rights specified in the constitution and in other laws require the timely provision of relevant information and compensation for damage caused by violation of environmental standards and regulations. Initially, the primary responsibility for enforcing environmental legislation was given to the Ministry for Environmental Protection and Natural Resources (Environmental Ministry), which had branches throughout Russia. It was later divided into the Ministry for Natural Resources and the State Committee for Environmental Protection. The Environmental Ministry had been empowered by its statutes 'to visit without impediment any facilities, offices and organizations (including those with restricted access), on the basis of established procedures, guarded areas and other sites, regardless of their departmental status . . . and conduct inspections, record their results in protocols, [and] develop binding instructions designed to rectify environmental violations'.[44] The Environmental Ministry was also empowered to suspend the operation of any facility, whether state or privately owned, if it violated environmental requirements and could instruct the Finance Ministry to cease funding a project which had violated environmental regulations. Environmental crimes are given high priority in the Criminal Code of the Russian Federation which entered into force on 1 January 1997. Articles 246 and 247 address violations of environmental standards and regulations during the conduct of work and the handling of dangerous substances and wastes and provide a punishment of up to 5 to 8 years imprisonment for such violations.

Despite the stringent environmental legislation which exists, it remains to be seen whether the new Environmental Committee will be able to prevail over the powerful Ministry of Defence—widely recognized as the largest violator and polluter but one that, for the most part, goes unpunished. The curtailment of the

[41] *Vedomosti Verkhovnogo Soveta* [Supreme Soviet Gazette], no. 10 (1992), art. 457.

[42] *Vedomosti Verkhovnogo Soveta* [Supreme Soviet Gazette], no. 15 (1992), art. 769–70.

[43] Presidential decree no. 2211, 18 Dec. 1993, *Sbornik Aktov Prezidenta i Pravitelstva RF* [Collection of acts by the RF President and Government], no. 29 (1993), art. 2675.

[44] Federal government edict no. 375, 23 April 1994, *Rossiyskaya Gazeta*, 17 May 1994 (in Russian).

powers of the Federal Nuclear and Radiation Safety Authority (Gosatomnad-zor) may set a precedent for chemical demilitarization efforts and illustrates how the military can resist civilian supervision. The MOD opposed Gosatom-nadzor's attempts to exercise its supervisory functions at military nuclear facilities. Yeltsin's presidential decree no. 350 of 26 July 1995 was surprising because it gave the MOD, rather than Gosatomnadzor, the task of implementing federal supervision of nuclear radiation safety as regards the development, manufacturing, testing, operation, storage and disposal of nuclear weapons and military nuclear power plants. The decree was a dramatic and controversial departure from the original objective of empowering Gosatomnadzor with uni-form supervisory functions applicable both to military and civilian nuclear facilities. Prior to the decree Gosatomnadzor inspectors were generally pre-vented by the MOD from visiting its facilities on the pretext that Gosatomnad-zor employees lacked appropriate military security clearance, despite the fact that Gosatomnadzor was legally empowered to carry out inspections. A similar response is feasible as regards chemical demilitarization.

Such clashes of departmental interests seemed more likely following the entry into force of the Law on Environmental Assessment.[45] The law was based on the assumption that any industrial or other project could be potentially haz-ardous to the environment, and initial approval of any project was contingent on a positive assessment by specially authorized experts of the Environmental Ministry (now the Environmental Committee). Under the law subsequent legis-lation or presidential decrees are subject to environmental assessment before they can enter into force. Under Article 18 if a draft international agreement does not comply with the requirement for mandatory environmental assessment it could be rendered invalid at a later stage.

An additional complication is provided by the fact that the law makes it pos-sible to launch a parallel 'public environmental assessment' involving non-governmental experts. If conducted in compliance with the relevant regulations, such an assessment would have the same impact as a government assessment. A public environmental assessment can be initiated by individuals and public organizations, including their local branches. However, a provision in Article 20 prohibits a public environmental assessment if the data involved are state or commercial secrets or classified information.

There is also controversy about how environmental jurisdiction is divided between the federal government and the subjects of the federation. The 1993 Constitution provides general guidelines which emphasize the exclusive role of federal jurisdiction in order to enable the government to pursue one environ-mental policy for Russia, but lack of details and clarification has led to over-lapping of numerous legislative initiatives. Moreover, prior to the signing of the Federation Treaty and adoption of the 1993 Constitution, the subjects of the federation had enacted their own environmental legislative acts, which conflict with federal laws in some instances. A similar problem is faced by the adminis-trations of the subjects of the federation because the governmental bodies often enact their own environmental acts without adequate regard for their legality and compatibility with existing regional or federal legislation.

---

[45] Law on Environmental Assessment [ekologicheskaya ekspertiza], 23 Nov. 1995, *Sobranie Zakono-datelstva RF* [Collection of RF legislation], no. 48 (1995), art. 4556 (in Russian).

The role of public organizations and local governmental bodies

There is a significant legal gap in the Russian CW demilitarization programme as regards the role of public organizations and local governmental bodies. As indicated above, the Law on CW Destruction no longer specifies the jurisdiction of local governmental bodies. The 1996 Federal Programme and the 1994 and 1995 government edicts on Gorny and Kambarka mention only the general concept of 'developing positive attitudes among the local population and public organizations toward the issue of CW destruction'.[46] However, confusion existed as to the specific agency responsible for this activity. The Federal Programme assigned responsibility to the Presidential Committee; government edicts assigned it to the MOD. Specific projects were not named, but dissemination of information and cooperation with regional media were encouraged.

Disregard for the role of public organizations and local governmental bodies had blocked earlier government efforts to initiate a nationwide chemical demilitarization programme. Attempts at totalitarian imposition of the will of the federal government on the local communities where chemical weapons were to be destroyed failed at least twice in the late 1980s (at Chapayevsk in the Samara oblast and, later, in Novocheboksarsk in Chuvashia). The local population was not informed about the planned CW destruction projects and protested so violently when it became known what the government intended that the government was forced to change its plans.

The growing body of relevant laws makes it imperative that recognition be given to the role of public organizations and local governmental bodies. The 1995 Law on Environmental Assessment first clarified their potential input to CW demilitarization efforts.[47] Opponents to the 1997 Law on CW Destruction claim that it was drafted and approved in violation of the 1995 law. Tamara Zlotnikova, Chairperson of the Duma Committee on Environment, has stated that the 1997 law 'is not only a threat to the country's ecological safety, but also a time bomb to the nation's genetic stock'.[48] She has stressed that the long-term implications of a large accident during CW destruction could be comparable to those of the Chernobyl disaster.

The Law on Public Associations is also relevant.[49] Its Article 17 stresses that issues affecting the interests of public associations are dealt with by state and local governmental bodies together with relevant public associations or in coordination with them. They have become powerful players under the law, which enables them to propose legislative and other initiatives, distribute publications, organize meetings, demonstrations and picketing, and so on. The Law on the General Principles of Organizing Self-Government in the Russian Federation specifies how local communities can express their wishes by legal acts, local referendums, citizen law-making initiatives (narodnaya pravotvorcheskaya initsiativa), and the like.[50] This law and the constitution define their area of juris-

---

[46] Notes 10 and 36.

[47] Note 45.

[48] Subbotina, Y. [We are threatened by a chemical Chernobyl], *Moskovskaya Pravda*, 28 Feb. 1997 (in Russian).

[49] [Law on public associations], Federal law no. 89-FZ, 25 May 1995, *Solidarnost*, no. 13 (1995) (in Russian)

[50] [Law on the general principles of organizing self-government in the Russian Federation], Federal law no. 154-FZ, 28 Aug. 1995, *Rossiyskaya Gazeta*, 1 Sep. 1995 (in Russian).

diction as *inter alia* 'local issues'. However, the presence of a CW destruction facility in a community could expand the meaning of 'local issues' to include the effect of chemical demilitarization on the local population. The mood in Shchuchye (Kurgan oblast) can be gauged by an April 1997 letter from local leaders to President Yeltsin expressing dissatisfaction with the way the 1350 citizens of Shchuchye had been treated by the federal government: 'It is depressing to feel like hostages without any rights'.[51]

VIII. Conclusions

Russia's efforts related to CW destruction have coincided with a dramatic societal transformation which has enabled chemical demilitarization to be structured in a democratic and open manner. However, the Russian legal system continues to undergo change and modernization. Evolution towards a society based on the rule of law and on democratic norms and standards is slow, and the work on legislation regarding chemical demilitarization reflects this.

The principal difficulty is the novelty of the exercise. Neither Russia nor its predecessor the USSR had ever undertaken such a large demilitarization project. Past such efforts were conducted on a smaller scale without the need for an elaborate legislative apparatus. The previous situation was characterized by highly centralized decision making, limited transparency, lack of involvement of local communities or the public and little concern for the environmental implications of the demilitarization activities.

The legal basis of CW demilitarization is constrained by serious gaps in other areas such as ambiguous power-sharing arrangements between the federal government and the subjects of the federation. Some of these gaps are being filled independent of the drafting and adoption of CW demilitarization legislation or concurrent with such activities. This can lead to the need for revision and updating and may create delays and confusion in implementation of laws.

Russia is a country with limited democratic legislation and institutions, and it must overcome numerous problems before the rule of law prevails. Officials often fail to recognize the need to implement enacted legislation and instead tend to base their actions on departmental instructions and similar types of guidance. There is a lack of civilian leadership and excessive secrecy in the military, which has led to a situation in which the Ministry of Defence is unenthusiastic about supporting effective and transparent CW destruction legislation. Lack of funding is also a factor, and even the best legal system will break down if inadequately funded.[52] Russia's financial problems have negatively affected the rule of law and the creation and implementation of legislation for orderly and safe disposal of the Russian chemical weapon stockpile.

---

[51] [Terrorism and chemical weapons: rather compatible things], *Obshchaya Gazeta*, 8–15 May 1997 (in Russian).

[52] According to Duma sources only approximately 5% of the 1996 budget allocation (less than 100 billion roubles, or $20 million) was spent on CW demilitarization projects. The 1997 budget originally provided approximately 120 billion roubles ($24 million)—prior to a mid-year across-the-board budget reduction of approximately 20% owing to a revenue shortfall. The Mar. 1996 Federal Programme for CW Destruction estimated total expenditures on CW demilitarization for 1996 and 1997 at 144 billion roubles and 2.096 trillion roubles, respectively (in Jan. 1995 prices, approximately $36 million and $524 million).

4. Chemical weapon destruction requirements of the CWC

JOHN HART

I. Introduction

The Chemical Weapons Convention consists of 24 articles and three annexes: the Annex on Chemicals, the Annex on Implementation and Verification (also called the Verification Annex) and the Annex on the Protection of Confidential Information (also referred to as the Confidentiality Annex).[1]

Paragraph 2 of Article I obliges each state party to destroy all chemical weapons[2] which it 'owns or possesses, or that are located in any place under its jurisdiction or control'. The declaration and destruction provisions for chemical weapons are located in Articles III and IV and Part IV(A) of the Verification Annex. The convention requires that chemical weapons be destroyed in 'an essentially irreversible way to a form unsuitable for production of chemical weapons'.[3] A party may not destroy chemical weapons through 'dumping in any body of water, land burial or open-pit burning'.[4]

Paragraph 10 of Article IV requires each party which is engaged in CW destruction activities to 'assign the highest priority to ensuring the safety of people and to protecting the environment'. International destruction requirements do not, however, supersede national environmental legislation. Paragraph 10 thus also states that 'Each State Party shall transport, store and destroy chemical weapons in accordance with its national standards for safety and emissions'.

The CWC creates an international body to organize and oversee its implementation, the Organisation for the Prohibition of Chemical Weapons (OPCW). It consists of three parts: the Conference of the States Parties, the Executive Council and the Technical Secretariat (TS).

The Conference of the States Parties (also know as the Conference) consists of members of the OPCW, that is, countries which have signed and ratified the CWC. The Conference is charged with overseeing the implementation of the CWC, reviewing and approving procedural rules or recommendations submit-

---

[1] The breakdown is as follows: Preamble; Article I, General Obligations; Article II, Definitions and Criteria; Article III, Declarations; Article IV, Chemical Weapons; Article V, Chemical Weapons Production Facilities; Article VI, Activities not Prohibited under this Convention; Article VII, National Implementation Measures; Article VIII, The Organization; Article VIX, Consultations, Cooperation and Fact-Finding; Article X, Assistance and Protection against Chemical Weapons; Article XI, Economic and Technological Development; Article XII, Measures to Redress a Situation and to Ensure Compliance Including Sanctions; Article XIII, Relation to other International Agreements; Article XIV, Settlement of Disputes; Article XV, Amendments; Article XVI, Duration and Withdrawal; Article XVII, Status of the Annexes; Article XVIII, Signature; Article XIX, Ratification; Article XX, Accession; Article XXI, Entry into Force; Article XXII, Reservations; Article XXIII, Depositary; and Article XXIV, Authentic Texts. The Convention on the Prohibition of the Development, Production, Stockpiling and Use of Chemical Weapons and on their Destruction (corrected version), 8 Aug. 1994, is reproduced on the SIPRI Chemical and Biological Warfare Project Internet site at URL <http://www.sipri.se/cbw/docs/cw-cwc-texts.html>.

[2] Annexe A in this volume provides the CWC definition of 'chemical weapons' and other terms.

[3] Part IV(A) of the Verification Annex, para. 12.

[4] Part IV(A) of the Verification Annex, para. 13.

ted to it by the Executive Council and reviewing scientific and technological developments which could affect the implementation of the CWC.[5]

The Executive Council is the executive branch of the OPCW. Among other activities, the Executive Council is responsible for concluding agreements or arrangements with states and organizations on behalf of the OPCW, considering and submitting draft programmes and budgets for the OPCW and overseeing implementation of the CWC.

The Technical Secretariat is headed by a Director-General and is responsible for carrying out inspections and verifying compliance with the CWC. As such it also oversees the destruction of chemical weapons.

Paragraph 1 of Article II of the convention defines a chemical weapon as consisting of one or more of the following: (a) toxic chemicals and their precursors except where intended for purposes not prohibited under the CWC, as long as the types and quantities are consistent with such purposes; (b) munitions and devices which are specifically designed to cause harm or death through the use of such toxic chemicals; or (c) any equipment which is specifically designed to be used directly in connection with the munitions and devices, as defined above.

Toxic chemicals and precursors are categorized in three 'schedules'. Each schedule in turn is divided into sections A and B. Section A consists of toxic chemicals, and section B lists their precursors. Chemicals were placed in schedules in an attempt to reflect the relative risk which each chemical poses to the convention in relation to its commercial utility.

Schedule 1 chemicals are chemicals which pose a high risk to the convention. Lewisite, sulphur and nitrogen mustard, and all nerve agents are included in Schedule 1. Two toxins, ricin and saxitoxin, are also included. The chemical components of binary weapons and nerve agent precursors are among the chemicals in section B.

Schedule 2 chemicals are chemicals which represent a significant risk to the convention. Some of them are precursors to Schedule 1 chemicals. Schedule 3 chemicals are chemicals which present some risk to the convention. Each of the toxic chemicals listed in part A of Schedule 3 was used as a chemical weapon in World War I.[6]

II. Obligations for parties after entry into force

A party is required *inter alia* to: (a) declare whether it owns or possesses chemical weapons in any place under its jurisdiction or control, (b) declare any direct or indirect transfer or receipt of chemical weapons at any time since 1 January 1946, and (c) submit a general destruction plan for all chemical weapons which it is obligated to declare within 30 days after the CWC enters into force for the party.[7] A party must submit annual detailed plans for chemical weapons to be

---

[5] Article VIII, para. 21.

[6] These chemicals were, however, originally developed for non-military purposes.

[7] Article III, para. 1. Declaration requirements can be found in Articles III and IV and Part IV(A) of the Verification Annex.

destroyed[8] as well as annual declarations on the implementation of destruction.[9] The party must also certify the completion of the destruction of chemical weapons to the Technical Secretariat within 30 days after it has been completed.[10] Some of the specific information which must be submitted to the TS includes: (*a*) the aggregate quantity of each chemical and the total weight of each chemical by storage site, (*b*) the name, geographic coordinates and a detailed map of each CW storage facility, (*c*) the International Union of Pure and Applied Chemistry nomenclature of all chemicals being declared (including chemical components to binary and multi-component weapons), and (*d*) the number of filled and unfilled munitions.

The Preparatory Commission[11] developed a Declaration Handbook which contains the forms that a state must submit to meet its declaration obligation. The appendices describe various codes. Appendix 2, for example, lists approximately 400 chemicals which fall under one of the three schedules. The molecular formulas of the chemicals and their Chemical Abstracts Service (CAS) registry numbers are also provided.[12] There are also specialized codes for chemical industry declarations, country codes and a data dictionary. Changes and additions to the format of the Declaration Handbook will continue, especially with respect to Appendix 2. Declarations may be marked as OPCW Restricted, OPCW Protected or OPCW Highly Protected, in that order of sensitivity.[13]

III. Order of destruction

The rate of destruction of chemical weapons is defined by an 'order of destruction' under which scheduled chemicals and their parts and components, as well as unfilled munitions, devices and equipment, are placed in one of three categories.[14] Category 1 chemical weapons consist of Schedule 1 chemicals, their parts and components. Category 2 chemical weapons are chemicals which are not on Schedule 1 and their parts and components. Category 3 chemical weapons are unfilled munitions, devices and equipment 'specifically designed for use directly in connection with employment of chemical weapons'.[15]

A different order of destruction applies to each category. During the Conference on Disarmament negotiations which resulted in the CWC a linear destruction timetable was initially envisaged. Progressive destruction timetables were later introduced for category 1 chemical weapons, however, in an attempt to

---

[8] Part IV(A) of the Verification Annex, Article IV, para. 7(a), 29.

[9] Article IV, para. 7(b). The first set of annual declarations must be submitted 60 days before the start of each annual destruction period. The second set of annual declarations are due no later than 60 days after the end of the annual destruction period.

[10] Article IV, para. 7(c).

[11] The Preparatory Commission (PrepCom) was established in Feb. 1993 to set up the infrastructure of the OPCW and develop implementation procedures. Stock, T., Geissler, E. and Trevan, T., 'Chemical and biological arms control', *SIPRI Yearbook 1995: Armaments, Disarmament and International Security* (Oxford University Press: Oxford, 1995), p. 729.

[12] Note by the Executive Secretary, PrepCom document PC-XIV/B/8, 26 July 1996.

[13] See, e.g., Marking of confidential information, PrepCom document PC-X/B/WP.2, 15 Dec. 1994, section 3.3.2.1, para. 1. The official OPCW policy on confidentiality, formally adopted by the First Conference of the States Parties (which met on 6–23 May 1997), is contained in OPCW document C-I/DEC.13, 16 May 1997.

[14] Part IV(A) of the Verification Annex, paras 15–23.

[15] Part IV(A) of the Verification Annex, para. 16.

Table 4.1. Destruction of category 1 chemical weapons

Phase	Time period[a]	Minimum amount of CW which must be destroyed (%)
1	Years 1–3	1 (by the end of year 3)
2	Years 3–5	20 (by the end of year 5)
3	Years 5–7	45 (by the end of year 7)
4	Years 7–10	100 (by the end of year 10)

[a] The years refer to time elapsed after entry into force of the CWC (29 April 1997), not to entry into force of the CWC for a particular state party.

Source: Part IV(A) of the Verification Annex of the Chemical Weapons Convention, para. 17(a).

help facilitate the destruction of chemical weapons in Russia.[16] It should be emphasized that certain provisions of the order of destruction became effective when the CWC entered into force on 29 April 1997 and are not affected by the date when the convention enters into force for a particular party.

The destruction of category 1 chemical weapons is divided into four 'phases' (see table 4.1).[17] Destruction must begin not later than two years after the convention has entered into force for the party.

Within the first year after the convention enters into force for a party, the destruction of category 2 and category 3 chemical weapons must begin. By the end of the fifth year after entry into force of the convention, all category 2 and 3 chemical weapons must be destroyed (see table 4.2).

Destruction must occur at a rate no slower than that which would occur if the category 2 chemical weapons were destroyed in equal increments over these five years. If a state has 5 tonnes of category 2 chemical weapons, for example, the amount destroyed cannot be less than 1 tonne in any given year. The same principle applies to category 3 chemical weapons. A party may also destroy category 2 and 3 chemical weapons in equal increments from the end of year 1 through the end of year 5. A party is not precluded from destroying its chemical weapons at a faster rate.

The unit of comparison for measuring the destruction of category 1 and 2 chemical weapons is based on chemical weight. The unit of comparison for measuring the destruction of category 3 chemical weapons is based on volume for 'munitions' and 'devices' and by number for 'equipment'.

Possibilities for extension of destruction deadlines

Modification of the destruction deadlines are envisaged in the CWC for category 1 chemical weapons only.[18]

---

[16] Krutsch, W. and Trapp, R., *A Commentary on the Chemical Weapons Convention* (Martinus Nijhoff: Dordrecht, 1994), p. 345.

[17] The phases are as follows: phase 1, the first 3 years after entry into force; phase 2, years 3–5; phase 3, years 5–7; and phase 4, years 7–10.

[18] The destruction deadline extension provisions are outlined in Part IV(A) of the Verification Annex, paras 20–28.

Table 4.2. Destruction of category 2 and 3 chemical weapons

Time period[a]	Destruction requirement
End of year 1	Destruction must have begun
End of year 5	100 % of all category 2 and 3 CW must be destroyed

[a] The years refer to time elapsed after entry into force of the CWC (29 April 1997), not to entry into force of the CWC for a particular state party.

Source: Part IV(A) of the Verification Annex of the Chemical Weapons Convention, para. 17(b).

Request for extension within 120 days after entry into force of the convention

A party may find that it will be unable to achieve the level of destruction required at the end of phase 1, 2 or 3 because of reasons beyond its control. In such a case it must submit a proposed change of an intermediate destruction deadline to the Technical Secretariat within 120 days after entry into force of the convention.[19]

Request for intermediate destruction deadline extension

A party may also request the Executive Council to grant an extension of an intermediate destruction deadline for category 1 chemical weapons if the request is made at least 180 days before the intermediate destruction deadline. The party is obliged to submit proposed changes individually. An extension of an intermediate destruction deadline does not change the overall obligation of the party to destroy its category 1 chemical weapons within 10 years after entry into force of the convention.

Request for extension of final destruction deadline

In addition, a party may request the Executive Council to extend the final destruction deadline for category 1 chemical weapons. Such a request must be submitted no later than 9 years after entry into force of the CWC.[20] In such cases, an extension of up to 5 years may be granted. If the extension is granted the party must also submit a report to the Executive Council on its destruction activities (in addition to the detailed annual destruction plans which are required regardless of whether or not an extension has been granted).

Binary and multi-component weapons[21]

The order of destruction for binary or multi-component chemical weapons is subject to additional provisions. A figure representing the total amount of the toxic product for such weapons is calculated on a stoichiometric basis which assumes 100 per cent yield. The chemical components of the chemical weapons must be destroyed in a manner which reduces the total amount of their toxic

[19] The time limit applies to entry into force of the CWC, not entry into force of the convention for the party.
[20] See note 14.
[21] Part IV(A) of the Verification Annex, paras 18–19.

end-products. The toxic end-products must be treated as if they were category 1 or 2 chemical weapons which are neither binary nor multi-component. This is accomplished by determining the actual weight ratio between a so-called 'key component' and the remaining components. If there is an excess amount of a 'non-key component' (on the basis of the actual weight ratio), the excess amount must be destroyed in the first two years after the start of destruction.

IV. Discussion

The purpose of an inspection regime is to determine the extent and nature of the CW stockpiles and to verify that they have been destroyed. Costs associated with implementation of the convention can be reduced to some extent in a number of ways. The inspected party is responsible for the direct costs of verification of the destruction of chemical weapons. In other words, the party is responsible for all additional costs incurred by each inspection.[22] Any measures which limit the level of verification therefore will tend to reduce overall costs. This can be achieved by designing CW destruction facilities bearing in mind that they will be subject to a verification regime. Such facilities should be designed to give maximum assurance that chemical weapons cannot be easily diverted during the destruction process. Maintaining a strict and transparent inventory of items from storage to ultimate destruction and allowing the inspectors to take samples throughout the destruction process would enhance confidence that diversion would be unlikely to occur. Efforts could be made to make CW destruction facility designs generally compatible with automatic monitoring equipment and verification measures. Increased use of continuous and automatic on-site monitoring would cost less than reliance on international inspectors, which would involve ensuring transport from the point of entry and other more costly measures.[23]

Chemical agents must be destroyed to such an extent that they can no longer be readily used as weapons.[24] Munitions, devices and equipment should also be destroyed in a manner which precludes their use for the purpose for which they were designed. Following their destruction, however, it should be possible to determine the original nature of the objects. Uncertainties regarding the original nature of destroyed items would probably lead to additional verification measures.

If the verification provisions of other disarmament agreements are deemed consistent with those of the CWC, the Executive Council may limit verification measures.[25] Such a situation might also allow for a reduction in the costs of

---

[22] In the case of Russia the cost of international inspections by the OPCW has been estimated at $3–4 million per year. It is unclear whether these cost estimates assume that a bilateral destruction agreement between Russia and the USA will be in effect at the time the OPCW implements a verification regime in Russia. Deen, T., 'EU nations will sponsor disposal of Russian arms', *Jane's Defence Weekly*, vol. 28, no. 20 (19 Nov. 1997), p. 5.

[23] The costs of verification which can be charged to the inspected party under Articles IV and V are listed in Decision, programme and budget and working capital fund, OPCW document C-I/DEC.74, 23 May 1997, pp. 59–61.

[24] Part IV(A) of the Verification Annex, para. 12.

[25] Article IV, para. 13.

verification under the provisions of the convention. However, opinions differ as to whether the overall costs would be less in such a case.[26]

Only those states which had ratified the CWC by the time it entered into force can maximize the time allotted to them for destruction. If a state ratifies the convention after the 10-year destruction period, it is obligated to destroy its weapons 'as soon as possible'. The Executive Council will also impose a 'stringent' verification regime on such states,[27] and because the inspected party must pay for all of the direct costs of inspection, the overall destruction costs will almost certainly be higher.

States which are not parties to the CWC face restrictions on chemical trade. Parties, for example, are prohibited from transferring Schedule 1 and Schedule 2 chemicals to states which are not parties to the convention.[28]

Following the entry into force of the CWC many technical difficulties in implementing the convention were experienced.[29] For example, there was a tendency by parties to mark all or most of the information contained in their initial declaration to the Technical Secretariat as Highly Protected, the highest security classification. Since only personnel with a P-3 or higher rank are allowed to process such information, this contributed to the increased workload which the TS experienced immediately after entry into force of the convention. In addition, a larger than anticipated number of declarations were submitted to the TS in paper form, rather than using the Electronic Document Managing System. Not all of the information was in the standardized format, which also caused delays in processing the information into a more usable form. A significant number of parties failed to designate a point of entry for the OPCW inspectors, communicate standing diplomatic clearance for non-scheduled aircraft to the Technical Secretariat, pay the full amount of their contribution to the OPCW, submit the initial declaration on time or pass all of the necessary domestic implementing legislation. In addition to hiring and training large numbers of new personnel, the TS spent substantial time concluding hundreds of facility agreements and conducting the required initial inspections. In general, such problems could only be fully resolved by the implementation of the

[26] There has been long-standing support of the view that, given the comparatively large number of CW-related facilities which must be inspected in Russia and the USA, other parties should not be obliged to pay the additional costs of verification to the OPCW of such facilities if a bilateral destruction agreement between Russia and the USA were not in force when the OPCW implements its verification regime. I.e., any difference in verification costs because of the absence of a Russian–US destruction agreement ought to be covered by the inspected parties. This view is reflected in a decision taken by the First Conference of the States Parties which states that the costs of recruitment, training and salaries for the additional inspectors which would be needed in the absence of such a bilateral destruction agreement 'can be attributed to Member States' obligations under Article IV, paragraph 16 or Article V, paragraph 19'. The decision makes clear, however, that this and other related language apply to the 1997 OPCW budget only and should not be understood as setting a precedent for future budgets. OPCW document C-I/DEC.74 (note 23), p. 61. The text of the Agreement between the United States of America and the Union of Soviet Socialist Republics on the Destruction and Non-Production of Chemical Weapons and on Measures to Facilitate the Multilateral Convention on Banning Chemical Weapons is reproduced in *SIPRI Yearbook 1991: World Armaments and Disarmament* (Oxford University Press: Oxford, 1991), pp. 536–39.

[27] Article IV, para. 8.

[28] Part VI of the Verification Annex, para. 3; and Part VII of the Verification Annex, para. 31. Parties may transfer Schedule 2 chemicals up to 3 years after entry into force of the CWC. Certain restrictions on the trade of Schedule 3 chemicals are likely since parties are obligated to ensure that such chemicals are not used for purposes prohibited by the CWC. Part VIII of the Verification Annex, para. 26.

[29] Draft report of the organisation on the implementation of the convention (29 April–28 October 1997), OPCW document C-II/2, EC-VI/2, 31 Oct. 1997; and Report of the Executive Council on the performance of its activities (13 May–31 October 1997), OPCW document C-II/3, EC-VI/4, 7 Nov. 1997.

CWC and were, in fact, to be expected as the day-to-day activities of the OPCW were normalized. At the time of writing, December 1997, there was no indication that any party had purposely acted to circumvent the convention. The CWC has acted as a catalyst to initiate destruction programmes for old and abandoned chemical weapons and has stimulated existing destruction efforts. If sufficient relevant information is made available to the OPCW there is little reason that the CWC cannot be effectively implemented.

5. Destruction or conversion of Russian chemical weapon production facilities

JOHN A. GILBERT, HARVEY W. HUBBARD,
ROBERT F. PRUSZKOWSKI and MARK FELIPE

I. Introduction

The Chemical Weapons Convention imposes a number of obligations on its parties in addition to the requirement to destroy all chemical weapon stocks. In particular, parties must cease CW production at the entry into force of the CWC,[1] close and inactivate all chemical weapon production facilities (CWPFs) and destroy all such facilities within defined time-limits. In exceptional cases, CWPFs may be temporarily converted for use as CW destruction facilities or may be converted to other purposes not prohibited under the convention. Production facility conversion must be approved on a case-by-case basis by the Conference of States Parties (CSP) on the basis of recommendations by the Executive Council and the Director-General of the Technical Secretariat (TS).

Each party must cease CW production at entry into force if production had not already terminated when the party signed the CWC. It must also submit a comprehensive initial data declaration not later than 30 days after entry into force for the party.[2] This declaration must specify: CWPF locations, the chemical weapons which were produced, the production processes used, production capacity, history of production, a detailed inventory of all specialized and standard equipment, and other information about each declared production facility.

In addition to factual data about each CWPF each party must also specify the measures taken to close and inactivate it. Detailed plans for the destruction of each CWPF must be submitted to the TS not later than 180 days before destruction begins. In addition to systematic inspections of closed and inactivated facilities, the process of destruction at each facility may be subject to extensive observation and documentation by inspectors of the Organisation for the Prohibition of Chemical Weapons (OPCW). The cost of these inspections must be borne by the affected party. Once a CWPF has been completely destroyed in accordance with approved plans it is no longer subject to systematic inspection and new buildings can be constructed and equipment installed for any purpose not prohibited by the convention.

If a party intends to request approval of conversion, that fact must be noted in the initial declaration for each facility (which must be submitted not later than 30 days after entry into force of the convention for the party), along with the intended dates of proposed conversions. In particular, specific justification and conversion plans for each facility that a party converted prior to entry into force must be submitted not later than 30 days after the CWC enters into force for the party. In the case of a facility that has not been converted to non-prohibited

---

[1] The CWC entered into force on 29 April 1997. The Convention on the Prohibition of the Development, Production, Stockpiling and Use of Chemical Weapons and on their Destruction (corrected version), 8 Aug. 1994, is reproduced on the SIPRI Chemical and Biological Warfare Project Internet site at URL <http://www.sipri.se/cbw/docs/cw-cwc-texts.html>.

[2] Article XXI of the CWC addresses entry into force.

uses at entry into force for the party, detailed justification and conversion plans must be submitted not later than 30 days after the party makes a decision to convert, but in any case not later than four years after the CWC enters into force for the party. In all cases the Annex on Implementation and Verification (known as the Verification Annex) requires such conversion to be complete not later than six years after entry into force of the CWC—*not* six years after entry into force for the party.[3]

If approval is granted to convert a CWPF to other uses, it will be subject to verification or confidence-building measures. This means that the converted facility may be subject to substantially more systematic inspections on an annual basis than the four inspections per year conducted at each inactivated CWPF awaiting destruction. As an additional condition of conversion, inspectors will be granted unimpeded access to converted facilities at any time for a period of at least 10 years after conversion is complete. Verification measures could be extended even beyond the end of this period. As with inactivated CWPFs, the cost of inspecting converted facilities must be borne by the affected party.

II. CWC requirements affecting production facility destruction or conversion

Production facility destruction

The CWC defines CW production facilities as consisting of any equipment, as well as any building housing such equipment, that was designed, constructed or used at any time since 1 January 1946 as part of the production stage where material flows would contain any Schedule 1 chemical or any other chemical that has no non-prohibited use above 1 tonne per year but can be used for CW purposes.[4] The definition of CWPFs also includes equipment and buildings used for filling Schedule 1 chemicals into munitions, filling chemicals into binary containers or submunitions, loading containers into binary munitions, and loading submunitions into munitions.

On the basis of this comprehensive set of definitions, each party which produced chemical weapons is obligated to immediately close and inactivate all CWPFs and to later destroy all specialized and standard equipment falling within the definition of production equipment, all munition filling and loading equipment, and the buildings in which these types of equipment are located.

For states which are parties to the CWC at the time of entry into force, destruction of CWPFs must begin not later than the end of the first year after entry into force. Schedule 1 facility destruction must be complete not later than 10 years after entry into force and destruction of other (non-Schedule 1) CWPFs must be complete not later than 5 years after entry into force. The order of destruction for a particular party may vary, but certain percentages of productive capacity must be destroyed at intervening times. For states which accede after entry into force of the convention, CWPF destruction must still be

---

[3] Verification Annex, Part V, para. 72.
[4] Chemical Weapons Convention, Article II, para. 8 (a).

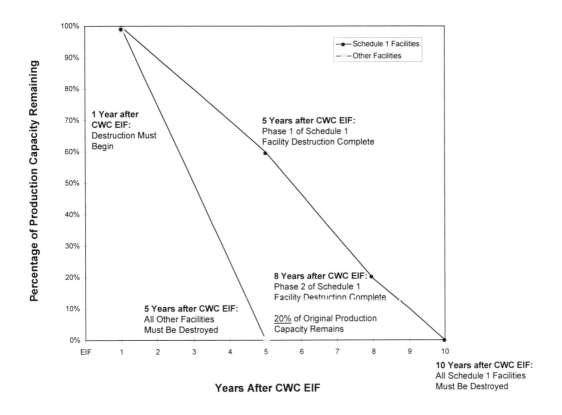

Figure 5.1. Representative order of destruction for an original party to the Chemical Weapons Convention

EIF = Entry into force.

Source: Based on analysis by the Science Applications International Corporation, McLean, Virginia, of the order of the destruction provisions outlined in the CWC Verification Annex, Part V, para. 30 (a).

completed at the end of 5 or 10 years, but the order and rate of destruction may be significantly compressed.

The order of destruction of CWPFs is based on the principle of 'levelling out'. This means that percentages of the original production capacity must be destroyed in three specified time intervals (years 2–5, 6–8 and 9–10 after entry into force of the convention). Key factors determining the actual rate of destruction are recognition of the fact that destruction efficiency is expected to increase over time and that sufficient production capacity must be destroyed during the first two periods to reach the residual level of production capacity agreed to remain undestroyed at the end of the second period (i.e. at eight years after entry into force of the CWC). Figure 5.1 illustrates this for an eighth-year residual level equal to 20 per cent of original production capacity. In this example, the affected party is required to destroy equipment and buildings representing varying proportions of production capacity each year, on average, to meet order of destruction requirements. This is shown in table 5.1.

Table 5.1. Average percentage of production capacity required to be destroyed per year after entry into force of the Chemical Weapons Convention

Years after entry into force of the CWC	Average % of other production capacity required be destroyed per year	Average % of Schedule 1 production capacity required to be destroyed per year
0–1	0	0
2–5	25	10
6–8	100	13.33
9–10	100	10

Source: Based on analysis by the Science Applications International Corporation, McLean, Virginia, of the order of the destruction provisions outlined in the CWC Verification Annex, Part V, para. 30 (a).

A state which accedes to the CWC after its entry into force is still required to complete equipment and building destruction by 5 and 10 years after entry into force, respectively. Accession delay can cause significant compression of the time allowed to complete destruction. Delay will also escalate the average yearly rate of required destruction prior to the 8-year point after entry into force of the CWC. Russia ratified the CWC on 5 November 1997 and became a party to it on 5 December 1997. Article V, paragraph 8 of the CWC requires a party to begin destruction of its CWPFs not later than one year after the convention enters into force for it. However, Russia's economic problems have delayed the destruction of its CWPFs and could delay the initiation of CWPF destruction beyond the one-year deadline. While such a delay would technically put Russia in non-compliance with the CWC here a case is illustrated in which Russia begins destruction of its CWPFs 2 years after entry into force of the convention. Figure 5.2 and table 5.2 illustrate the effects on the rate of production facility destruction using an assumed two-year delay in initiating destruction of Russian CWPFs.

For this case, where Russia begins destroying its CWPFs two years after entry into force of the convention, the rate of production facility destruction is 100 per cent greater in the second and third years after accession than the rate required in those years if Russia had been an original party to the convention and had begun destroying its CWPFS one year after entry into force of the CWC. As an added complication, the required rate of destruction of Schedule 1 production facilities in years 4–6 after Russian accession is one-third less than the rate required in years 2 and 3 after accession. This will complicate programme management, may lead to inefficient resource utilization in the critical mid-stage of Russia's CWPF destruction programme and could lead to an increase in the total cost of production facility destruction compared to the cost if Russia had been an original party. Obviously, further analysis is required before drawing firm conclusions, but Russia should carefully consider the effect of the delay in the start of destruction on total production facility destruction programme costs.

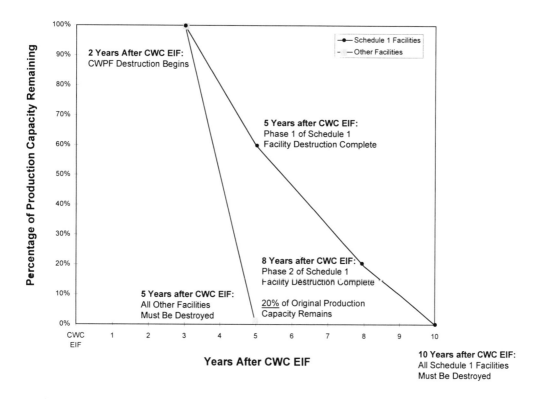

Figure 5.2. Representative order of destruction for a party to the Chemical Weapons Convention that begins destruction of chemical weapon production facilities two years after entry into force of the convention

EIF = Entry into force.

Source: Extrapolation by the Science Applications International Corporation, McLean, Virginia, of the percentage of capacity that must be destroyed to be in compliance with CWC requirements to destroy all CWPFs within 10 years after entry into force of the CWC.

Table 5.2. Average percentage of production capacity required to be destroyed per year after accession by a party to the Chemical Weapons Convention

Years after entry into force of the CWC[a]	Average % of other production capacity required be destroyed per year	Average % of Schedule 1 production capacity required to be destroyed per year
0–1	0	0
2–3	50	20
4–6	100	13.33
7–8	100	10

[a] Assuming that destruction of chemical weapon production facilities begins 2 years after entry into force of the CWC

Source: Based on analysis by the Science Applications International Corporation, McLean, Virginia, of the percentage of capacity that must be destroyed to be in compliance with CWC requirements to destroy all CWPFs within 10 years after entry into force of the CWC.

Conversion to non-prohibited uses

A party may request approval to convert CWPFs for purposes not prohibited by the convention. Article V of the CWC and the Verification Annex describe the process in as much detail as can be determined, but several factors following directly from CWC provisions are particularly important for Russia to consider in making decisions to pursue conversion versus destruction of its CWPFs. Some of the factors are discussed below.

Production facility conversion not a right. In fact, the CWC explicitly states that a party may request permission to convert a CWPF in 'exceptional cases of compelling need'.[5] Permission must also be sought on a case-by-case basis to operate a facility which may have been converted to non-prohibited uses prior to entry into force. Even if Russia submits all the required justifications and descriptions of steps to be taken to convert versus destroy a given CWPF, there can be no guarantee that the Conference of States Parties of the Organisation for the Prohibition of Chemical Weapons will approve such a request.

Approval of CWPF conversion requires preparation and submission of detailed plans in advance. If Russia intends to convert a CWPF, it must submit detailed plans in advance. Even in cases where a facility may have been converted to non-prohibited uses prior to entry into force, detailed plans must be prepared and submitted 30 days after entry into force for Russia. The information required for approval by the CSP may be in addition to the internal planning and programmatic information (such as schedules and plans for installation of new process equipment) necessary for the party to manage and carry out a conversion.

Converted facilities may be subject to more rigorous verification than inactivated facilities awaiting destruction. Article V, paragraph 15 of the CWC specifies that 'converted facilities shall be subject to systematic verification through on-site inspection and monitoring with on-site instruments'. Similar language in Article V, paragraph 3 applies to CWPFs in general. However, the Verification Annex makes a definitive statement that inspectors must be granted 'unimpeded access to the facility at any time' and also have a right to managed access to the entire plant site at which the facility is located for 10 years after the Director-General of the TS certifies that conversion is complete at each facility.[6] Even after 10 years, verification activities could continue indefinitely at the initiative of the Executive Council. By contrast, each inactivated CWPF awaiting destruction is subject to only four inspections per year.

The cost of verification will be borne by the party owning the affected CWPFs. Article V, paragraph 19 of the CWC specifies that each party must pay the cost of verification of CWPF inactivation, destruction or conversion. In practical terms, this means that the total cost of inspection activity must be added to the cost of conversion of the affected facilities in order to perform cost–benefit analyses of the economic viability of conversion versus destruction. Only in cases where complementary verification by the OPCW is in progress, such as if a bilateral agreement were in place with another CWC party,

---

[5] Chemical Weapons Convention, Article V, para. 13.
[6] Verification Annex, Part V, section D, para. 85.

would Russia be able to offset verification costs at its converted facilities, which would then be apportioned under the United Nations scale of assessment.

Production facility conversion is subject to time constraints. A party must submit a request for approval of conversion of CWPFs that are being used for non-prohibited purposes at entry into force not later than 30 days after entry into force for the party. For any facility a party desires to convert after entry into force for it, detailed plans must be submitted not later than 30 days after the decision is made to convert the facility. Both types of requests are subject to a period of review and consideration of the request and associated verification provisions. It is possible that the review and approval process alone could exceed 360 days for each request. Of additional importance is the fact that all requests for conversion must be submitted not later than four years after entry into force for the party. Furthermore, Part V, paragraph 72 of the Verification Annex requires all conversion to be completed not later than six years after CWC entry into force—*not* entry into force for the affected party.

In general, it appears reasonable to conclude that the CWC provisions affecting production facility conversion to non-prohibited uses are burdensome, time-consuming and potentially costly, and there is considerable uncertainty as to whether or not any specific request will be approved by the CSP.

Conversion to CW destruction facilities

CSP approval is not required for conversion of CWPFs to CW destruction facilities, and the process follows a less rigorous time-line for consideration. In such cases, only the TS and the party need to agree on the details of conversion, operation and verification. Although all facilities converted to CWPFs must be destroyed when CW destruction operations are complete (but not later than 10 years after entry into force of the CWC), there are no specific intermediate time-limits for conversion, such as the 6-year deadline after CWC entry into force for conversion to other non-prohibited uses. In fact, a party could legitimately decide several years after entry into force to convert a production facility to destroy chemical weapons, complete the process by 6 or more years after CWC entry into force, operate for a short period, then shut down and destroy the facility not later than 10 years after CWC entry into force.

Time-lines for approving destruction or conversion plans

The time-lines in figure 5.3 illustrate key milestones involved in the process of submitting, reviewing and approving plans for CWPF destruction or conversion. Part V of the Verification Annex specifies time-lines for submitting declarations for CWPFs that are to be destroyed. It also establishes the schedule for submission of plans for converting CWPFs to destruction facilities, or to facilities for non-prohibited uses. The time-line for conversion to non-prohibited use is particularly long. Not later than 30 days after the CWC enters into force for a party an initial conversion plan must be submitted to the Director-General of the TS. Conversion plans will be reviewed by the TS and submitted to the Executive Council, which then has 30 days to review them. The CSP will subsequently review the conversion plans *as soon as possible* after receiving the

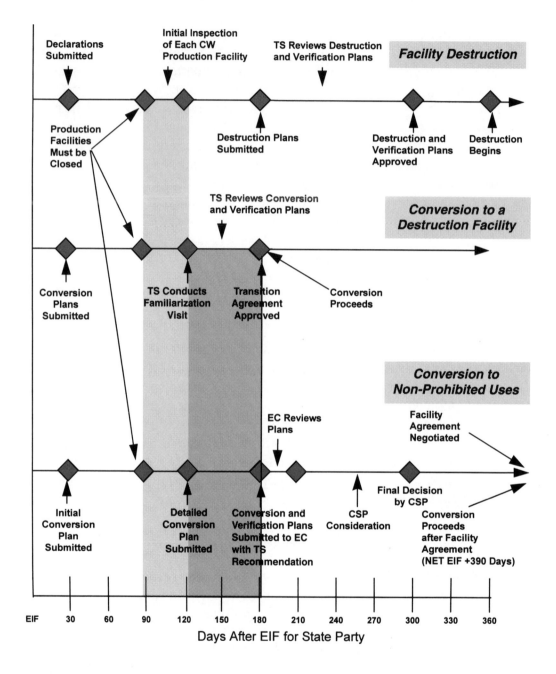

Figure 5.3. Time-lines for approval of individual chemical weapon production facility destruction and conversion plans

EIF = Entry into force.

Source: Based on the time-lines outlined in the Verification Annex, Part V.

Director-General's report on their feasibility. While the Verification Annex stipulates that consultations within the CSP regarding such conversion plans may take up to 90 days,[7] actual approval of such plans may be delayed, as the CSP meets only once a year unless it decides to hold extra sessions.

III. Key factors affecting the Russian CW production facility destruction programme

A number of factors can be expected to heavily influence the Russian CWPF destruction programme. Among them are technical, political and economic considerations, verification, time and international assistance. Any decisions to convert facilities to destroy chemical weapons or for other purposes not prohibited by the convention should take them fully into consideration.

In particular, Russia may want to consider the availability of international assistance and its potential for accelerating compliance with Russia's obligations under the CWC as well as providing reasonable economic payoffs for states or commercial firms which provide assistance and for Russia itself. Each major factor is discussed briefly in the following paragraphs, and some judgements are made as to how they could affect the Russian programme.

Technical considerations

Safe and efficient CWPF destruction or conversion involves many technical aspects. The following subsections discuss some of those that may have the greatest influence on destruction or conversion.

Contamination of process equipment and buildings

Based upon US experience with CWPF destruction, most equipment previously used to manufacture Schedule 1 material, all CW filling equipment and major portions of process buildings are likely to be unusable for any commercial purposes because of residual contamination. Decontamination of specialized and standard equipment and building materials to a degree which would permit safe disposal is generally feasible, and a number of technologies have been evaluated for decontamination effectiveness and environmental impact. Russia could save money by limited decontamination of surplus equipment, but this would add long-term risk if not done adequately. The most effective decontamination technologies result in destruction of equipment or application of decontamination procedures which would make any future reuse questionable from a safety and performance perspective.

Equipment condition, age and configuration

Russian CW production facilities probably contain equipment that was used exclusively for the production of toxic and highly corrosive material. Much of the equipment may have been built and installed 20 or more years ago. While the age of the equipment may not determine its economic viability, the installed

---

[7] Verification Annex, Part V, para. 75.

equipment may be of outdated design and unable to operate economically or efficiently. Furthermore, its exposure to corrosive materials over long periods of time may also render it unusable for commercial applications. In addition, these facilities were probably constructed to optimize CW production and may not be in suitable condition to support non-prohibited production without major refurbishment or reconfiguration.

Building condition and configuration

Chemical weapon production facility buildings were probably purpose-built for CW production and contain features that could make other uses difficult or inefficient. In particular, special negative-pressure, containment or high-efficiency filtration systems may be difficult to maintain and are unnecessary for the type of activity that would probably be permitted in converted buildings. Buildings that were not built with special features to support CW production may still be in poor condition if they have not been in regular use and/or maintained well.

Overall, these and other technical issues will generally be easier to deal with at facilities that are to be destroyed because the primary emphasis will be on safe and rapid decontamination, dismantlement and destruction. For converted facilities, additional complications will be the need to conduct extensive surveys to identify salvageable equipment and infrastructure, develop a technical plan to thoroughly decontaminate the facility and its equipment, dispose of unusable material and rebuild or extensively reconfigure the facility and equipment. In addition, as a precondition for conversion all specialized equipment at CWPFs must be destroyed and all special features of buildings that are associated with Schedule 1 production must be eliminated.[8]

Political considerations

As noted above, conversion of any CWPFs must be approved by the CSP, and approval is expected to be granted only in cases of compelling need following a careful review of conversion plans, verification measures to be applied and justification for each conversion request.

Most parties to the CWC have never produced chemical weapons and have no facilities to destroy or convert them. It may therefore be difficult to gain the approval of the CSP, whose members could view conversion as an attempt to subvert one of the CWC's fundamental obligations in order for the converting state to gain economic advantage. This was discussed by many parties and was one of the reasons that it has been difficult for the Preparatory Commission (PrepCom) and the OPCW to reach consensus on which conversion approval criteria will be used. If this rationale is adopted or accepted by a significant number of parties, approval of any conversion request may require exceptional justification, well-presented programme plans and extremely intensive verification—to be paid for by the party requesting approval to convert.

It is important to note that if even one party to the convention objects to approval of a conversion request, consultations must be held and the request

---

[8] Verification Annex, Part V, para. 70.

and any associated conditions must be taken as a matter of substance by the CSP. This means that consensus must be reached or, if consensus is not achieved, a two-thirds affirmative vote is required to approve each conversion request. Conversion requests made by a state which was not an original party or did not accede shortly after entry into force of the CWC might be particularly difficult to approve by consensus.

Economic considerations

The destruction of production facilities requires removal, decontamination and disposition of processing equipment followed by decontamination and dismantlement of production buildings and disposition of building materials. Conversion would still require extensive decontamination of process equipment and buildings, and residual equipment and infrastructure may not be able to be optimized for non-prohibited uses. This could lead to a situation in which initial expenses for decontamination, reconfiguration, and disposal of unserviceable equipment and building materials would be considerable for converted facilities, and it may be difficult to operate such facilities profitably once conversion is complete.

Verification

Verification of production facility closure, inactivation and destruction is expected to be relatively straightforward, and the number, duration and intensity of inspections will be somewhat predictable at facilities awaiting destruction. Although the direct inspection costs are borne by the affected party under the 'possessor pays' principle, the total cost of initial inspections and up to four systematic or routine inspections per year until each facility is destroyed will be controllable to some degree by the possessing party, which can choose to destroy facilities more rapidly than required. Of course, once a CWPF has been destroyed and the destruction is confirmed by the OPCW, systematic inspections—and their associated costs—will cease.

On the other hand, verification of conversion may be much more difficult since considerable activity may continue at and around affected facilities. As a result, inspections may take longer, be more intrusive, require extensive sampling and analysis to identify or confirm the absence of Schedule 1 or 2 material or other prohibited activity, and be conducted frequently since the number of inspections per year at converted facilities is not limited to four. Inspectors will also have a right to observe the entire plant site where the converted facility is located and conduct inspection activities under managed access. Although the OPCW's confidentiality policy will be in force, the extensive and intrusive presence of inspectors may lead to increased concerns over the inadvertent loss of confidential business information at converted facilities. This increased concern could make investment in converted facilities less attractive for some investors than similar investments made at facilities which have been destroyed and are no longer subject to inspection.

Time

The time required to destroy CWPFs may be much shorter than the time required to convert them. This is because facility-specific destruction plans are subject to review over a 180-day period before destruction begins at the affected facilities, while conversion requires submission of more detailed plans, at least one inspection, review by the Director-General of the Technical Secretariat, an affirmative recommendation by the Executive Council, and consideration and approval by the CSP. The conversion review process may take one year or more in each case and approval is not certain. In fact, disapproval of a conversion plan would require the subsequent destruction of facilities whose conversion was not approved, force at least a 180-day wait for approval of destruction plans and require additional time to complete. Overall, disapproval of conversion could force a heavy resource commitment by the affected party in order to meet its order of destruction requirements within required time-limits.

International assistance

Many states may be willing to assist Russia in meeting its CW stockpile and production facility destruction requirements. The United States has already committed over $134 million to assist the Russian CW stockpile destruction programme[9] and more money could be provided to assist in other ways, such as by helping to finance CWPF destruction. Other states, particularly Finland, Germany, the Netherlands and Sweden, have offered additional destruction and environmental protection assistance in the form of grants, credits, and access to technology.

No state has yet made or implied a public commitment to provide financial or technical support for Russian CWPF conversion programmes, even if they are approved by the CSP. In addition, recent statements by prominent US political figures have indicated that future US assistance may be contingent upon Russian ratification and implementation of strategic nuclear arms reduction treaties, full compliance with the CWC and assurances that certain other weapon programmes have been terminated. Given this environment, it is not possible to predict whether or not conversion of Russian CWPFs could attract US Government financial or technical support. However, private investors could be a source of funds to support Russian CWPF destruction and/or conversion. Their potential imperatives and expectations in offering such assistance are examined in more detail in sections VI and VII of this chapter.

IV. Potential solutions

There are a range of possible courses of action for Russia to consider in deciding how best to deal with the issue of CWPF destruction or conversion. Some of the options are: (*a*) destruction of all facilities in accordance with the order of destruction; (*b*) destruction of some facilities and conversion of others to CW destruction facilities; (*c*) destruction of some facilities and conversion of

---

[9] US Cooperative Threat Reduction Program, URL <http://www.ctr.osd.mil/17frame.html>, version current on 2 Mar. 1998.

others to non-prohibited uses; (*d*) destruction of some facilities, conversion of some to CW destruction facilities and conversion of others to non-prohibited uses; (*e*) conversion of all facilities; and (*f*) accelerated destruction of all facilities and subsequent use for non-prohibited purposes.

All of these alternatives can be fully compliant with the CWC, support the CWC's objective of preventing future CW production and are technically feasible if done properly. However, some can be approved and completed much sooner than others. The difficulty for Russia is in selecting the preferred alternative, which will require careful balancing of a number of factors, extensive analysis of each affected facility, evaluating economic aspects of the various courses of action and determining the degree to which international assistance or direct investment might be provided to assist in implementing Russia's preferred strategy.

V. Verification of production facility destruction and conversion

One important consideration in any decision to destroy or convert CWPFs is verification. The requirements for verification of production facility closure, inactivation and destruction are relatively clear and designed not to burden or unnecessarily delay the destruction process. On the other hand, verification activities related to converted facilities are far more rigorous, potentially more intrusive and may continue indefinitely at the option of the Executive Council, on the basis of recommendations of the Technical Secretariat. This is because of concern among the negotiators of the CWC regarding potential non-compliance at converted facilities, since some of the equipment and infrastructure remaining in place could facilitate such illegal activity. This section summarizes the inspection requirements for destroyed and converted facilities, notes the cost implications for Russia and the OPCW, and proposes a verification scheme intended to provide high confidence in the OPCW's ability to detect indications of non-compliance at converted facilities.

Inspection requirements

Some important requirements for inspecting destroyed and converted CW production facilities are summarized in table 5.3.

Verification cost considerations

As noted, inspections of converted CWPFs are expected to be more frequent, much more intensive, and to occur over a much longer time period than those of facilities which are destroyed. Each inspection of a CWPF in Russia may cost several tens of thousands of dollars and numerous inspections will be conducted every year at each facility. In particular, inspections of converted facilities will undoubtedly be far more expensive because inspection teams may be larger and will require more time to conduct each inspection. More samples will be collected and analysed, and inspections will probably occur more frequently than the four times per year expected for each facility awaiting destruction.

Table 5.3. Comparison of inspection requirements for CW production facilities awaiting destruction and for converted facilities

Key inspection requirements	Facilities awaiting destruction	Converted facilities
Inspections objectives	Confirm closure Confirm inactivation Review destruction plans Observe destruction activity Confirm facility destruction	Confirm closure Confirm inactivation (if applicable) Review proposed conversion plans Observe conversion activity Confirm conversion completion Confirm absence of Schedule 1 chemicals, by-products and degradation products Confirm absence of Schedule 2 chemicals Confirm continued compliance with approved conditions for conversion
Representative inspection activities	Visual observation Photography Limited sampling and analysis Installation of seals and tags Installation of continuous monitoring instruments	Visual observation Photography Extensive sampling and analysis Installation of seals and tags Installation of continuous monitoring instruments Record reviews Personnel interviews
Sampling and analyses	Generally limited in accordance with Facility Agreement	Generally unlimited
Number of systematic inspections per year at each site	Four	Unlimited
Inspector access within declared facility	Generally unlimited, but may be addressed in Facility Agreement	Unlimited
Inspector access to surrounding plant site	Not provided for	Yes, subject to managed access
When inspections cease	Upon confirmation of destruction	Not earlier than 10 years after conversion but could continue indefinitely

Source: Based on the inspection requirements outlined in the Verification Annex, Part V, C, paras 43–63.

As specified in the CWC[10] and in the Verification Annex,[11] the full costs of destruction, conversion and verification must be borne by the affected party unless the Executive Council decides otherwise. Obviously, the total verification cost for converted facilities will be much greater than for facilities that are destroyed.

If a complementary mechanism, such as a bilateral agreement, were in place that provided effective verification and high confidence in compliance, the

[10] Chemical Weapons Convention, Article V, para. 19.
[11] Verification Annex, Part V, para. 86.

OPCW could decide to limit its own verification activities. In this case, the OPCW would only monitor implementation of the agreement. This would greatly reduce the overall cost of verification and any remaining costs would be assessed proportionately among all parties in accordance with the UN scale of assessment, rather than being paid by Russia alone.[12]

The bilateral agreement on destruction and non-production of chemical weapons (BDA), which was signed in June 1990 between the Soviet Union and the USA, contains a strong verification regime and also provides that the inspecting party—not the state possessing CW facilities—will pay most of the cost of inspections.[13] Russia subsequently agreed to become party to the BDA as a successor to the Soviet Union. However, the BDA has not entered into force, and the outlook for entry into force is uncertain. Russia could realize considerable economic benefit from proceeding with the BDA, but until this happens there is no alternative which would reduce the direct cost of verification of production facility destruction or conversion, particularly conversion, under the CWC.

An effective verification strategy for converted facilities

An effective verification strategy for converted CWPFs must meet several requirements. For example, in order to be acceptable to the CSP it must deter non-compliance, provide high confidence that non-compliance would be detected, ensure that conditions of conversion approval are met, allow the TS and the Inspectorate to meet all other requirements, avoid unduly increasing the fixed costs of operating the OPCW, and preserve security and the other interests of all parties to the convention. In addition, so as not to unduly penalize a party that chooses to convert CWPFs, the strategy should also allow CSP-approved non-prohibited activities to be conducted, preserve the confidentiality of proprietary processes and other confidential business information, and minimize intrusiveness and disruption of ongoing activity.

A well-crafted array of complementary measures could be extremely effective in achieving both sets of requirements. This could include (among other activities) frequent inspections with minimal notice, an intensive sampling and analysis regime involving both on-site and off-site analysis, photographic documentation of equipment configuration, full accountability of installed process equipment, and spot checks of portions of record sets and periodic reviews of all relevant records, particularly those critical to providing material accountability.

Ideally, inspections should not be able to be predicted by the affected party, and the activities actually planned to be conducted during each inspection could be varied at the discretion of the Team Leader or the Head of the Inspectorate. Additionally, the team size and composition should be the same for all inspections, as should the deployed equipment set. In this situation, each inspection team would be fully equipped to conduct the full range of required inspection

[12] Chemical Weapons Convention, Article V, para. 19 and Article VIII, para. 7.

[13] Agreement between the United States of America and the Union of Soviet Socialist Republics on Destruction and Non-Production of Chemical Weapons and on Measures to Facilitate the Multilateral Convention on Banning Chemical Weapons, *SIPRI Yearbook 1991: World Armaments and Disarmament* (Oxford University Press: Oxford, 1991), pp. 536–39.

Table 5.4. A proposed inspection scheme to provide high-confidence verification of compliance at converted CW production facilities[a]

Systematic inspections	Full inspections	Abbreviated inspections
Number per year	3–4	6–9
Team size	6–8	6–8
Duration	2–4 days	1–2 days

[a] The entries refer to activities conducted on an annual basis, except where noted.

Source: Based on an inspection scheme proposed independently by the authors.

activities but may not actually carry out all of them during each inspection in order to save time and cost (e.g., the cost of collecting samples and having them analysed at accredited laboratories).

Continuous monitoring with instruments could provide data on activities and conditions at a converted facility. However, the cost and complexity of this aspect of verification are considerable, and there is no consensus that it is of high utility or desirable for converted CWPF verification. For this reason, continuous monitoring with instruments is not recommended as a primary verification tool in this scheme. Instead, such monitoring should be reserved only for particularly difficult situations requiring constant information collection. Table 5.4 briefly outlines a proposed verification scheme that meets the requirements noted above, will be sustainable over a long period of time, can be conducted in Russia with minimal manpower, and will have minimal impact on the OPCW's budget and its equipment inventory. In implementing this proposed scheme, two types of systematic inspections are envisioned: full inspections, which will employ all applicable procedures and equipment, and abbreviated inspections, which will selectively employ procedures and equipment as determined on a case-by-case basis.

VI. International assistance

As Russia proceeds with its national assessment of how to meet CWC requirements for CWPF destruction or conversion, major factors in the decision process could be the availability of international assistance and the willingness of governments or private investors to provide help. Potential sources of assistance are the governments of the United States, Western Europe and other states; private industry; consultancies; and investors or investment funds. In this process, a number of alternatives must be analysed, cost estimates compiled, economic reviews conducted and decisions made. This process is critical now that the CWC has entered into force.

Meeting Russia's requirements

Russia will need to meet a number of requirements in order to successfully complete a destruction or conversion programme within the required time-limits. In order to attract interest in providing assistance, it will be important for Russia to fully comply with CWC provisions and develop plans that provide an opportunity for future economic success after destruction or conversion is complete. Some of the more important requirements are the following:

1. The planning process and programme execution must be fully compliant with the CWC.
2. Destruction and conversion plans must meet required time-lines.
3. Rapid agreement must be achieved with the OPCW on closure, inactivation and verification measures.
4. Profitable uses must be identified for converted facilities and at locations where facilities are destroyed.
5. Technical issues must be resolved.
6. Environmental protection and safety must be ensured.
7. Adequate funding must be provided for destruction or conversion.

An effective international assistance programme

Many aspects of a CWPF destruction or conversion programme can benefit from international assistance, and such assistance can be provided in many forms. Several categories of assistance may be helpful in creating and implementing an effective programme. Some of the more important ones are: (*a*) financing for all phases; (*b*) technology for such purposes as decontamination, rapid removal and disposition of equipment and building components and economical production of viable product; (*c*) programme planning assistance to help gather data, conduct market surveys, review alternatives, develop schedules and prepare required destruction or conversion plans; (*d*) programme management assistance in such areas as environmental protection planning, resource allocation, progress tracking and problem solving; (*e*) facility destruction assistance in areas such as decontamination, dismantlement, disposition of equipment and building materials; (*f*) facility conversion assistance in areas such as equipment re-engineering, selecting appropriate new equipment, process optimization, construction and installation; (*g*) facility reconstruction assistance in designing and constructing new facilities at locations where production facility destruction has been completed; and (*h*) facility operation assistance covering a wide range of activities to support operations at converted facilities or at newly constructed facilities which replaced destroyed CWPFs. Some probable categories and sources of assistance are summarized in table 5.5.

VII. Preparing an effective destruction programme

In order to meet its requirements, minimize cost and disruption to ongoing programmes and identify promising sources of assistance Russia will need to prepare a comprehensive programme plan. In particular, an effective review should be conducted of all aspects of destroying or converting each existing CW production facility. This should be started as soon as possible or accelerated if it has already begun. In conducting this review, it is important for Russia to consider the factors discussed above that will affect the environment in which this process will occur.

Table 5.5. Potential categories and sources of international assistance for destruction or conversion

Category	Government	Private investors	Investment funds	Private industry	Consultancies
Financing	√	√	√	√	
Technology	√			√	√
Programme planning	√	√	√	√	√
Programme management	√			√	√
Facility destruction	√			√	√
Facility conversion	?	?	?	√	√
Facility reconstruction	√	√	√	√	√
Facility operation	?			√	√

? = Possibility of involvement is uncertain.

Source: Sources of funding and international assistance derived from independent analysis by the authors.

Once an effective programme plan has been prepared and implementation has begun, meeting deadlines for submission of the initial data declaration and required conversion and destruction plans will be particularly important. In addition, early agreement with the OPCW on facility closure, inactivation and verification measures will probably be read by potential sources of assistance as indicators of a Russian commitment to meet CWC obligations and deadlines. On the other hand, inability to come to quick agreement with the OPCW on these key aspects of destruction and conversion programme implementation could be seen as major risk factors in investors' decision-making processes and may make it more difficult for Russia to attract assistance in completing its destruction/conversion programme.

Figure 5.4 is a flowchart that outlines an example of a process for conducting a thorough review of alternatives for destruction and conversion as part of an integrated programme plan that would be attractive to investors and others who can provide assistance. In particular, this example emphasizes a number of steps that could be conducted in parallel to expedite early decision making and programme completion as soon as it is practical. The intent is not to advocate this as the only way to carry out the required planning process but rather to present a basis for discussion and consideration of ways to assess all of the factors that will affect national and individual facility destruction and conversion decisions. In conducting this review and planning process, several important assumptions should be considered such as:

1. The entry into force of the CWC occurred in April 1997, and Russia became a party in December 1997.

2. Russia has declared a significant number of CW production facilities.

3. Economic returns from each facility should be maximized as soon as possible.

4. New facilities can be constructed at the sites of all destroyed CW production facilities as soon as the OPCW has conducted its final post-destruction inspection.

5. Verification costs will be particularly significant for converted facilities.

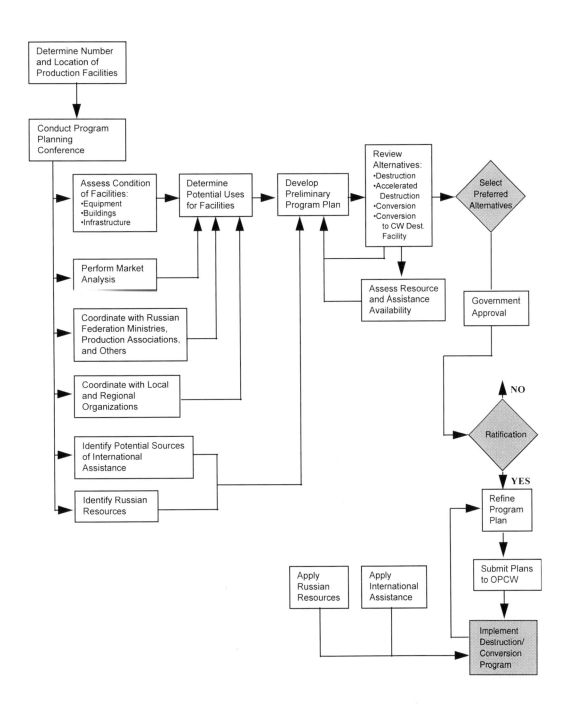

Figure 5.4. A process for developing an effective chemical weapon production facility destruction or conversion programme

Source: Illustration of the process proposed by the authors.

6. Verification costs at destroyed facilities can be minimized by accelerated destruction.

7. The total cost of the destruction/conversion programme should be minimized. This means that the costs of individual programme elements do not need to be minimized if increased expenditures can produce offsetting savings elsewhere.

VIII. Conclusions

The entry into force of the CWC brings with it a requirement to destroy all CW production facilities or—in exceptional cases—may permit approval of plans to convert individual production facilities. Russia has indicated that it intends to convert at least some of its CW production facilities to non-prohibited uses because of economic needs.

The process of approving destruction and conversion plans is lengthy and, in the case of conversion, the result is uncertain. In any case, destruction and conversion must be completed by certain deadlines that are generally based on entry into force of the CWC. Some intermediate deadlines can be adjusted for a party that accedes after CWC entry into force but all Schedule 1 production facilities must be destroyed not later than 10 years after entry into force of the convention. All other CW production facilities must be destroyed not later than five years after the convention enters into force, and all conversion must be completed not later than 6 years after CWC entry into force. Late accession will compress this process. For example, the required annual rate of facility destruction may be increased by 50 per cent in some years if CWPF destruction is delayed until 2 years after entry into force of the CWC.

Russia will soon be faced with a complicated situation. There may be long-term economic benefits to conversion, but the initial costs, uncertainty over whether or not the OPCW will approve any specific conversion request and the high continuing cost of verification activities at converted facilities may make it difficult to attract international assistance. In order to help resolve this situation, a comprehensive programme plan should be developed as soon as possible. This plan should consider a range of alternatives and factor in projected market conditions, national and site-conversion versus destruction costs, and the likelihood of attracting international assistance.

A Russian national programme of accelerated CW production facility destruction, completed well ahead of CWC-required time-lines, would make it possible to begin constructing new chemical or other industrial facilities soon after destruction is completed at each location. This would provide new infrastructure and efficient modern equipment, avoid the cost of ongoing verification and might have considerable appeal to potential investors and other providers of assistance.

Comprehensive analysis of cost–benefit alternatives and programme management options should begin as soon as possible. Early completion may also be attractive to potential sources of international assistance for Russia's preferred CW production facility destruction or conversion programme.

6. Chemical weapon destruction technologies for the Russian CW stockpile

THOMAS STOCK*

I. Introduction

The destruction of chemical weapons in Russia is both a political and a technical challenge. The Russian CW stockpile is composed of lewisite, mustard, mustard–lewisite mixtures, phosgene, sarin (GB), soman (GD) and V-agents. The total quantity of CW agents is estimated at approximately 40 000 tonnes. The agents are stored at seven sites in munitions and bulk storage containers.

Approximately 7500 agent tonnes, 18.8 per cent of the stockpile, are blister agents (lewisite, mustard and their mixtures) that are stored in bulk containers or filled munitions. This figure also includes approximately 5 agent tonnes of phosgene which is said to be weaponized (i.e., prepared to be delivered as weapons). Approximately 32 500 agent tonnes, 81.2 per cent of the total stockpile, are weaponized organophosphorus agents (sarin, soman and V-agents). Table 6.1 shows the distribution of the CW agents by type of storage.

The Special Federal Programme for Chemical Weapons Destruction, which was adopted in March 1996,[1] outlines the principal objectives of CW destruction: *(a)* destruction of chemical weapon stockpiles in accordance with the Chemical Weapons Convention, *(b)* preparation of draft federal laws and other legislative acts on CW destruction, *(c)* adoption of measures to protect the environment at CW storage and destruction sites, and *(d)* recognition of the need to address what it terms 'psychosocial aspects' for the people living near the CW storage sites.[2] The edict presents the general framework for CW destruction but does not prescribe the use of specific destruction technologies. The only obligation is that the technologies must be environmentally safe.

In the aftermath of the cold war the changed political climate has made available more information on Russia's CW stockpile. This chapter presents an overview of some CW destruction technologies and assesses the ones which may be used in Russia. Information is available about some of the technologies that have been considered, but because a final decision has not been taken on the technology or technologies to be used, there has been a debate on the value of the various methods. Although uncertainty remains about some aspects of the Russian CW destruction programme, a comprehensive destruction act has been signed into law.[3]

---

[1] 'Federalnaya tselevaya programma' [Special federal programme], Federal government edict no. 305, 21 Mar. 1996, *Rossiyskaya Gazeta*, 2 Apr. 1996, pp. 5–6; and Russian Federation, Special federal programme, destruction of chemical weapons stockpiles in the Russian Federation, Preparatory Commission document PC-XIV/B/WP.7, 25 June 1996, pp. 19–20.

[2] Psychosocial aspects is the term used for the social and psychological behaviour of the people living near the CW storage sites, including their reactions to knowledge of the risks associated with CW storage.

[3] 'Ob unichtozhenii khimicheskogo oruzhiya' [On the destruction of chemical weapons], Federal Law no. 76-FZ, 25 Apr. 1997, *Krasnaya Zvezda*, 17 May 1997.

* The views expressed here are those of the author and do not necessarily represent those of Mannesmann Demag, Germany.

Table 6.1. Distribution of Russian CW agents by type of storage

Type of CW	Weaponized (%)	Bulk (%)
V-gas	100	–
Sarin	100	–
Soman	100	–
Mustard	–	100
Lewisite	2	98
Mustard–lewisite mixture	40	60
Phosgene	100	–

Source: 'Federalnaya tselevaya programma' [Special federal programme], Federal government edict no. 305, 21 Mar. 1996, *Rossiyskaya Gazeta*, 2 Apr. 1996, pp. 5–6; and Russian Federation, Special federal programme, destruction of chemical weapons stockpiles in the Russian Federation, Preparatory Commission document PC-XIV/B/WP.7, 25 June 1996, pp. 19–20.

II. CWC requirements for chemical weapon destruction

The conditions for the destruction of chemical weapons are outlined in the Verification Annex of the Chemical Weapons Convention:

'Destruction of chemical weapons' means a process by which chemicals are converted in an essentially irreversible[4] way to a form unsuitable for production of chemical weapons, and which in an irreversible manner renders munitions and other devices unusable as such.

Each State Party shall determine how it shall destroy chemical weapons, except that the following processes may not be used: dumping in any body of water, land burial or open-pit burning. It shall destroy chemical weapons only at specifically designated and appropriately designed and equipped facilities.

Each State Party shall ensure that its chemical weapons destruction facilities are constructed and operated in a manner to ensure the destruction of the chemical weapons; and that the destruction process can be verified under the provisions of this Convention.[5]

The CWC also provides guidance for activities related to the transport, sampling, storage and destruction of chemical weapons: 'Each State Party, during transportation, sampling, storage and destruction of chemical weapons, shall assign the highest priority to ensuring the safety of people and to protecting the environment. Each State Party shall transport, sample, store and destroy chemical weapons in accordance with its national standards for safety and emissions'.[6]

---

[4] The CWC does not specify the meaning of 'essentially irreversible'. In principle, all chemical reactions can be reversed.

[5] Part IV(A) of the Verification Annex, paras 12–14. The Convention on the Prohibition of the Development, Production, Stockpiling and Use of Chemical Weapons and on their Destruction (corrected version), 8 Aug. 1994, is reproduced on the SIPRI Chemical and Biological Warfare Project Internet site at URL <http://www.sipri.se/cbw/docs/cw-cwc-texts.html>.

[6] Part IV(A) of the Verification Annex (note 5).

III. Options for CW disposal

The destruction of CW is challenging in terms of the technical and organizational operations involved. The technology and expertise necessary for destroying CW agents and munitions exists,[7] and several countries have destroyed chemical weapons in the past (see table 6.2). The USA has the most experience in the destruction of CW agents and munitions, especially those manufactured after 1945 (see table 6.3).[8]

Prior to the destruction of chemical weapons it is necessary to identify and categorize the material which is awaiting disposal (e.g., bulk agents, munitions filled with CW agents, contaminated material). On the basis of the evaluation the appropriate technology and procedure must be developed to meet the requirements of the disposal operation. While incineration may be the primary means of destruction the method to be used for each category of material will need to be determined individually. Some of the methods of CW disposal are discussed in the following subsections.

Land burial

Land burial of chemical agents was viewed as a quick and cheap solution for many years. Although burial may be unacceptable to environmentalists it is the method of disposal which many countries currently use to deal with hazardous material from commercial and municipal sources. As noted in section II, the CWC does not allow land burial.[9] Burial which occurred before 1 January 1977 is not affected by the CWC because there is no obligation for a party to the convention to declare such disposal activities.[10]

Sea disposal

When conducted properly, dumping at sea is a quick and relatively safe method for the disposal of CW munitions. The principal toxicity threats posed by chemical weapons that have been dumped at sea stem from the arsenic-

---

[7] USA, Verification of chemical weapons stockpile destruction, Conference on Disarmament document CD/424, 20 Jan. 1984; Conference of the Committee on Disarmament documents CCD/324, 360, 366, 367, 381, 403, 434, 436, 485, 497, 498, 506, 538 and 539; Committee on Disarmament, Working Group on Chemical Weapons, Conference on Disarmament document CD/CW/CTC/18, 3 Aug. 1982; USA, Demilitarization and disposal of US chemical warfare agent and munitions, Conference on Disarmament document CD/CW/WP. 265, 11 Dec. 1989; Program Manager for Chemical Demilitarization, *Chemical Stockpile Disposal Program: Final Programmatic Environmental Impact Statement,* vols 1–3 (US Army: Aberdeen Proving Ground, Edgewood, Md., Jan. 1988); *Chemical Weapons: Obstacles to the Army's Plan to Destroy Obsolete US Stockpiles, Report to Congressional Requesters,* GAO/NSLAD-90-155 (US General Accounting Office: Washington, DC, May 1990); and Committee on Demilitarizing Chemical Munitions and Agents, Board on Army Science and Technology, Commission on Engineering and Technical Systems, National Research Council, *Disposal of Chemical Munitions and Agents* (National Academy Press: Washington, DC, 1984).

[8] Conference of the Committee on Disarmament document, CCD/436, 16 July 1974; Program Manager for Chemical Demilitarization (note 7), vol. 3; SIPRI, *Chemical Weapons: Destruction and Conversion* (Taylor & Francis: London, 1980); and Committee on Alternative Chemical Demilitarization Technologies, Board on Army Science and Technology, Commission on Engineering and Technical Systems, *Alternative Technologies for the Destruction of Chemical Agents and Munitions* (National Research Council: Washington, DC, 1993).

[9] Part IV(A) of the Verification Annex (note 5).

[10] Part IV(A) of the Verification Annex (note 5).

Table 6.2. Overview of CW destruction campaigns, 1967–94

Country	Agent	Amount (tonnes)	Method	Period
Indonesia[a]	Sulphur mustard	c. 45	I	1979
USA, RMA	Sulphur mustard	3071	I	1969–74
USA, Tooele	Sarin	4188	N	1973–76
USA, Tooele	Sarin	38	I	1981–86
USA, JACADS	Sarin	40	I	1991
USA, Tooele	VX	8	I	1984
USA, JACADS	VX	54	I	1992
USA, JACADS	Sulphur mustard	56.5	I	1992
Canada, DRES	Sulphur mustard	700	N/I[b]	1974–76
Canada, DRES	Sulphur mustard	12	I	1990–91
Canada, DRES	VX, sarin, tabun	0.3	N/I[b]	1990–91
FRG, Munster	Sulphur mustard and other agents	73	I	1980–93
Soviet Union, Shikhany, etc.	Sarin, soman, Sulphur mustard	300	N/I[b]	1980–90
Soviet Union, Shikhany, etc.	VX	30	N/I[b]	1980–90
UK, Porton Down	Sulphur mustard	Small amounts	N	1967–68
UK, Nancekuke	Sarin	20	N	1967–68
UK	Sulphur mustard	6 000	I	1958–60
Italy	Mixture of sulphur, sulphur mustard and phenyl-dichloroarsine	> 1.5	N	1990
Iraq (UNSCOM)	Sulphur mustard	600	I	1992–94
Iraq (UNSCOM)	Tabun	30	N	1992–94
Iraq (UNSCOM)	Sarin, mixture sarin/cyclosarin	70	N	1992–93

[a] Letter dated 31 March 1982 from the heads of the delegations of Indonesia and the Netherlands transmitting a document entitled 'Indonesia and the Netherlands: working document, destruction of about 45 tons of mustard agent at Batujajar, West-Java, Indonesia', Conference on Disarmament document CD/270, 31 Mar. 1982.

[b] The destruction operations were conducted in 2 steps: hydrolysis, followed by incineration of the reaction products.

[c] The operations of the mobile destruction unit KUASI are described in Union of Soviet Socialist Republics, Complex for the destruction of faulty chemical munitions (KUASI), Conference on Disarmament document CD/CW/WP.369, 8 Oct. 1991; and Union of Soviet Socialist Republics, Letter dated 16 December 1987 from the representative of the Union of Soviet Socialist Republics addressed to the President of the Conference on Disarmament transmitting a working paper entitled 'Information on the presentation at the Shikhany military facility of standard chemical munitions and of technology for the destruction of chemical weapons at a mobile unit', Conference on Disarmament document CD/789, 16 Dec. 1987.

I = incineration; RMA = Rocky Mountain Arsenal, Colorado, USA; N = neutralization; JACADS = Johnston Atoll Chemical Agent Disposal System; and DRES = Defence Research Establishment Suffield, Canada; and UNSCOM = United Nations Special Commission on Iraq.

Source: Compiled by the author.

Table 6.3. Summary of US Army chemical agent and munition destruction, 1972–98

Operation	Description	Date	CW agent	Site	Process	Quantity (1000 kg)
Project Eagle Phase I	Ton containers	July 1972–Mar. 1974	H	R	I	2 008.5
Project Eagle Phase I	Ton containers	July 1972–Mar. 1974	HD	R	I	777.5
Project Eagle Phase II[a]	M34 cluster bombs	Oct. 1973–Nov. 1976	GB	R	N/I	1 873.2
Project Eagle Phase II	Underground storage tanks	Sep.–Nov. 1974	GB	R	N	171.5
Project Eagle Phase II	Ton containers	May–Nov. 1975	GB	R	N/I	1 635.0
Project Eagle Phase II	Honest John warheads (M139)	Apr. 1975–Nov. 1976	GB	R	N/I	34.7
Chemical agent identification set disposal	Chemical agent identification sets	May 1981–Dec. 1982	(C)	R	I	16.6
M55 rocket disposal	..	Sep. 1979–Apr. 1981	GB	C	N/I	58.1
Agent injection incineration tests	..	Apr. 1981–Jan. 1984	GB	C	I	5.1
Agent injection incineration tests	Ton containers	June 1981–Aug. 1984	VX	C	I	3.6
155-mm projectile disposal	..	July 1981–July 1982	GB	C	N	27.4
105-mm projectile disposal	..	Mar.–July 1982	GB	C	I	..
In-situ agent incineration	..	Oct. 1982–Dec. 1983	GB	C	I	8.0
M55 rocket incineration	..	Nov. 1985–Nov. 1986	GB	C	I	1.0
Liquid incineration test	..	Aug. 1985–Aug. 1986	GB	C	I	17.2
Agent BZ disposal	..	May 1988–Sep. 1989	BZ	P	I	42.6
Liquid incinerator test	..	Sep.–Oct. 1989	VX	C	I	18.1
Operational verification test I	M55 rockets	July 1990–Feb. 1991	GB	J	I	35.1
Operational verification test II	M55 rockets	Nov. 1991–Mar. 1992	VX	J	I	61.2
Operational verification test III	Ton containers	Aug.–Sep. 1992	HD	J	I	51.2
Operational verification test IV	105-mm projectiles	Oct. 1992–Mar. 1993	HD	J	I	16.1
JACADS	8-inch, 105-mm, 155-mm projectiles 500, 750-lb bombs M-55 rockets/warheads, ton containers	1993–9 Aug. 1998	GB, VX, HD	J	I	1 514.0

Table 6.3 *contd*

Operation	Description	Date	CW agent	Site	Process	Quantity (1000 kg)
TOCDF	750-lb bombs, ton containers, M-55 rockets/warheads	Aug. 1996– 9 Aug. 1998	GB,	T	I	1 996.0
Total						**10 371.7**

a For additional information, see *Project Eagle Phase II: Demilitarization and Disposal of the M34 GB Cluster at Rocky Mountain Arsenal: Final Environmental Impact Statement* (US Army Materiel Command: Aberdeen Proving Ground, Edgewood, Md., Feb. 1973)

CW agents: H = early production mustard gas; HD = distilled mustard gas; GB = sarin; (C) = chloropicrin, cyanogen chloride, lewisite, mustard, nitrogen mustard, phosgene and sarin; VX = O-ethyl-S-(2-diisopropylaminoethyl) methylphosphonothiolate; and BZ = 3-quinuclidinyl benzilate (psychochemical); *Sites*: R = Rocky Mountain Arsenal, C = Chemical Agent Munitions Disposal System, P = Pine Bluff Arsenal, J = Johnston Atoll Chemical Agent Disposal System; and T = Tooele Chemical Agent Disposal Facility; and *Processes*: I = incineration of agent and explosive (and/or thermal decontamination of metal parts), N/I = agent neutralization and explosive incineration (and/or thermal decontamination of metal parts), and N = neutralization.

Sources: Disposal of Chemical Agents and Munitions Stored at Anniston Army Depot, Anniston, Alabama: Final Environmental Impact Statement (US Army: Aberdeen Proving Ground, Edgewood, Md., May 1991), table 2.6; *Project Eagle Phase II: Demilitarization and Disposal of the M34 GB Cluster at Rocky Mountain Arsenal: Final Environmental Impact Statement* (US Army Materiel Command: Aberdeen Proving Ground, Edgewood, Md., Feb. 1973); Program Manager for Chemical Demilitarization, *Chemical Stockpile Disposal Program: Final Programmatic Environmental Impact Statement,* vol. 3 (US Army: Aberdeen Proving Ground, Edgewood, Md., Jan. 1988), p. D-4; US Army, Program Manager for Chemical Demilitarization, 'Johnston Atoll Island Chemical Agent Disposal System (JACADS)', URL <http://www-pmcd.apgea.army.mil/text/aag_jacads.html>, version current on 9 Aug. 1998; and US Army, Program Manager for Chemical Demilitarization, 'Tooele Chemical Agent Disposal Facility', URL <http://wwwpmcd.apgea.army.mil/text/aag_tocdf .html>, version current on 28 July 1998.

containing products of hydrolysis and the slowly dissolving mustard agents.[11] Old chemical weapons are defined by the CWC as those produced before 1945, and dumping them at sea was common practice from the end of World War II until the late 1960s. The only know problems associated with sea disposal occurred after dumping was carried out in relatively shallow waters, such as the Baltic Sea. Fishermen have been severely hurt when dumped munitions have been brought aboard their ships. The impact of these CW agents on the marine environment is uncertain.[12] The USA used this disposal method extensively until 1972, but as early as 1969 a National Academy of Sciences report recom-

---

[11] In general, all arsenic-containing compounds have a relatively high toxicity. If mustard agent is exposed to cold water a polymer crust forms on the exterior of the droplets of the agent while the interior remains viscous and toxic for decades. Injury can occur if the outer crust is broken. In addition, the rate of hydrolysis of sulphur mustard in cold water is very slow.

[12] Laurin, F., 'The Baltic and North Sea dumping of chemical weapons: still a threat?'; and Fonnum, F., 'Investigation of ships filled with chemical munitions which were sunk off the Norwegian coast after World War II', eds T. Stock and Kh. Lohs, *The Challenge of Old Chemical Munitions and Toxic Armament Wastes*, SIPRI Chemical & Biological Warfare Studies, no. 16 (Oxford University Press: Oxford, 1997), pp. 263–78 and pp. 279–90, respectively.

mended that sea disposal be avoided and that new, safe and environmentally acceptable methods be sought.[13]

The 1972 Oslo Convention for the Prevention of Marine Pollution by Dumping from Ships and Aircraft and the 1975 Convention on the Prevention of Marine Pollution by Dumping of Wastes and Other Matter stipulated that the disposal of material such as chemical weapons cease at the end of 1992.[14] In addition, the CWC prohibits sea disposal of chemical weapons.[15] However, chemical weapons that were dumped at sea before 1 January 1985 are not affected by the CWC because there is no obligation for a party to the convention to declare such disposal.[16]

Open burning

Open-pit, or tray, burning was used often in the past, particularly in the period just after World War II. However, it can result in the release into the atmosphere of considerable quantities of combustion products (e.g., acid compounds in the case of mustard). The only method which might be considered technically and environmentally acceptable is open-air explosive demolition in cases where the relocation of CW munitions is likely to be hazardous. The United Nations Special Commission on Iraq (UNSCOM) used this particular type of open-pit burning in Iraq to destroy 122-mm rockets that contained nerve agents and were equipped with fuses and explosives and those damaged in air raids. UNSCOM employed this method because there was no other safe means of destruction. However, the CWC does not allow open-pit burning.[17]

Chemical degradation

Chemical degradation can be used to destroy or reduce most CW agents to a negligible level of toxicity. Nerve agents, for example, can be neutralized by treatment with a 10–20 per cent (by volume) aqueous solution of sodium or potassium hydroxide. However, as is generally the case for neutralization reactions, a major disadvantage of using hydrolysis is the production of large volumes of hydrolysates (salts).[18]

This type of disposal may not meet the CWC requirement that destruction should be 'essentially irreversible' and result in a product that cannot be readily reconstituted into a CW agent or a key precursor. Hydrolysis is based on the shift of a chemical equilibrium, and in principle the hydrolysate can be reacted so that the CW agent is recreated. In order to comply with the CWC additional

[13] Ad Hoc Advisory Committee of the National Academy of Sciences, *Disposal of Certain Chemical Warfare Agents and Munitions* (National Academy of Sciences: Washington, DC, 24 June 1969).

[14] The Convention for the Prevention of Marine Pollution by Dumping from Ships and Aircraft entered into force on 6 Apr. 1974; there are 13 parties. The Convention on the Prevention of Marine Pollution by Dumping of Wastes and Other Matter (London Dumping Convention) entered into force on 30 Aug. 1975; there are 74 parties. The Convention on the Prevention of Marine Pollution from Land-Based Sources (Paris Convention) entered into force on 6 May 1978; there are 12 parties. See also Heintze, J.-H., 'Legal problems related to old chemical munitions dumped in the Baltic Sea', Stock and Lohs (note 12), pp. 255–62.

[15] Part IV (A) of the Verification Annex, para. 13.

[16] CWC, Article III, para. 17.

[17] Part IV (A) of the Verification Annex, para. 13.

[18] For GB which can be neutralized by $Ca(OH)_2$ the maximum total of dry waste salts is 4.6–18 kg per 1 kg of agent.

steps must be taken after hydrolysis. The following subsections outline methods which can be used to dispose of CW neutralization wastes.

Chemical degradation followed by sea disposal

If chemical degradation is followed by disposal at sea the hydrolysates are diluted to reduce the acid ion concentration to the required environmental limit. The solution is then discharged into the sea via normal effluent outfall. Whether or not this process is acceptable depends in part on the geographical location of the disposal site and also on international environmental conventions.

Chemical degradation followed by incineration

The hydrolysate can be further degraded by high-temperature incineration. However, if sodium or potassium hydroxide has been used to carry out the hydrolysis the low caloric value and high salt content of the product make this a demanding, expensive process. There is also a need to dispose of the inorganic salts that are recovered from the incinerator's effluent-gas cleaning plant.

Chemical degradation followed by land burial after concentration

If the hydrolysate is to be buried after concentration it is first placed in open-air evaporation pans. The liquid is allowed to evaporate, and the residual salts are collected and buried in an environmentally safe and secure landfill. This option is regarded as safe, cheap, energy-efficient and essentially environmentally acceptable.

Chemical degradation followed by biodegradation

Laboratory investigations have demonstrated the feasibility of biodegradation of hydrolysate products, and its possible industrial application has been studied, especially in the USA.[19] The hydrolysis of sulphur mustard under alkaline conditions results in the formation of thiodiglycol as the main product. Species which can immobilize[20] this substance are under investigation.[21] For nerve agents species have been studied that use carbon for growth.[22]

The US Army officially decided to abandon neutralization in favour of incineration in 1982, citing the following reasons:

1. The by-product of neutralizing mustard was hazardous and had to be disposed of by incineration anyway.

2. The chemical required to neutralize mustard has a low flashpoint and had caused a laboratory explosion.

---

[19] National Research Council, Panel on Review and Evaluation of Alternative Chemical Disposal Technologies, Board on Army Science and Technology, Commission on Engineering and Technical Systems, *Review and Evaluation of Alternative Chemical Disposal Technologies* (National Academy Press: Washington, DC, 1996).

[20] National Research Council (note 19), pp. 120–30. In the CWC 'immobilize' means that it is not possible to reverse the hydrolysate. Micro-organisms will oxidize the thiodiglycol, which will result in carbon dioxide, water and sulphate.

[21] Species is used here to mean a chemical entity, such as a particular atom, ion or molecule.

[22] National Research Council (note 19), p. 150; and Picardi, A., Johnston, P. and Stringer, R., *Alternative Technologies for the Detoxification of Chemical Weapons: An Information Document* (Greenpeace International: Washington, DC, 24 May 1991), pp. 22–25.

3. The neutralization reaction can be difficult to control, resulting in more waste product—from 2.6 to six lbs [1.2–2.8 kg] of salt per pound [0.45 kg] of GB (sarin) neutralized.

4. The neutralization reaction could be very slow—only 50 percent of the agent was neutralized within twenty-four hours, while other batches took between five and sixteen days and one required forty-eight days of processing.

5. Neutralization can be reversed to reform the original chemical agent.

6. Neutralization is not applicable to all agents in the stockpile.[23]

However, the discussion of alternative technologies which has taken place in recent years has led to reconsideration of neutralization. On the basis of recommendations from the National Research Council and the US Army, US research and development will focus on two technologies: stand-alone neutralization, and neutralization followed by biodegradation.[24] These technologies will be used instead of incineration at two sites where only bulk agents are stored.

Incineration

Most CW agents, with the exception of sarin, are flammable and have relatively high calorific values that make them good candidates for incineration.[25] In properly designed incineration plants a destruction efficiency of 99.99999 per cent can be obtained.

Direct incineration has been used for sulphur mustard disposal in Canada and the United Kingdom. Direct high-temperature incineration can also be used for the destruction of G-agent (nerve agents), but their higher vapour pressure and greater inhalation toxicity pose greater difficulties related to the design and operation of an incineration plant. The main problem is not the incineration, but rather the handling and feeding of the material into the furnace and the containment requirements (protection of personnel).[26]

The USA currently is destroying nerve agents in specially designed incineration plants at the Johnston Atoll Chemical Agent Demilitarization System (JACADS), located south-west of Hawaii, and at the Tooele Chemical Agent Disposal Facility (TOCDF). Plants for the incineration of mustard can be

[23] Quoted in Smithson, A. E. and Lenihan, M., *The U.S. Chemical Weapons Destruction Program: Views, Analysis, and Recommendations* (Henry L. Stimson Center: Washington, DC, Sep. 1994).

[24] Committee on Alternative Chemical Demilitarization Technologies (note 8).

[25] A calorific value is the heat per unit mass produced by complete combustion of a given substance.

[26] Incineration of chemical agents always creates exhaust gases which must be passed through a pollution abatement system. Chlorinated dioxins, a class of highly toxic compounds which can be formed by recombination of incineration products, are of particular concern in the exhaust treatment process. Chlorinated dioxins may form in an exhaust gas stream if the temperature is 180–400°C and if chlorine and reactive hydrocarbons are present. Such a reaction is more likely to occur if inorganic molecules such as iron and aluminium are present. These molecules act as catalysts for the formation of chlorinated dioxins. Sarin and V-agents do not, however, contain chlorine atoms. Mustard contains chlorine and its incineration can be a major source of chlorinated dioxins. Even small quantities of chlorine may be sufficient to cause the formation of chlorinated dioxins. The destruction process therefore should minimize the period during which the incineration 'off-gases' are heated to 180–400°C. Subsequent processing of these gases must include the removal of any chlorinated dioxins which have formed. At JACADS the pollution abatement systems are designed so that the incineration off-gases are rapidly cooled (quenched) by water to c. 60°C. The HCl and Cl_2 then are removed by contact with a sodium carbonate solution. Activated charcoal filters are also used to treat the gases before they are released into the atmosphere. Continuous monitoring is maintained to ensure that no dioxins are released into the atmosphere. Committee on Alternative Chemical Demilitarization Technologies (note 8).

VX-type V-gas

$$2 (C_2H_5O)PO(CH_3)SCH_2CH_2N(iPr)_2 + 39.5O_2 \longrightarrow 2 NO_2 + P_2O_5 + 2 SO_2 + 22 CO_2 + 26 H_2O$$

Sarin

$$2 (CH_3)_2CHOP(O)F(CH_3) + 13 O_2 \longrightarrow 8 CO_2 + 9 H_2O + P_2O_5 + 2 HF$$

Soman

$$2 (CH_3)_3C(CH_3)CHOP(O)F(CH_3) + 22 O_2 \longrightarrow 14 CO_2 + 15 H_2O + P_2O_5 + 2 HF$$

Mustard

$$2 (ClCH_2CH_2)_2S + 13 O_2 \longrightarrow 8 CO_2 + 2 SO_2 + 4 HCl + 6 H_2O$$

Lewisite

$$2 ClCH = CHAsCl_2 + 6 O_2 \longrightarrow As_2O_3 + 4 CO_2 + 2 HCl + H_2O + 2 Cl_2$$

Figure 6.1. Chemical formulas of Russian CW agents that can be incinerated

constructed from commercially available components. It may be possible for commercial plants that incinerate municipal and toxic wastes to also incinerate chemically degraded nerve agents. However, environmental and safety standards must be met. Figure 6.1 shows the chemical formulas of the CW agents that are stockpiled in Russia which can be destroyed by incineration.[27]

IV. Designing a disposal operation

General disposal strategies

The selection of any destruction technology is restricted by the provisions of the CWC. Determining whether a candidate technology meets these criteria depends on the chemical and physical state of the final destruction product and its toxicity (the level of toxicity must be in accordance with national hazardous waste disposal standards). The CW agent must be 'transformed' in an irreversible way so that it is not possible to reconstitute it.

No single technology can produce waste materials that meet the requirement of both the CWC and hazardous waste disposal criteria. Incineration alone does not adequately treat the acid gases for release into the air. Neutralization requires subsequent treatment of the detoxification products in order to meet the CWC irreversibility criterion. The most stable final products resulting from the destruction of chemical agents and munitions are metal parts that are completely decontaminated and products that do not contain any complex organic molecules. Examples of such basic chemical products are the gases carbon

[27] Russian V-gas is not identical with US VX. It is an isomer of VX in which the phosphor-alkoxy is isobutyl and the dialkyl amine is diethyl. Its chemical name is S-2-diethylaminoethyl O-isobutyl methylphosphonothioate. In this chapter, however, VX is used instead of the isomer.

dioxide, water and nitrogen and various salts such as calcium, sodium, or potassium salts of phosphate, chloride, sulphate, carbonate and fluoride.

Chemical weapon disposal operations may involve bulk agent, filled CW munitions and contaminated equipment, munitions and soil. The type of disposal technique depends on the amount of CW material to be destroyed. Major problems are more likely to arise in the pre-destruction activities than during the final destruction operation. Such problems include detection, unearthing, cleaning and identification, transport, interim storage, dismantling and preparation for destruction. The following subsections address the problems associated with destroying various types of CW materials.

Bulk CW agents

On-site destruction of bulk CW agents is unlikely to create significant problems. The choice of an appropriate destruction technique depends on the type of CW agent to be destroyed. The main concerns are related to the level of containment and the protection of personnel. Few countries have experience in destroying bulk agents.[28] If the bulk CW agents are moved to a central destruction site the primary problem is their safe transport. Appropriate packaging, preparation for emergencies and safe transport techniques are vital.

CW munitions

CW munitions can be divided into two categories: munitions without an explosive or propellant component, and munitions with such a component. Munitions without explosives or propellants can be handled more easily, although corrosion and leakage can create difficulties during dismantling. High levels of containment are needed for draining and emptying munitions and adequate protection must be provided for the destruction personnel.

CW munitions that contain explosives or propellants present a different challenge, and their safe destruction presents major problems. There are two options for handling such munitions. Either the explosive component must be separated from the CW-containing component and both parts then destroyed separately, or the explosive component and the CW agent-containing component must be treated as a whole. The first approach is the most common.

The munition is moved to a specially designed chemical-containment facility. After it is drilled or cut open by the use of remote-controlled instruments the CW agent is drained. Three separate wastes result: the drained CW agent, the explosive component and the casing. The destruction process is relatively cheap but slow, and the disposal rate is low. Automation could accelerate the process, but there are limitations because the individual munitions vary as a result of corrosion, external factors and different CW fill. Environmental and safety standards also demand that certain measures be taken (e.g., negative pressure, ventilation, closed-circuit monitoring, continuous automatic agent monitoring and passive detection). In addition, safety procedures are required to meet the danger created by explosives.

[28] Canada, Germany, the UK, the USA and those countries which participated in UNSCOM destruction activities are among those which have such experience.

The less common approach, in which the CW-filled munition and the explosive or propellant are treated simultaneously, requires technology that curtails the risk of explosions. Such a system must be designed so that there is near total containment of the chemicals and explosives. For this type of destruction it may be possible to use the cryofracture technique, in which the complete munition is cooled in liquid nitrogen and then mechanically fractured into small pieces. The pieces are thermally treated in an incineration plant which has been designed to cope simultaneously with CW agents, explosives or propellants and metal from munitions. Cryofracture plants can process a relatively large number of munitions but are extremely expensive. If there is a large variety of types of CW agent in munitions the demands on the process will increase. This is especially true of arsenic compounds.

Contaminated equipment and munitions

Contaminated equipment and emptied munitions can be decontaminated by chemical or thermal treatment. Chemical treatment uses neutralization solutions. Metal that has been exposed to a CW agent for a long period will have absorbed significant amounts of it. The decontaminant solution must therefore be kept in contact with the contaminated material for a long time and the equilibrium between desorption and adsorption regulated by the addition of fresh decontaminant solution, which can later be buried or incinerated.[29]

The absorbed CW agent molecules are desorbed at specific temperatures when thermal treatment is used for decontamination. The temperature must be high enough to allow desorption of the CW agent from the munition, and the thermal treatment must be continued long enough to ensure 100 per cent desorption. The hot desorption air must then be incinerated in order to destroy all volatized CW agents and related by-products. Experience has shown that thermal treatment is efficient in dealing with a variety of feedstock material that has been contaminated to various degrees.

Dismantling of chemical weapons

When CW munitions are dismantled the fuses, bursters and boosters (i.e., explosive) charges are removed, and the chemical fill is drained. In most cases special remote-controlled dismantling equipment is used, such as defusing tools, machines for drilling, milling and sawing, and chopping benches. The dismantling step normally governs the speed of the entire disposal process.

There are several dismantling techniques. If there is a wide variety of munitions to be processed, several dismantling workshops are required. The following subsections discuss the various types of dismantling that have been used.

Mechanical dismantling

Mechanical dismantling is the removal of the fuse from a munition. The fuse is unscrewed by the use of power tools.

---

[29] An excess amount of the chemical decontaminant must be added continuously in order to shift the desorption/adsorption equilibrium towards desorption.

Drilling

In drilling a drill bit is used to penetrate the shell casing, and the contents are then extracted for processing. This technique is used for munitions that contain a liquid. Some drilling tools have an expansion chamber to contain any compressed gas that escapes from inside the projectile, which enables the dismantling of munitions that contain compressed gas, such as phosgene. This operation can be made completely automated.

Sectioning

When sectioning is employed the munition is cut into two or more parts, allowing access to its internal components. Sectioning can be used for all types of munition and is especially useful for those that contain solid CW agent. However, the number of munitions which can be processed in this manner is low.

Chemical dissolution

In chemical dissolution a corrosive agent is used to dissolve the shell casing. This technique enables simultaneous removal of the energetic compounds,[30] decontamination of the casing and destruction of the CW agent. The time needed for chemical dissolution and the behaviour of the explosive in a corrosive bath must be known before processing can begin.

Electrochemical dissolution

Electrochemical dissolution can be used to neutralize or destroy explosives or CW agents. A soluble anode, consisting of a carefully selected part of the munition, is reacted with an electrolyte whose composition is appropriate to neutralize or destroy the explosives or chemical agents.

Casing

The munition can be cut open by using an abrasive jet of water or decontaminant in order to extract the energetic compounds. The casing process limits the damage caused by an explosion because the cutting is done while the munition is immersed. This also allows the CW agent to be immediately neutralized.

Penetration using a hollow charge

A munition can be penetrated by a small hollow charge. This dismantling method can be used for any munition that contains an unpressurized, noninflammable liquid. This induces an explosion of an already primed fuse chain.

Cryofracture option

In cryofracture dismantling a munition is immersed in liquid nitrogen. The munition becomes brittle and ruptures or fragments when external force is applied by a hydraulic press. This process can be used for most munition types.

---

[30] Energetic compounds are explosives and propellants, including fuses, boosters, bursters and solid rocket propellants. The energetics and associated metal parts are often contaminated with CW agent.

Combining cryofracture with follow-on incineration is an attractive dismantling option. However, frozen 'lumps' can create problems of uneven combustion and erratic furnace operation.

Designing the CW destruction operation

The destruction of CW munitions involves CW agents, energetic compounds, contaminated metal parts from munitions and containers, and dunnage.[31] Some of the metal parts may contain significant amounts of CW agents that have gelled and therefore cannot be drained readily. The dunnage material may not contain CW agents, but if mixed wastes are to be treated the most stringent safety precautions must be used and the wastes treated as if they were contaminated with CW agents. In addition, as a result of normal decontamination activities the dismantling process produces decontamination fluids that may contain minor residual CW agent decontamination and ventilation air that may contain CW agent vapours.

CW munition destruction at JACADS

The Johnston Atoll Chemical Agent Disposal System is the US destruction facility where large-scale CW destruction operations were first carried out as part of the programme to dispose of the US CW stockpile.[32] JACADS uses a three-step process: (a) storage, transport to the disposal building and unloading; (b) disassembly and draining; and (c) destruction and decontamination. The disassembly and draining of the munitions is, second to transport, the most time-consuming element. The result is three separate streams of material of varying toxicity and physical properties: (a) CW agents; (b) a mixture of energetic compounds, small metal components and residual CW agents; and (c) large metal parts with residual CW agents but no energetic compounds. The separation into three streams creates technological advantages for subsequent destruction or decontamination, but the greatest achievement is higher safety. The disposal system for each stream is specifically designed for the properties of the particular stream.

At JACADS the CW munitions are placed in an explosion-containment room which has an atmosphere that is below atmospheric pressure (to prevent leakage of CW agents) and constructed to withstand overpressure in the event of the explosion of a munition. The ventilation air passes through charcoal filters. If bulk storage containers are processed a special bulk drain station is used. The CW agent is removed from the munitions or containers by automated machinery. If possible, containers (rockets, landmines, bombs, spray tanks and ton containers) are simply punched (perforated) and drained of CW agent. Artillery

---

[31] Dunnage is miscellaneous waste from the dismantling process, including packing material, protective clothing, storage material, and the like.

[32] As of 12 July 1998 the following had been destroyed at JACADS: 13 020 GB, 8-inch nerve agent-filled projectiles; 49 360 GB, 105-mm nerve agent-filled projectiles; 107 197 GB, 155-mm nerve agent-filled projectiles; 2570 MK-94 (500 lb) bombs filled with GB nerve agent; 3047 MC-1 (750 lb) bombs filled with GB nerve agent; 72 242 M-55 GB and VX nerve agent-filled rockets and warheads; 45 108, 105-mm blister agent-filled projectiles; 68 blister agent-filled ton containers; and 66 GB nerve agent-filled ton containers. US Army, Program Manager for Chemical Demilitarization, 'Johnston Atoll Island Chemical Agent Disposal System (JACADS)', URL <http://www-pmcd.apgea.army.mil/text/aag_jacads.html>, version current on 28 July 1998.

projectiles (with heavy-walled steel) are disassembled before being drained of CW agent. The disassembly operation begins with the removal of the explosive elements if these are present in the projectile. In general, the extraction of the burster tube is the means of gaining access to the CW agent. These operations result in the three streams of material mentioned above.

After the CW agent is drained from the munitions and stored in tanks it is destroyed by incineration. The liquid incinerator consists of two sequential combustion chambers and a pollution-abatement system. Gases from the first chamber are transferred into the second chamber for the final burn.

The energetic compounds are burned in a counterflow rotary kiln for 15 minutes at 1000°F (538°C). Gases from the rotary kiln that are contaminated with CW agent are treated in an after-burner for approximately 1 second at 1200°C. The metal parts, which have been drained of CW agent, are heated to 538°C and maintained for approximately 15 minutes in a fuel-fired, metal-parts furnace. Gases discharged from these metal parts are passed through an after-burner at 1200°C. All three furnace systems are equipped with a pollution-abatement system. Dunnage is treated in a primary chamber, and the resulting gases are transferred into an after-burner.

All of the resulting gases and other products of incineration from the entire system are treated with a variety of pollution-abatement equipment (quench tower, venturi scrubber, scrubber tower, demister, and so on). The brine produced by the scrubbers is evaporated and the final salts are packed in drums.

V. Options for the destruction of Russian CW agents

This section outlines options for the destruction of Russia's CW agents, based on the composition of the stockpile. The nature of the Russian CW stockpile and its composition (bulk or munitions) is significant for the choice of technology. Some of the reactions shown below have been tested only on the laboratory scale, and full-scale testing remains to be done.

Lewisite destruction

There are several options for the destruction of lewisite. Lewisite is stockpiled at Gorny (293 tonnes), Kambarka (6349 tonnes) and Kizner (129 tonnes);[33] 98 per cent is stored in bulk and only 2 per cent is weaponized. In 1994 an evaluation was conducted in Russia of the most preferable technology for lewisite destruction. Alkaline hydrolysis followed by electrolysis was determined to be the most promising technology. The resulting metallic arsenic could serve as the basis for a future arsenic industry. If an alloy is reacted with sulphur at 160–180°C at a 30-40-minute interval, the resulting polymer can be buried. Figure 6.2 presents the chemical formulas that relate to the destruction of lewisite.

---

[33] Hart, J., 'The concept of "order of destruction" and resulting implications for destruction of chemical weapons in Russia', Paper presented at the NATO Advanced Research Workshop Chemical and Biological Technologies for the Detection, Destruction and Decontamination of Chemical Warfare Agents, Moscow, 12–15 May 1996.

Reaction of alloy with sulphur at 160–180°C at 30–40-minute interval

$$ClCH = CHAsCl_2 + S \rightarrow polymer + HCl$$

Interaction with monomethacrylate at 60–90°C at 60–80-minute interval

$$ClCH = CHAsCl_2 + CH_2C(CH_3)CO(O)CH_2CH_2OH \rightarrow polymer + HCl$$

Chlorination reaction at 110–130°C at 2-hour interval

$$ClCH = CHAsCl_2 + Cl_2 \rightarrow AsCl_3 + ClCH = CHCl$$
$$Cl_2$$
$$\rightarrow Cl_2CHCHCl_2$$

Alkaline hydrolysis reaction at 103–110°C at 1-hour interval

$$2 ClCH = CHAsCl_2 + 6 NaOH + 2 H_2O \rightarrow As + 0.5 H_2 + O_2 + 2 CH \equiv CH + AsH_3 + 3 (NaOCl + NaCl + H_2O)$$

Alcoholysis reaction at 50–80°C at 2–3 hour interval

$$ClCH = CHAsCl_2 + 3 RONa \rightarrow (RO)_3 As + 3 NaCl + CH \equiv CH$$

Hodrogenolysis

$$5 ClCH = CHAsCl_2 + 7 H_2 \rightarrow AsCl_3 + 12 HCl + CH \equiv CH + As_4 + C_2H_4 + C_2H_6 + 4 C$$
$$900°C$$
$$CH \equiv CH + H_2 \rightarrow C_2H_2 \rightarrow C_2H_6$$
$$800–1000°C$$
$$4 AsCl_3 + 6 H_2 \rightarrow As_4 + 12 HCl$$

High-temperature oxidation

$$> 600°C$$
$$ClCH = CHAsCl_2 + C_3H_8 + 7.75 O_2 \rightarrow 0.5 As_2O_3 + 5 CO_2 + 2 HCl + 0.5 Cl_2 + 4 H_2O$$

Ammonia reduction at 1000–1100°C at 2-hour interval

$$ClCH = CHAsCl_2 + 6NH_3 \rightarrow As + 3 NH_4Cl + 1.5 N_2 + 2 CH_4$$
$$AsCl_3 + 4 NH_3 \rightarrow As + 3 NH_4Cl + 0.5 N_2$$

Figure 6.2. Chemical formulas for lewisite destruction

Source: Petrov, S. V., Kholstov, V. I. and Zoubrilin, V. P. 'Practical actions of Russia on preparations for destruction of stockpiled lewisite and "mustard"', eds J. F. Bunnett and M. Mikolajczyk, *Arsenic and Old Mustard: Chemical Problems in the Destruction of Old Arsenical and 'Mustard' Munitions*, NATO ASI series, vol 19 (Kluwer Academic Publishers: Dordrecht, Boston, London, 1998), pp. 79–90.

Hydrolysis

$$(ClCH_2CH_2)_2S + Ca(OH)_2 \rightarrow (HOCH_2CH_2)_2S + CaCl_2$$

Two-stage reaction with monoethanolamine at 100–110°C at 1-hour interval

Stage 1

$$(ClCH_2CH_2)_2S + 2HOCH_2CH_2NH_2 \rightarrow S(CH_2CH_2)_2N^+H(CH_2CH_2OH) + Cl^-$$
$$+ (H_2NCH_2CH_2OH)HCl$$

Stage 2

$$3 S(CH_2CH_2Cl)_2 + 10 HOCH_2CH_2OH \rightarrow 6 ClCH_2CH_2OH + 6 H_2O +$$

$$S(CH_2CH_2OCH_2CH_2OCH_2CH_2SCH_2CH_2CH_2CH_2OH)$$

Figure 6.3. Chemical formulas for mustard agent destruction

Mustard destruction

Mustard is stockpiled at Gorny (680 tonnes) in bulk form, and there are several options for its destruction. The most promising destruction option now seems to be the reaction with monoethanolamine in a two-stage process, which will lead to a product that can be reacted further with bitumen to form solid blocks which can then be buried. Figure 6.3 presents the hydrolysis of mustard and the two-stage reaction with monoethanolamine.

Nerve agent destruction

The Russian CW stockpile contains approximately 32 000 agent tonnes of the nerve agents sarin, soman and V-agent. The nerve agents are stockpiled at Kizner, Leonidovka, Maradikovsky, Popchep and Shchuchye. All these nerve agents are weaponized. Nerve agents can be destroyed by chemical reaction or incineration. The chemical reactions are illustrated in figure 6.4. In addition to chemical treatment, nerve agents can be destroyed by thermal treatment such as pyrolysis (incineration followed by pollution abatement). Pyrolysis and incineration of sarin, soman and VX are presented in figure 6.5.

Option for nerve agent destruction

The reaction with monoethanolamine is especially suited for destruction of G-type nerve agents. It involves two steps: (*a*) destruction of the agent via neutralization with monoethanolamine at 100–110°C, and (*b*) further destruction of the reaction mass to a bitumen and calcium hydroxide mixture at 130–140°C. When cooled the final product is a solid 'bitumen salt mass'.[34]

---

[34] Bechtel National, Inc. and US Army Program Manager for Chemical Demilitarization, Office of the Product Manager for Cooperative Threat Reduction (PM-CTR), *Joint Evaluation of the Russian*

Hydrolysis

$$(CH_3)_2CHOP(O)F(CH_3) + 2\ NaOH \rightarrow (CH_3)_2CHOP(O)(CH_3)(ONa) + NaF + H_2O$$

Acid-catalysed hydrolysis

$$H^+$$
$$(CH_3)_2CHOP(O)F(CH_3) + H_2O \rightarrow (CH_3)_2CHOP(O)(CH_3)(OH) + HF + H_2O$$

$$\overset{H^+,\ H_2O}{\longrightarrow}\quad HOP(O)(CH_3)(OH) + (CH_3)_2CHOH$$

Reaction with monoethanolamine at 100–110°C

$$2\ (CH_3)_2CHOP(O)F(CH_3) + 3\ HOCH_2CH_2NH_2 + H_2O \rightarrow$$

$$(CH_3)_2CHO(CH_3)P(O)(OCH_2CH_2NH_2) + (CH_3)_2CHO(CH_3)P(O)(OH)$$

$$2\ HOCH_2CH_2NH_3{}^+F^-$$

Oxidation

$$(C_2H_5O)PO(CH_3)SCH_2CH_2N(iPr)_2 + 3\ HSO_5{}^- + H_2O \rightarrow (C_2H_5)OPO(CH_3)OH +$$

$$O_3SCH_2CH_2NH(iPr)_2{}^+ + 3\ HSO_4{}^-$$

Figure 6.4. Chemical reactions for nerve agent destruction

In the 1980s a reaction with ethylene glycol and phosphoric acid was used for V-agents.[35] Russia now plans to use a process for V-agent destruction that will employ the Russian decontaminating solution RD-4, which is principally composed of a mixture of potassium isobutylate and isobutyl alcohol (75 per cent by weight) and N-methyl pyrrolidine (25 per cent by weight).[36] The main component is potassium isobutylate, which reacts with the V-agent. The reaction temperature is approximately 90°C. In a second step the reaction mass is added to the bitumen at approximately 140°C.

VI. Conclusions

The destruction of the 40 000-tonne Russian CW stockpile requires the invest-ment of large amounts of money and major technical and technological efforts. The necessary technologies for these activities exist and have been proven effective and applicable to the situation in Russia. In recent years the discussion on various destruction options has accelerated. Russia's ratification of the CWC

Two-Stage Chemical Agent Destruction Process, Final Technical Report: Phases 1 & 2 (Bechtel National, Inc. and US Army PM-CTR, July 1996 revision), p. 16; and chapter 8 in this volume.

[35] Committee on Alternative Chemical Demilitarization Technologies (note 8), p. 68.

[36] Bechtel National, Inc. and US Army Program Manager for Chemical Demilitarization (note 34).

Pyrolysis

$$(CH_3)_2CHOP(O)F(CH_3) + 6.5\ O_2 + 4\ NaOH \rightarrow 4\ CO_2 + 7\ H_2O + NaF + Na_3PO_4$$

Incineration of sarin

$$2\ (CH_3)_2CHOP(O)F(CH_3) + 13\ O_2 \rightarrow 8\ CO_2 + 9\ H_2O + P_2O_5 + 2\ HF$$

Incineration of soman

$$2\ (CH_3)_3C(CH_3)CHOP(O)F(CH_3) + 22\ O_2 \rightarrow 14\ CO_2 + 15\ H_2O + P_2O_5 + 2\ HF$$

Incineration of VX

$$2\ (C_2H_5O)PO(CH_3)SCH_2CH_2N(iPr)_2 + 39.5O_2 \rightarrow 2\ NO_2 + P_2O_5 + 2\ SO_2 + 22\ CO_2 + 26\ H_2O$$

Figure 6.5. Thermal reactions for nerve agent destruction

is a commitment to CW destruction. The governmental programme on CW destruction must be implemented without delay, and construction of the CW destruction facilities must start soon.

Hesitation with respect to the choice of destruction technology will create further delay. The various technologies have been evaluated and must now be implemented. In order to facilitate implementation more information on the technical aspects of CW destruction should be made available to concerned legislators and citizens so that they more fully understand the advantages and disadvantages of each technology. The citizens of Russia are aware of the need to destroy the Russian CW stockpile, and their support will be crucial to the success of the CW destruction programme.

7. Risks posed by the chemical weapon stockpile in the Udmurt Republic

VLADIMIR KOLODKIN

I. Introduction

A relatively small area of the Ural region contains nearly one-half of the total Russian stockpile of chemical warfare agents.[1] Of the total stockpile, 15.9 per cent is located in Kambarka in the Udmurt Republic;[2] 14.2 per cent in Kizner, also in the Udmurt Republic;[3] and 17 per cent in Maradikovsky in the Kirov region. These chemical agents and the CW destruction facilities to be constructed at each stockpile site pose a potential threat to humans and the environment, and the residents of these areas are therefore anxious that adequate precautions be taken to ensure their safety and the protection of the environment. Various aspects of the potential problems associated with these facilities must be analysed. The decisions regarding the construction and operation of CW storage and destruction facilities require prior analysis of potential hazards (i.e., risk assessment).

II. Risk assessment

A risk assessment of the CW stockpile in the Udmurt Republic was carried out under the aegis of Green Cross International.[4] The following were created or developed for that purpose: (*a*) an information database, including the physical and chemical properties of the CW agents; (*b*) a geographical information system (GIS) for the stockpile sites;[5] (*c*) physical, chemical and mathematical models of the nature and origin of potential threats related to chemical weapons; (*d*) dispersion models of toxic substances in the environment; and (*e*) a computer-based forecasting system. The risk-assessment programme

---

[1] The Ural Mountains extend *c*. 2000 km from the Kara Sea to the border with north-western Kazakhstan. The CW storage facilities are located in the mid-southern Ural region. The Udmurt Republic is located *c*. 1000 km east of Moscow.

[2] Kambarka is located *c*. 1300 km east of Moscow. The CW storage facility is *c*. 3000 metres from the centre of Kambarka. The lewisite, which has been stored at the facility since 1951, is in 8 buildings that have stone walls and wooden roofs. There are 16, 50-m^2 steel tanks in each building. The tanks are 'filled to varying levels'. 'West to help in safe but costly disposal of Russia's CW stocks', *Jane's Defence Weekly*, vol. 26, no. 6 (7 Aug. 1996), p. 15.

[3] Munitions filled with lewisite, sarin, soman and VX are stored at Kizner. The total amount of CW agents at the Kizner storage facility is 5600 tonnes. The CW munitions were transported to Kizner for storage in 1954–87.

[4] Green Cross International is an environmental organization founded by former Soviet President Mikhail Gorbachev. Its headquarters are in Geneva, Switzerland, and its activities include disseminating information on CW destruction.

[5] GIS is a database developed and administered by the Institute of Nature and Technogenic Disasters at Udmurt State University. It is open to the public and was established to support the development of a computer-based modelling system for creating CW-related risk assessments, which is also under development at the institute. That system contains the quantitative information upon which the computer model risk assessments are based. Financial support for it and for the database was provided by Green Cross International. The institute provides information on CW storage and destruction to the press, federal and local officials, students and academics. Institute of Nature and Technogenic Disasters, 'Information sheet', URL <http://wing.uni.udm.ru/intd/kurs.html>, version current on 13 Nov. 1997.

received financial support totalling approximately $120 000 from Green Cross Switzerland and organizational support from Green Cross Russia. It was also supported by the Russian Ministry of Defence, the Headquarters on Civil Defence and Emergencies of the Udmurt Republic, and the Committee on Problems of Chemical and Biological Weapon Conventions of the Government of the Udmurt Republic. The work resulted in the publication of a report on the results of the risk assessment conducted at the Kambarka CW storage facility.[6]

These activities assist the organizations that are responsible for the safety of the local population and the protection of the environment in the vicinity of the CW storage sites by indicating the most likely accident scenarios. This is accomplished by analysis of the main potential hazards and by modelling the behaviour of toxic substances in a contaminated environment.[7] Information is made public in the belief that the local population can be more easily convinced of the need for CW destruction if the potential threat posed by the chemical weapons is demonstrated.

Types of risk

Chemical weapon risk assessments are a quantitative measure of the level of potential hazard posed by such weapons. The assessments may focus on the source of the hazard (e.g., fire or explosion) or on the entity that is affected by it (e.g., humans, air, water). Risks can be classified as active/operational (e.g., accidents that occur during the operation of an industrial chemical facility) or passive/catastrophic, such as catastrophic but relatively unlikely events (e.g., earthquakes, a meteorite or aircraft crash, the spontaneous detonation of a munition or terrorist activities). The risk posed by CW destruction facilities is an example of an active risk while CW storage facilities pose a passive risk. Various types of activities, including those of facility personnel, can also create risks that may fall into either category.

Assessing the degree of risk

The degree of risk associated with the operation of a CW storage facility is not greater than for a comparable industrial chemical facility. There is currently no evidence that the operation of CW storage facilities adversely affects either the health of the people living near them or the environment. As regards the CW storage facilities in the Udmurt Republic, this statement is supported by the results of independent medical examinations of the local population that have

---

[6] Green Cross Russia, *Prognoz Posledstvii Avarii na Obekte Khraneniya Boevykh Otravlyayushchikh Veshchestv v Rayone g. Kambarka Udmurtskoi Respubliki* [Prognosis on accident consequences at the chemical weapon storage facility in the Kambarka region, Udmurt Republic] (Green Cross Russia: Izhevsk, Mar./Nov. 1995).

[7] Modelling is the devising of a mathematical model of a phenomenon, system, etc.

Table 7.1. Predicted frequency of accidents at chemical weapon storage facilities

Type of event	Predicted frequency (year^{-1})^a
Earthquake (Ural Region)^b	10^{-12}
Violent storm (Ural Region)^b	10^{-4}
Aeroplane crash (Kambarka storage facility)^c	10^{-8}
Fire in conjunction with leak of chemical agent^d	10^{-5}

^{a} E.g., 10^{-4} = 1 accident per 10 000 years.

^{b} According to the Ministry of Defence of the USSR (see table sources).

^{c} See note a. Aircraft flights are banned over the Kambarka and Kizner CW storage facilities.

^{d} According to Kholstov et al. (see table sources).

Sources: Ministry of Defence of the USSR, 'Problemy unichtozheniya khimicheskogo oruzhiya' [Chemical weapon destruction problems], *Sbornik Nauchnikh Trudov*, no. 1 (1990), p. 108; and Kholstov, V. I. et al., Puti resheniya problemy bezopasnosti obektov po unichtozheniya khimicheskogo oruzhiya [Ways of resolving the problem of safety at chemical weapon destruction facilities], *Rossisskii Khimicheskii Zhurnal*, vol. 39, no. 4 (1995), pp. 65–73.

been carried out by various organizations[8] and the results of spot checks of the environment.[9] These storage facilities have operated for several decades.

Various factors (e.g., particular threats to the environment or humans, the characteristics of a potential hazard) affect risk assessment. The key elements are the properties and the volume of the chemical agents. An accurate prediction of the extent of risk can be made only after the location, destruction technology and the like have been determined. In general, CW storage facilities can be assumed to be more hazardous than CW destruction facilities. This is because of the greater volume of CW agents at the storage facilities. At CW destruction facilities the quantity of chemical weapons decreases progressively as they are destroyed.

Predicting accidents

Table 7.1 presents an estimate of the probability of events that can cause accidents at CW storage facilities. The frequency of the predicted events varies widely. In table 7.1 the frequency of a given scenario occurring at a CW storage site is indicated numerically (i.e., 10^{-4} per year indicates one accident per 10 000 years). The assessment does not take into account illegal acts such as theft or terrorism.

The probability of an accident caused by a catastrophic, natural occurrence is statistically insignificant. However, the consequences of such an accident would be serious, and a risk assessment is therefore warranted. The effects of catastrophes can be modelled with a much higher degree of certainty than in the

[8] Danilov, G. E. et al., 'Assessment of the state of health of the population of the Kambarka region based on the results of investigations carried out by NIIGTP, VNCMDL and ISMI', and Danilov, G. E. et al., 'The state of health of children living in the vicinity of the lewisite stockpile', *Vtoriye Publichnyie Slushaniya po Probleme Unichtozheniya Khimicheskogo Oruzhiya* [Second public hearings on the problem of chemical weapon destruction] (GRC and Udmurt State University: Izhevsk, Russia, May 1996), pp. 83–86 and 93–95, respectively (in Russian).

[9] Ionov, L. B. et al., 'Results of work on a series of investigations on the state of the environment', *Vtoriye Publichnyie Slushaniya po Probleme Unichtozheniya Khimicheskogo Oruzhiya* (note 8), pp. 51–58 (in Russian).

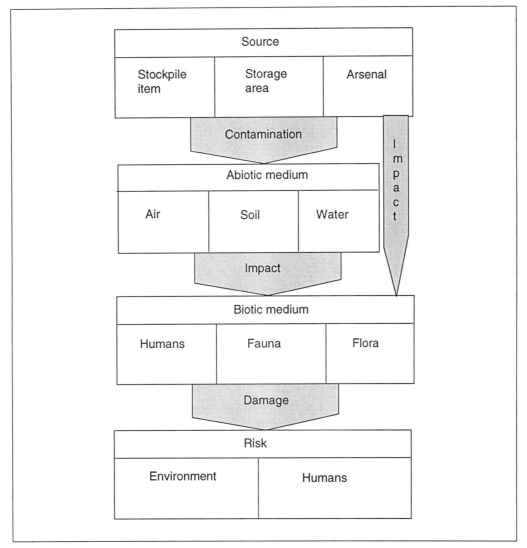

Figure 7.1. General scheme for predicting the consequences of an accident

Source: Author's research.

case of risk associated with normal operations. The assessment of risk should focus on the effect that highly toxic materials can have on humans and the environment. Defining the consequences of an accident is easier than quantifying the likelihood of naturally occurring catastrophes which may never or rarely occur. Because there is no 10 000-year historical record of CW storage facilities it is difficult to exactly determine the probability of accidents.

A general scheme for forecasting the consequences of an accident is shown in figure 7.1. An accident causes contamination of the elements of the abiotic medium (air, soil, water) which transmits the impact to the recipient of the risk.

Defining risk

The source of a hazard, its potential toxic impact on the environment or humans, and the consequences of such an accident can be described by mathematical modelling of the agents' physical and chemical properties. The models

Table 7.2. Models to assess risk of accident

Model	Examples
Source	Explosion of storage tank, fire in building, burning of liquid (e.g., lewisite), depressurization of shell caused by fire or explosion
Abiotic medium	Atmospheric turbulence, evaporation, soil filtration, transport of admixture by stream or river, spread of liquid
Biotic medium	Reaction of humans, fauna or flora to toxic substance
Level of potential hazard	Mathematical presentation of accident risk assessment for humans, flora and fauna

Source: Author's research.

for the region where the CW destruction and storage facilities are located take into account existing conditions, the behaviour of the chemical agent in the environment, the state of health of the local population and the number of people living in the region. Table 7.2 presents a risk model for the CW stockpile in the Udmurt Republic.

The consequences of an accident depend, in particular, on the climatic conditions at the time of the accident. When a risk assessment of a potential accident is made its severity is averaged as a function of time (usually one year). R indicates the magnitude of risk posed to humans or the environment. In table 7.3 the prediction is averaged over a year so that varying meteorological conditions in the different seasons can be taken into account. The proportion of the population that actually will be affected may be higher or lower than R.

The extent of the hazard can be predicted on the basis of analysis of the results of a computer simulation of an accident, the dispersion of the chemical agents into the environment, and the resulting effect on humans and the environment. The reliability of the prediction is primarily determined by how well the physical–chemical–mathematical model corresponds to the circumstances described above. Its validity is affected by how well the model corresponds to the actual reactions of the recipients of risk. The magnitude of risk may be several times higher or lower than the values predicted.

III. Accident scenarios

Predictions of the effect of various accident scenarios in the CW storage facilities at Kambarka and Kizner are presented in tables 7.3–7.11. The value of R depends on the distance from the accident of the object or person affected. The analysis of the consequences of each accident is limited to one hour. In general, the magnitude of risk decreases as the distance from the source increases. The effects of CW exposure can be divided into three categories: lethal effect (death), temporary physical incapacitation and eye irritation.

Table 7.3. Radii of area of lethal effect at an R = 10^{-6} magnitude of risk at the Kambarka CW arsenal

Volume of spill (m^3)	Radius (m)
80	430
320	680
640	870
960	920

Source: Author's research.

Table 7.4. Radii of the area affected by a 320 m^3 lewisite spill at various magnitudes of risk at the Kambarka CW arsenal

Distances are in metres.

Magnitude of risk	R = 10^{-2}	R = 10^{-4}	R = 10^{-6}
Lethal effect	200	450	680
Temporary physical incapacitation	250	850	1 400
Eye irritation lasting up to 30 minutes	350	950	1 500

Source: Author's research.

Table 7.5. Radii of area of lethal effect at R = 10^{-2} and R = 10^{-6} magnitudes of risk when sarin and soman are released from artillery shells of various calibres at the Kizner CW arsenal

Distances are in metres.

Quantity of shells	122-mm	130-mm	152-mm	240-mm
R = 10^{-2} magnitude of risk				
1	1.7	1.5	1.5	2.0
5	1.5	1.5	2.0	3.0
R = 10^{-6} magnitude of risk				
1	4.0	4.0	5.0	7.0
5	5.0	6.0	7.0	12.0

Source: Author's research.

CW agent spill scenario

The Kambarka CW arsenal

In accidents involving spills of CW agents the volume of the spilled agent can vary greatly. The impact of such accidents on humans and the environment will therefore also vary widely. Tables 7.3 and 7.4 illustrate the magnitude of risk for various types of spills at the Kambarka CW arsenal.

The Kizner CW arsenal

Artillery shells filled with sarin and soman are stored at the Kizner CW arsenal. Table 7.5 presents data on the consequences of the release of sarin and soman

Table 7.6. Quantity of storage tanks destroyed in an explosion at the Kambarka CW arsenal

Kilograms of explosive agent	Number of tanks destroyed
1	1
5	4
10	11
50	16

[a] The explosive used was trinitrotoluene, trotyl in Russian.

Source: Author's research.

Table 7.7. Area of lethal effect in an explosion at the Kambarka CW arsenal at various magnitudes of risk

Kilograms of explosive agent	Radius of magnitude of risk (m)	
	$R = 10^{-2}$	$R = 10^{-6}$
10	300	700
20	400	1 000
50	680	1 800

Source: Author's research.

into the atmosphere from these munitions at two magnitudes of risk ($R = 10^{-2}$ and $R = 10^{-6}$).

Explosion in a CW arsenal scenario

The Kambarka CW arsenal

Trinitrotoluene (TNT) units are used to designate the quantity of explosives. In tables 7.6 and 7.7 it is assumed that the explosive agent is located below a storage tank containing lewisite and that all of the explosive agent is destroyed in the blast. The assumption is also made that part of the chemical agent is dispersed into the atmosphere and part spilled onto the ground. Tables 7.6 and 7.7 present data on the scenario of an accidental explosion at the Kambarka CW arsenal.

In such a scenario the neighbouring storage tanks may also be damaged, which would cause additional spillage. The destruction of all of the tanks in one storage building could occur if the equivalent of 25 kg of TNT were to be exploded in the centre of the building (see table 7.7).

The Kizner CW arsenal

The extent of the environmental contamination caused by an explosion would be increased if burster charges ignite as a result of the shock wave that results from the initial explosion. Such 'sympathetic' explosions would cause the

Table 7.8. Characteristics of contaminated areas in an explosion at the Kizner CW arsenal

Kilograms of explosive agent	Radii of area of contamination (m)	Remaining kg of chemical agent in area of contamination
10	50	139
50	340	633
100	620	1 237

Source: Author's research.

Table 7.9. Area of lethal effect in an explosion at the Kizner CW arsenal at various magnitudes of risk

Figures in parentheses represent the area where temporary physical incapacitation would occur.

Kilograms of explosive agent	Radius of magnitude of risk (m)		
	$R = 10^{-2}$	$R = 10^{-4}$	$R = 10^{-6}$
10	1 500	2 500 (3 000)	3 000
20	2 300	4 400 (5 000)	5 000
50	3 000	5 400 (5 600)	5 600
100	3 300	5 500 (5 700)	5 600

Source: Author's research.

Table 7.10. Area of lethal effect in a fire at the Kambarka CW arsenal at various magnitudes of risk

Volume of spill (m³)	Radius of magnitude of risk (m)		
	$R = 10^{-2}$	$R = 10^{-4}$	$R = 10^{-6}$
80	500	1 750	2 300
320	700	2 300	2 800
640	750	2 500	3 200

Source: Author's research.

shells to scatter and the area of contamination to be extended. Tables 7.8 and 7.9 present data on an explosion at the CW arsenal at Kizner.

Fire in a CW arsenal scenario

The Kambarka CW arsenal

The rupture of a storage tank that is filled with a chemical agent in combination with a fire is another possible hazard at a CW arsenal. The consequences of lewisite leaking from a ruptured tank followed by a fire in the centre of a storage building are presented in tables 7.10 and 7.11. In this scenario the assumption has been made that the leak occurred independently, before the fire began.

Table 7.11. Area where human activity would be affected in a fire at the Kambarka CW arsenal at R = 10^{-4} magnitude of risk[a]

Distances are in metres.

Volume of spill (m³)	Radius of area of temporary physical incapacitation	Radius for temporary eye irritation lasting up to 30 minutes
80	2 000	2 400
320	2 700	2 800
640	2 800	3 100

[a] Data on the area of lethal effect are presented in table 7.10.

Source: Author's research.

IV. Conclusions

Risk assessments can be used to determine the best strategy to ensure the safety of humans and the protection of the environment at CW storage and destruction facilities. The results of the assessments can be used to: (*a*) estimate the potential harm posed by operations at these facilities; (*b*) determine the relative efficacy of various protective measures and the extent to which these measures are employed; (*c*) establish an information system (e.g., software for accident and emergency planning and for training the personnel who would be involved in such incidents) to assist in decision making related to safety measures; and (*d*) provide information so that the people, especially those living near the facilities, are provided with the data they need to address their concerns about the facilities.

8. The Russian–US joint evaluation of the Russian two-stage process for the destruction of nerve agents

IRINA P. BELETSKAYA

I. Introduction

The governments of Russia and the United States have concluded a number of bilateral agreements which establish a basis for joint efforts to destroy chemical weapons.[1] The 30 July 1992 bilateral agreement set up a plan of work for providing assistance to the Russian CW destruction programme, and an addendum was agreed to in 1994 which provided for a joint Russian–US evaluation of the Russian two-stage process for the destruction of nerve agents.[2]

A programme for joint evaluation of the Russian two-stage process on a laboratory scale was approved by both Russia and the USA in January 1995 after a meeting between Russian and US specialists in Edgewood, Maryland.[3] Russia agreed to supply detailed information on its proposed destruction process for organophosphorus CW agents, and an evaluation of the process, largely funded by the USA, was scheduled. In part the evaluation was intended to serve as a basis for determining the possibility of further assistance from the USA, including financial assistance for the design and construction of Russian CW destruction facilities.

II. Two-phase evaluation of the Russian process

The evaluation was performed on a laboratory scale and conducted in two phases. In the first phase, the process was carried out jointly by a group of Russian and US scientists at the Chemical–Biological Defense Command (CBDCOM) laboratories in Edgewood, Maryland. Before the start of work agreement was reached on plans, procedures and analytical methods. The joint work was conducted from May to July 1995.

[1] Agreement between the United States of America and the Russian Federation Concerning the Safe and Secure Transport, Storage and Destruction of Weapons and Prevention of Weapons Proliferation, 17 June 1992; and Agreement between the Department of Defense of the United States of America and the President's Committee for Conventional Problems of Chemical and Biological Weapons Concerning the Safe, Secure and Ecologically Sound Destruction of Chemical Weapons, 30 July 1992.

[2] The 1995 Plan of Work for Assistance to the Russian Program for the Destruction of Chemical Weapons within the Framework of the Bilateral Destruction Agreement of 30 July 1992 and the Addendum to para. 12 of the 1994 Plan of Work for Assistance to the Russian Program for the destruction of Chemical Weapons within the Framework of the Bilateral Destruction Agreement.

[3] Program Plan for the Russian–American Experiment on the Joint Evaluation of the Two-Stage Destruction Process of Organophosphorus Agents, 17 Feb. 1995. The Russian participants were the Ministry of Defence of the Russian Federation, the Russian Federation President's Committee on Problems of Chemical and Biological Conventions, the Saratov Higher Military Engineering School of Chemical Defence and the Russian Federation State Scientific Research Institute for Organic Chemistry and Technology (GosNIIOKhT). The US participants were from the Cooperative Threat Reduction programme office of the US Department of Defense; the Program Manager for Chemical Demilitarization and the Edgewood Research, Development and Engineering Center of the Chemical–Biological Defense Command; the On-site Inspection Agency, Washington, DC; and the Edgewood, Md. offices of the non-governmental organization Battelle Memorial Institute.

US chemical warfare agents of high purity (95–99 per cent) were used for most of the experiments. Laboratory operations with undiluted agents were carried out by US specialists, with Russian experts observing both directly and via closed-circuit video. Once the chemical agents had been diluted and the reaction process had begun, laboratory activities were conducted jointly.

The second phase of the programme was carried out in September–November 1995 at the laboratories of the Saratov Higher Military Engineering School of Chemical Defence. Russian munition-grade chemical warfare agents were used to provide a more difficult challenge for the Russian two-stage destruction process. As in the first phase, all laboratory operations with undiluted agents were carried out by specialists from the host nation, with personnel from the United States observing directly and via closed-circuit video.

In addition to the laboratory investigations, specialists from both nations participated in other joint activities to enhance their technical skills and understanding of methods peculiar to each nation. Russian specialists trained US personnel in biochemical analysis methods using equipment and materials provided by Russia. US specialists trained Russian personnel in the use of modern gas chromatographic instrumentation and in the use of nuclear magnetic resonance (NMR) spectrometers.

The facilities at Saratov were refurbished with US funding to bring them into compliance with US safety and operating requirements and to accommodate the modern instrumentation provided by the United States. Identical equipment was used in both phases with the exception of the NMR spectrometer which was used only in the USA.

The experiments in both phases were conducted on four types of agents,[4] two classes of purity (high purity and munition-grade) and two quantities. The work in phase one involved highly pure sarin (GB), soman (GD) and US VX. In the USA two experiments were also performed using 200 grams of munition-grade GB and VX. In phase two munition-grade sarin, soman and Russian VX were used. In both phase one and two approximately 50 grams of each agent were used in each experiment. The favourable results obtained were an important step towards use of the process on a larger scale.

During both phases, to the extent possible, the methods of conducting the experiments and the materials and equipment were identical. Such commonality assured comparable test results in both phases. Four types of materials were used: *(a)* chemical agents, *(b)* special reactants, *(c)* standard laboratory reagents and *(d)* laboratory animals. Sarin, soman and VX with a purity of 98, 99 and 95 per cent, respectively, and munition-grade sarin and VX were used in the first phase. The Russian munition-grade chemical warfare agents sarin, soman and VX were used in the second phase. Four types of chemical agent detoxification reagents were provided by Russia.

In the first stage of the Russian two-stage destruction process the chemical warfare agents are neutralized using an organic reagent. For the G-agents (sarin and soman) the organic reagent is an aqueous solution of monoethanolamine (MEA), approximately 80 per cent by weight with the residual content being water. For the V-agents (Russian and US VX) the organic reagent is the

---

[4] The agents were sarin, soman, US VX and Russian VX, a structural isomer of US VX.

Table 8.1. Criteria for judging the success of phases 1 and 2 of the Russian–US joint evaluation programme

Criteria	Standards

Technology must destroy chemical warfare agent
  Irreversible
  Using solely Russian process
  For US agents sarin (GB), soman (GD), VX
  For Russian agents sarin, soman, Russian VX
	>99.99% destruction efficiency
	  (equivalent to a residual agent of
	  ~100 ppm)
	On laboratory scale

Technology must be safe	No extremely toxic or hazardous products Products must fall into the Russian State Standard Level IV
Results must be scientifically credible	Stand up to independent peer review

Source: Reproduced from Bechtel National, Inc. and US Army Program Manager for Chemical Demilitarization, Office of the Product Manager for Cooperative Threat Reduction (PM-CTR), *Joint Evaluation of the Russian Two-Stage Chemical Agent Destruction Process, Final Technical Report: Phases 1 & 2* (Bechtel National, Inc. and US Army Program Manager for Cooperative Threat Reduction, July 1996 revision), p. xiv.

Russian decontaminating solution RD-4. RD-4 is a brownish liquid which the Russian literature describes as 25 per cent (by mass) N-methyl pyrrolidinone and 75 per cent a mixture of potassium isobutylate and isobutyl alcohol.[5] Potassium isobutylate is the ingredient which reacts chemically with the V-agents. In the second stage of the destruction process the materials produced in the first stage (the 'reaction mass') are mixed with either bitumen[6] and calcium hydroxide ($Ca(OH)_2$), for G-agents, or bitumen alone, for V-agents.

Special attention was given to the qualifications of the participants in planning both phases of the programme. The members of both teams possessed special capabilities, knowledge and expertise for work with chemical weapons. The Russian specialists had in-depth knowledge of the Russian two-stage CW destruction technology because some of them had developed it. The US specialists had worked extensively with modern analytical equipment while the Russian specialists had not. A useful and mutually beneficial exchange of expertise and experience took place during the joint work.

The specialists faced a complex task. Work with chemical weapons is fundamentally risky and requires specially trained personnel and strict control to avoid contamination by toxic agents. The difficulties in this particular situation were increased because of differences in language, training and other factors. None the less, good relations and mutual understanding prevailed among the participants during activities at both Edgewood and Saratov.

III. Criteria for the Russian process and the evaluation programme

Fulfilment of established criteria was essential if the Russian process were to be used for CW destruction. Success depended on demonstrating the effectiveness

---

[5] Russian State standard TU 6-57-71-92.
[6] Bitumens are inflammable substances composed principally of mixtures of hydrocarbons.

Table 8.2. Evaluation of the Russian two-stage CW destruction technology

Characteristic	Conclusion
Destruction efficiency	>99.9999%
Reaction time	Relatively rapid
Operating conditions	Mild, stage 1 operates at moderate temperatures, atmospheric pressure; ordinary process equipment used throughout
Phosphorus–fluorine and phosphorus–sulphur bonds	Broken in stage 1, thus lowering the hazards posed by the reaction mass
Phosphorus	Most remains bound up in the bitumen–salt mass
Amount of waste	Low (for G-type agent: 4–7 times starting mass; for V-type agent: ~3 times)
Safety of reaction products	Merely 'slightly dangerous'

Source: Reproduced from Bechtel National, Inc. and US Army Program Manager for Chemical Demilitarization, Office of the Product Manager for Cooperative Threat Reduction (PM-CTR), *Joint Evaluation of the Russian Two-Stage Chemical Agent Destruction Process, Final Technical Report: Phases 1 & 2* (Bechtel National, Inc. and US Army Program Manager for Cooperative Threat Reduction, July 1996 revision), p. xvi.

of the process to completely, irreversibly and safely destroy chemical weapons, create products unsuitable for CW production, produce compounds of low toxicity and obtain reliable results (see table 8.1).

The two-phase evaluation determined that the Russian two-stage technology met these criteria. It guaranteed up to 99.9999 per cent safe CW destruction, and the resulting decomposition products were of low toxicity (Level IV, the lowest level on the stringent Russian toxicity standards scale).[7] This indicated a high level of detoxification.[8]

The results which were obtained are both reproducible and reliable. An independent technical review produced a report showing that the process met the standards and criteria outlined above, thereby demonstrating the effectiveness of the Russian destruction technology under laboratory conditions (see table 8.2).The report noted the following characteristics of the process: high effectiveness; large, fast reactions at moderate temperatures; complete cleavage of the phosphorus–fluorine (P–F) and phosphorus–sulphur (P–S) bonds (thought to be essential given the high toxicity of the molecules); comparatively low amount of waste; and negligible toxicity of the reaction products.

IV. Plans for further optimization of the CW destruction process

As a part of the Russian CW destruction programme the Russian and US specialists developed principles for optimization[9] of the destruction technology to be implemented after agreement on a future plan of work.[10] Various areas

---

[7] According to the Russian scale of toxicity, there are 4 levels of LD_{50} toxicity for reaction products: Level I, extremely dangerous (2–15 mg/kg); Level II, highly dangerous (15–150 mg/kg); Level III, moderately dangerous (150–5000 mg/kg); and Level IV, slightly dangerous (> 5 000 mg/kg).

[8] Russian state standard 12.1.007-76.

[9] 'Optimization' refers to use of the process on a larger scale.

[10] At the time of writing (Sep. 1997) it appeared that agreement on such a plan might be reached in 1998.

require additional work so that the destruction technology can be utilized effectively on a larger scale. For the neutralization stage work is needed on: the order of mixing the reagents and the speed of addition; the composition and amount of reagents; the temperature inside the reactor vessel; and the rate of mixing and reaction time. For bituminization, the process by which a bitumen is formed, the following have to be addressed: the type and amount of bitumen; the amount of calcium hydroxide and the sequence of its addition; the temperature and pressure inside the reactor; the construction of the reactor and the rate of mixing; and the reaction time. It was proposed that an evaluation be made of the effect the optimization process will have on toxicity levels and that experiments be conducted with larger quantities of chemical agents.

These issues, which are fundamental to the successful use of the Russian destruction technology, will be dealt with in the future.[11] Additional data must be obtained as the destruction technology is 'scaled up' for use in large-scale CW destruction activities. Many technological aspects (e.g., the nature of the reagent used for neutralization) require further study. Any questions of a technological nature which remain must be investigated using a structured scientific approach to ensure that the results are reliable and have been arrived at by the use of proper methodology.

V. The Russian two-stage CW destruction process

In the initial stage of the Russian destruction process the chemical weapons are destroyed by the action of a specific reagent which neutralizes them. The highly toxic chemical weapons are transformed into a reaction mass of low toxicity. Although its toxicity is low, the resulting product is not discarded but instead undergoes further treatment. In the second stage of the destruction process the reaction mass is treated with calcium hydroxide and bitumen for G-agents or bitumen alone for V-agents. The bituminization occurs at high temperatures (200°C for G-agents, 180°C for V-agents). Any CW which remain in the reaction mass after neutralization are destroyed. The decomposition products formed in the first stage are bound into a bitumen–salt mass.[12] Volatile organic compounds are distilled from the mixture during bituminization. The resulting product is a hard, black solid which is disposed of by burial in special containers.[13]

Detoxification of G-agents

The Russian two-stage destruction process for sarin and soman consists of neutralization by monoethanolamine in the presence of water at moderate temperature (approximately 110°C). The resulting reaction is depicted in figure 8.1. (The complete reaction may be significantly more complex.) It is important that the G-agents are transformed almost completely to products of low toxicity or significantly lowered toxicity.

[11] At the time of writing (Sep. 1997) it was not possible to say when this would occur.
[12] The bitumen–salt mass is a form of asphalt which contains hydrocarbons that boil at high temperature, alkaline salts and earths, and metals. It presents a low hazard of flammability because of the nature of hydrocarbons.
[13] The substance is a form of asphalt (note 12).

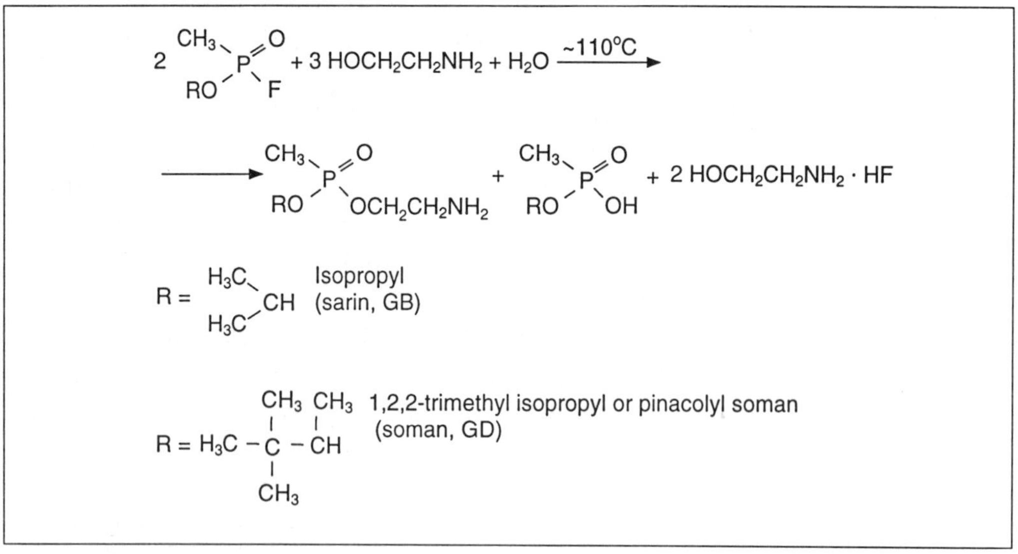

$$2 \; \underset{RO}{\overset{CH_3}{\diagdown}} \underset{F}{\overset{O}{P}} + 3 \; HOCH_2CH_2NH_2 + H_2O \xrightarrow{\sim 110^\circ C}$$

$$\longrightarrow \underset{RO}{\overset{CH_3}{\diagdown}} \underset{OCH_2CH_2NH_2}{\overset{O}{P}} + \underset{RO}{\overset{CH_3}{\diagdown}} \underset{OH}{\overset{O}{P}} + 2 \; HOCH_2CH_2NH_2 \cdot HF$$

$$R = \underset{H_3C}{\overset{H_3C}{\diagdown}} CH \quad \begin{array}{l} \text{Isopropyl} \\ \text{(sarin, GB)} \end{array}$$

$$R = H_3C - \overset{CH_3}{\underset{CH_3}{\overset{|}{C}}} - \overset{CH_3}{\overset{|}{CH}} \quad \begin{array}{l} \text{1,2,2-trimethyl isopropyl or pinacolyl soman} \\ \text{(soman, GD)} \end{array}$$

Figure 8.1. Neutralization of G-agents

The MEA employed in the Russian destruction process consists of 15–20 per cent water, by weight or mass. The molar ratio of reagents is approximately 1.0 : 2.3 : 1.5 (CW : MEA : H$_2$O).[14] The reaction is exothermic, and the resulting solution is referred to as the reaction mass.

In the second stage a hot mixture (130–140°C) of bitumen and calcium hydroxide is added to the reaction mass at atmospheric pressure. The resulting mixture is then heated to approximately 200°C at lowered pressure—approximately 0.10 atmospheres (atm) or 10 100 pascals (Pa)—for about one hour. The composition of the mixture is roughly the following: 35–37 per cent reaction mass, 12–14 per cent calcium hydroxide and 50–55 per cent bitumen.[15] Hardening occurs during cooling, resulting in the bitumen–salt mass. These bituminization conditions are needed in order to destroy any possible trace amounts of G-agents which may have remained after treatment with MEA. Destruction is achieved both by thermal treatment and the reaction with calcium hydroxide. The resulting product has a toxicity that places it at Russian Level IV, 'slightly dangerous', and it is less toxic than Category III of the US Department of Transportation guidelines.[16]

The calcium hydroxide treatment is important because the calcium hydroxide combines completely with the fluoride ions formed during neutralization into insoluble calcium fluoride. In this way it removes the fluoride ions from the reaction medium, essentially guaranteeing the irreversibility of the process and the impossibility of CW re-formation. The calcium hydroxide is also able to break the P–OR ester bond, leading to the formation of an associated ROH alcohol and insoluble calcium methylphosphonate (MeP(O)O$_2$Ca). The alcohols formed, together with a significant amount of 'unreacted' MEA (i.e., which did

---

[14] A mole is 1 of 7 base units of the Système International d'Unités, also know as the International System of Units. It is a unit of quantity equal to 6.02 x 10^{23} particles. It is equivalent to the amount of substance equal to the quantity containing as many elementary units as there are atoms in 0.012 kg of carbon-12.

[15] The percentages are by mass.

[16] Code of Federal Regulations, CFR 49, 'Transportation', paragraph 173.132, Class 6, Division 6.1, pp. 500–501, 1 Oct. 1993 edn.

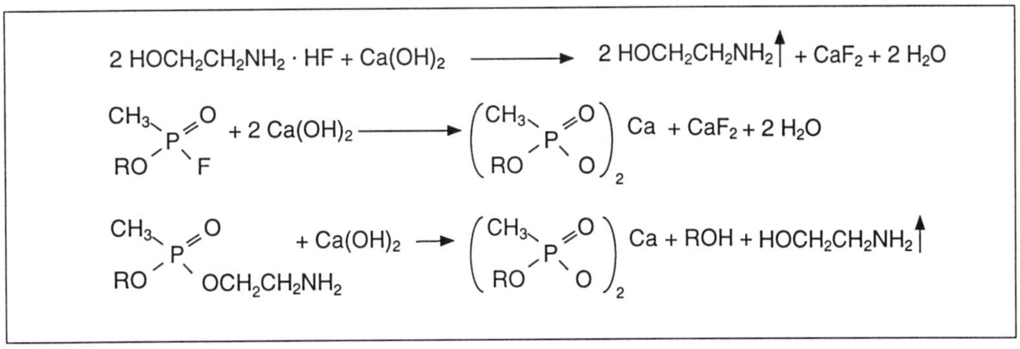

Figure 8.2. Bituminization of G-agents

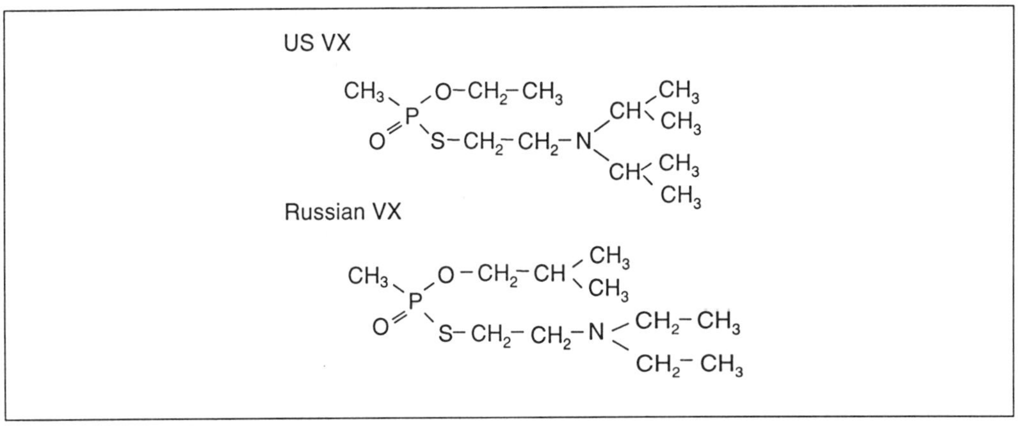

Figure 8.3. US and Russian VX

not participate in the reaction), are distilled off as the bitumen mass is heated at lowered atmospheric pressure. The distilled material can be reused. (The reactions which occur are shown in figure 8.2.)

The distillation of alcohol during bituminization increases the stability of the bitumen–salt mass and makes it resistant to leaching. Testing conducted during the 1995 Russian–US joint evaluation suggested that the products of the reaction are essentially environmentally safe. More extensive testing, which is needed to validate the results, will be conducted in the optimization programme.

Detoxification of V-agents

The first stage of the Russian two-stage V-agent destruction process involves a reaction with the special decontamination reagent RD-4 at a moderate temperature (approximately 90°). The ratio of V-agent to RD-4 is approximately 1 : 2, and the reaction is exothermic (see figure 8.3). In the reaction with RD-4, the phosphorus–sulphur bond is broken and methylphosphonate esters and alkyl salts of the corresponding aminoethanolamine are formed (see figure 8.4). This bond is responsible for the lethal action of VX.

The resulting reaction mass is subjected to bituminization. Bitumen is heated to 130–140°C and then added to an amount of reaction mass approximately equal to 60 per cent (by mass) of the bitumen (i.e., 6 grams of reaction mass would be added to 10 grams of bitumen). The temperature is raised to approximately 180°C for 30–45 minutes. The pressure is then reduced to approxi-

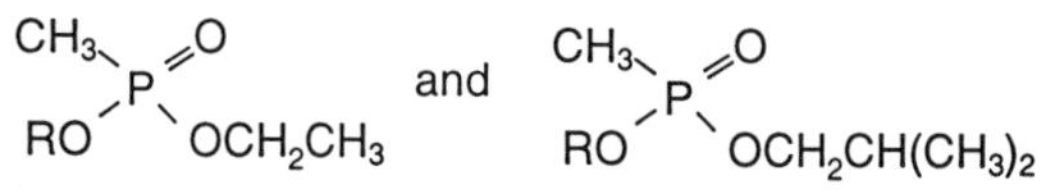

$$CH_3 \diagdown \overset{O}{\underset{\diagup}{P}} \diagdown OCH_2CH_3 \qquad \text{and} \qquad CH_3 \diagdown \overset{O}{\underset{\diagup}{P}} \diagdown OCH_2CH(CH_3)_2$$

Figure 8.4. Methylphosphonate esters formed during the reaction of RD-4 with US and Russian VX, respectively

mately 0.2 atm (approximately 20 200 Pa), and the volatile components (alcohols) are distilled off. They are recovered by condensation and can be reused. As in the case of the G-agents, the removal of alcohols increases the physical stability of the bitumen–salt mass and makes it more resistant to leaching. When the reaction is completed the bitumen–salt mass is poured out of the reactor vessel and allowed to cool. A hard, black solid is formed which is disposed of by burial in special containers.

Bituminization of V-agents differs from that of G-agents. Calcium hydroxide is not used because the phosphorus–fluoride bond is absent in V-agents and no fluoride ions are formed by its breakup, as is the case with the G-agents. Calcium hydroxide is used when destroying the G-agents since it reacts with the fluoride ions that are liberated during neutralization. Its use is unnecessary for V-agents. As with the G-agents, the second stage of V-agent destruction must ensure the destruction of any trace amounts of CW, in the event that destruction in the first stage was not total. The second stage ensures the transformation of the reaction mass to a product with low volatility and toxicity, corresponding to Level IV of the Russian toxicity scale.[17]

VI. Analysis methods

The most important aspect of CW destruction is credible analytical determination of the concentrations of toxic compounds. Only modern physico-chemical methods can quickly and precisely ascertain the completeness of the CW destruction and be used to accurately interpret the nature of the products formed. Modern analytical methods and the most up-to-date equipment with high resolution capabilities were used in both stages of the joint evaluation programme.

Russian and US specialists agreed on the application of analytical methods and corresponding equipment in May–August 1995. The equipment and methods included: (a) a biochemical analyser developed by the State Scientific Research Institute for Organic Chemistry and Technology (GosNIIOKhT); (b) Hewlett–Packard 5890 Series gas chromatographs of four detector types (atomic emission, mass spectrometric, Fourier transform infrared and flame photometric); and (c) nuclear magnetic resonance (NMR) spectrometry. In the USA the NMR spectra were determined using a Bruker Avance spectrometer DRX-300 megahertz (MHz) instrument measuring ^{1}H, ^{13}C, ^{19}F, and ^{31}P, and in Russia a Varian VXR-300 MHz instrument at Moscow State University measuring ^{1}H, ^{13}C, and ^{31}P was used. Using the same method but different types of NMR spectrometers did not distort the results.

[17] Note 7.

Analyses using various gas chromatographic and NMR spectral techniques demonstrated that the CW agent was not detectable in the stage one product (the reaction mass) or in the distillates produced in the second stage when the reaction mass was mixed with bitumen. The chemical agent was either absent or its concentration was below the detection limits of these methods. These data agreed with biochemical analysis which indicated that the remaining amount of chemical agent from sarin after the first stage of destruction was less than $2–4 \times 10^{-4}$ mg/ml. Destruction efficiency after the first stage therefore was 99.940–99.912 per cent and greater than 99.999 per cent after the second stage. For VX biochemical analysis revealed that the trace content of chemical agent was $2.2–9.0 \times 10^{-4}$ mg/ml, which corresponds to a destruction efficiency of 99.37–99.43 per cent. After the second stage, the efficiency increased to more than 99.999 per cent.

Toxicological investigations were conducted on laboratory animals.[18] Veterinarians monitored all work using laboratory animals, cared for the animals and prepared them for toxicological investigations.

After the first stage analysis showed that the reaction mass corresponded to Level III of the Russian toxicity scale,[19] the category to which the detoxification reagent MEA belongs. (As mentioned above, the bitumen–salt mass meets the criteria of Level IV of the Russian toxicity scale.[20]) Analysis also showed a destruction efficiency of greater than 99.999 per cent for all of the types of CW agents on which experiments were conducted, whether pure or munition-grade. In addition, the products that were formed were essentially safe (i.e., were not more toxic than laboratory reagents).

VII. Independent peer review of the results

When the joint evaluation programme was established it was decided that both the results and the methods of achieving them should be reviewed by an independent group of specialists with high qualifications in their fields. Their task was to evaluate the scientific credibility of the results. This was of key significance in order to demonstrate the effectiveness of the technology, and because the results of the appraisal were to be presented to a larger community in both Russia and the USA. A positive evaluation by independent experts with acknowledged achievements in their fields—but without personal, organizational or financial interest in the Russian CW destruction programme—was needed to inspire confidence in government and scientific circles and to address the concerns of those sceptical of the effort.

An independent Peer Review Committee (PRC) of three Russian and three US scientists was established to conduct the joint evaluation. The results are to be made accessible as part of the open archival documents on the joint evaluation programme. The author of this chapter was chosen to serve as the Russian co-chairman of the committee, and Professor Joseph Bunnett was chosen as the

---

[18] Male Sprague-Dawley albino rats from the Charles River Laboratories in Raleigh, N.C., were used in the 1st stage, and male Fisher-Strain albino rats from the Stolobovaya Russian Academy of Medical Sciences (Rossisskaya Akademiya Meditsinskick Nauk) laboratory animal nursery near Moscow were used in the 2nd stage.

[19] Note 7.

[20] Note 7.

US co-chairman.[21] The PRC familiarized itself with the work performed and its results. The PRC report on the Russian CW destruction process deemed it sufficiently successful and made a number of recommendations, some of which were adopted in later experiments.[22] Most of the recommendations remain to be implemented. The PRC evaluated the effectiveness and reliability of the chemical agent destruction method but did not compare it with other CW destruction methods. No evaluation was made of the costs involved or of the economic feasibility of the method.

VIII. Conclusions

It is important to emphasize both that the laboratory-scale investigations were carried out successfully and that they were conducted in two phases. In the two phases the US specialists familiarized themselves with the Russian destruction methods for two types of chemical agents and with Russian biochemical analysis methods, and the Russian specialists were able to acquaint themselves with the use of modern analytical equipment. The experiments in the USA were conducted with highly pure chemical agent, so-called standard analytical reference materials (SARM). In Russia the experiments were conducted with munition-grade chemical agents which are less pure than chemical agent standard analytical reference materials (CASARM) and may contain decomposition products, various mixtures formed during manufacture or transport, and special additives (e.g., stabilizers and thickeners). It is significant that the results of the experiments revealed no difference between laboratory and munition-grade chemical agents.

Experiments with munition-grade chemical agents require specialized equipment and laboratories with modern control and analysis technology. The establishment of a central analytical laboratory is a necessary first step towards chemical agent destruction operations. The modern equipment provided by the USA for the joint evaluation in Russia was left in Russia for use in such a laboratory.[23] This is positive considering the economic difficulties that Russia is currently experiencing. It is highly desirable that the promising cooperation which has begun between Russian and US specialists and to which substantial resources and efforts have been committed continues to be developed.

---

[21] Professor Bunnett and the present author were chosen as co-chairmen because they are chairman and co-chairman, respectively, of the International Union of Pure and Applied Chemistry Committee on Chemical Weapons Destruction. The co-chairmen selected the remaining members of the PRC: Professor Alexander Chimiskyan (Russia), Professor Matthew Meselson (USA), Dr George Parshall (USA) and Professor Sergey Varfolomeev (Russia).

[22] Bechtel National, Inc. and US Army Program Manager for Chemical Demilitarization, Office of the Product Manager for Cooperative Threat Reduction (PM-CTR), *Joint Evaluation of the Russian Two-Stage Chemical Agent Destruction Process, Final Technical Report: Phases 1 & 2* (Bechtel National, Inc. and US Army Program Manager for Cooperative Threat Reduction, July 1996 revision).

[23] It is located at GosNIIOKhT in Moscow.

9. The role of GosNIIOKhT in the Russian chemical weapon destruction programme

VLADISLAV SHELUCHENKO and ANTON UTKIN

I. Introduction

The State Scientific Research Institute for Organic Chemistry and Technology (GosNIIOKhT) was founded in 1924. GosNIIOKhT is well known for its research and development (R&D) work in the field of organic synthesis, including work with application to the Russian chemical industry. One of its notable developments was a method for large-capacity production of phenol and acetone through oxidation of isopropyl benzene.[1] This technique has also been used in other countries, including the United States.[2] GosNIIOKhT has significant research and production capabilities and currently conducts R&D on pharmaceuticals. The GosNIIOKhT facilities include a pilot plant where technologies can be tested from the laboratory- to pilot-plant scale. There are also laboratories where research is carried out on highly toxic agents. GosNIIOKhT subcontracts with established R&D organizations in Russia.

Under the Special Federal Programme for Chemical Weapons Destruction,[3] the Committee on Chemical and Petrochemical Industry is responsible for R&D related to CW destruction technology, and GosNIIOKhT is the leading organization within that committee. The institute analyses and tests existing methods and technologies, develops the most promising ones, provides data for the design of destruction facilities, makes available scientific support and supervision during the design and operation of such facilities, and refines CW destruction processes.

In addition, GosNIIOKhT develops methods for munition disassembly, including access to and removal of CW agents. It also develops methods for the decontamination of equipment, buildings, CW packaging materials and protective equipment, and for CW decontamination and thermal treatment of munitions. The institute is responsible for the development of the monitoring methods to be used during CW destruction. It has developed systems for pollution abatement and the treatment of waste water. In short, GosNIIOKhT is involved in all the activities that comprise the technology of CW destruction.

---

[1] Isopropyl benzene is also known as 2-methelethyl benzene. Its common name is cumene.

[2] Development of this process initially took place at GosNIIOKhT and was provided to the USA as partial compensation for US Lend Lease assistance to the Soviet Union in World War II. Western sources refer to the cumene oxidation process as the Hoch Process and credit US sources for its development. However, Karrer, P., *Course of Organic Chemistry* (GosKhimIzdat: Moscow, 1960), p. 224, fn (in Russian) refers to a cumene process developed by P. G. Sergeev, B. D. Kruzhatov and R. Yu Udris. The basic patents for the Hoch Process were granted to Allied Chemical & Dye Corporation, Inc., US patent no. 2 613 227, granted 7 Oct. 1952, Crane, E. J. *et al.*, *Chemical Abstracts* (American Chemical Society, Ohio State University: Columbus, Ohio, 10 Nov.–10 Dec. 1953), col. 11246; and Hercules Powder Company, US patent no. 2 484 841, granted 18 Oct. 1949, Crane, E. J. *et al.*, *Chemical Abstracts* (American Chemical Society, Ohio State University: Columbus, Ohio, 10 May.–25 Aug. 1950), col. 5908.

[3] 'Federalnaya tselevaya programma' [Special federal programme], Federal government edict no. 305, 21 Mar. 1996, *Rossiyskaya Gazeta*, 2 Apr. 1996, pp. 5–6; and Russian Federation, Special federal programme, destruction of chemical weapons stockpiles in the Russian Federation, Preparatory Commission document PC-XIV/B/WP.7, 25 June 1996, pp. 19–20.

At GosNIIOKhT, the scientist who develops a particular technology has the right and responsibility to ensure that its design and operation conform with the criteria and requirements for the technology and to design documentation. The scientist also has the right to suspend work until any problem or defect in a technological process is corrected.

II. Requirements for destruction technology and design criteria

The development of CW destruction technology must take into account such factors as the safety of the personnel and protection of the environment, the standards for allowable CW agent residue in the discharge streams, design criteria, cost, and availability of relevant experience in industry.

Russia has strict standards for the concentration of residual CW agent in discharge streams. Table 9.1 presents the Russian and US standards for maximum allowable concentrations in the air at working areas and for the general population. It shows that the norms in Russia are higher by at least one order of magnitude than in the USA. This means that the technology which is used in the USA is not necessarily applicable to Russia.

Design criteria must be established for any given CW destruction technology, and Russian design criteria specify that 'agents which are in the process of being destroyed and their solutions should be transferred through pipelines by vacuum or gravity'.[4] This requirement rules out the use of all technologies which operate at high pressure (i.e., above atmospheric pressure) as well as most technologies which operate at high temperatures.[5] The processes proposed for or in use by the United States (direct incineration, supercritical water oxidation, wet air oxidation and high-temperature hydrogenation) are therefore inconsistent with the Russian requirements for gravity or vacuum feed.

In order to develop CW destruction technology and establish principles and approaches that meet the Russian design criteria, GosNIIOKhT has conducted experiments into various agent detoxification methods including chemical liquid phase methods,[6] incineration, plasma arc methods, thermodegradation and polymerization. More than 40 technical methods have been tested by GosNIIOKhT, and technologies which for various reasons were not tested were nevertheless subjected to careful analysis and consideration. During this work 'discreteness', batch-mode and two-stage destruction were determined to be the key factors for the development of CW destruction technology.

Discreteness

'Discreteness' means that only a strictly limited quantity of a highly toxic CW agent is involved in the technological process. This quantity should correspond to the volume of agent in one or several munitions. The CW agent is immedi-

---

[4] Committee of the Russian Federation on Chemical and Petrochemical Industry, *Normi po Proektirovanii i Eksplutatsii Proizvodstv po Unitchtozheniu Khimicheskogo Oruzhiya* [Design and operation criteria for chemical weapon destruction facilities] (Ministry of Defense of the Russian Federation: Moscow, 1995), p. 9.

[5] This is because agent vaporization at high temperatures makes the application of vacuum methods for agent transfer more difficult.

[6] Such methods include oxidation, chlorination, hydrolysis, base- and acid-catalysed hydrolysis, reduction, alcoholysis, ammonolysis and the like.

Table 9.1. Russian and US standards for maximum allowable concentration of various CW agents (mg/m³) in air

Chemical agent	Russia		USA	
	Work area limit	GPL[a]	Work area limit	GPL[a]
Sarin (GB)	2×10^{-5}	2×10^{-7}	1×10^{-4}	3×10^{-6}
Soman (GD)	1×10^{-5}	1×10^{-7}	2×10^{-5}	3×10^{-6}
VX	5×10^{-6}	5×10^{-8}	1×10^{-5}	3×10^{-6}
Mustard (HD)	2×10^{-4}	2×10^{-6}	3×10^{-3}	1×10^{-4}
Lewisite (L)	2×10^{-4}	4×10^{-6}	3×10^{-3}	3×10^{-3}

[a] General population limit, the contamination limits for the general population as opposed to the limits for the facility.

Source: Kalinina, N., 'K voprosu o standartakh bezopasnosti pri unichtozhenii khimicheskogo oruzhiya' [Towards the issue on safety standards during chemical weapon destruction], *Toksikologicheskii vestnik*, no. 3 (1994), pp. 6–9.

ately subjected to treatment without first being collected in intermediate tanks. It is evacuated, transferred by pipeline into the reactor and then immediately detoxified (thus avoiding the need for additional storage space). This is an important safety principle because it allows emergency situations to be localized more easily (i.e., through the relatively small amount of agent being processed). The severity of CW-related accidents is directly related to the quantity of CW agent involved. The principle of 'discreteness' is in complete accordance with the Russian design criteria requirements.[7]

Batch mode

The batch-mode CW destruction method assumes that no additional CW agent will be added for detoxification before the initial amount has been completely processed. The completeness of agent detoxification must be confirmed by analytical methods. Continuous processes require constant, real-time monitoring to ensure that the maximum allowable concentrations of pollutants are not exceeded. Most continuous monitoring devices require three to five minutes before a reading can be taken, and excess emissions may go undetected during this period. Although the overall process design determines the level of risk of the pollution emission, batch-mode processes are inherently preferable to continuous processes because of their simpler design. Safety and reliability issues are best addressed during the initial development of the process rather than at the design stage.

Batch mode and discreteness are interrelated. For example, the US technology of direct incineration is a batch-mode–continuous process hybrid. CW agents from many different munitions are first accumulated in intermediate tanks—up to five tonnes at the Johnston Atoll Chemical Agent Disposal System (JACADS)—to maintain the continuous phase of direct incineration. When the batch-mode method is used the discharge of the products of incomplete detoxification into the environment can also more easily be avoided.

[7] Committee of the Russian Federation on Chemical and Petrochemical Industry (note 4).

However, if the CW agent is not completely oxidized during incineration it will nevertheless be discharged into the atmosphere through the stack, a fact which has been demonstrated in practice during operations at the JACADS facility. The batch-mode method meets the requirements of the Russian design criteria.[8]

Two-stage destruction

Two-stage destruction means that the agent must be destroyed twice—both times with 'completeness of destruction'.[9] Detoxification is accomplished at each stage with a high degree of destruction efficiency.

III. Two-stage technology

The GosNIIOKhT two-stage technology for destroying nerve agents is based on the above principles. It benefits from the experience gained from the construction of the pilot training facility at Chapaevsk, work on the destruction of leaking munitions with the Complex for the Destruction of Faulty Chemical Munitions (KUASI) mobile destruction unit and other research which resulted in the elimination of 5000 munitions of various calibres that contained approximately 200 tonnes of organophosphorus CW agents.[10] GosNIIOKhT supervised the construction of the Chapaevsk destruction facility, which began in 1986 and was completed in 1989. The facility has a design throughput of 350 tonnes of CW agent per year,[11] but it was never put into operation because of local protests. The KUASI destruction technology was designed to destroy non-explosive CW munitions that contain sarin, soman or VX. In the first stage the CW agent is treated with monethanolamine. The reaction products and munition body are then treated thermally.[12] The KUASI mobile destruction unit alone destroyed 4000 munitions of various calibres that contained approximately 280 tonnes of organophosphorus CW agents.[13]

The two-stage destruction technology is characterized by the simplicity of the main technological unit and chemical process, the availability of relevant experience from industry, its relatively low cost and the fact that it meets the Russian design criteria.

---

[8] Committee of the Russian Federation on Chemical and Petrochemical Industry (note 4), p. 11.

[9] Completeness of destruction is used to describe the extent to which the agent has been destroyed.

[10] Letter dated 16 December 1987 from the representative of the Union of Soviet Socialist Republics addressed to the President of the Conference on Disarmament transmitting a working paper entitled 'Information on the presentation at the Shikhany military facility of standard chemical munitions and of technology for the destruction of chemical weapons at a mobile unit', Conference on Disarmament document CD/789, 16 Dec. 1987; Union of Soviet Socialist Republics, Complex for the Destruction of Faulty Chemical Munitions (KUASI), Conference on Disarmament document CD/CW/WP.369, 8 Oct. 1991; and *An Important Confidence-Building Step: Foreign Observers Visit the Shikhany Military Area in the Soviet Union* (Novosti Press Agency Publishing House: Moscow, 1988).

[11] Petrov, S. V., 'Osnovnye problemy unichtozheniya khimicheskogo oruzhiya v Rossiyskoi Federatsii' [Fundamental problems of chemical weapon destruction in the Russian Federation], *Rossiyskii Khimicheskii Zhurnal*, vol. 37, no. 3 (1993), pp. 5–7.

[12] Union of Soviet Socialist Republics (note 10).

[13] Koshelev, V.M. *et al.*, 'Metody unichtozheniya fosfororganicheskikh otravlyaushchikh veshchestv' [Methods for the destruction of organophosphorus CW agents], *Rossiyskii Khimicheskii Zhurnal*, vol. 37, no. 3 (1993), pp. 22–25.

Chemical reaction

The first stage of CW destruction is a chemical reaction which transforms highly toxic CW agents into compounds of lower toxicity. Sarin, for example, is reacted with monoethanolamine, which results in a reaction mass with a toxicity of less than 2000 mg/kg. In other words, the first stage reduces the level of toxicity of the sarin 20 000 times. The toxicity level of the resulting reaction mass corresponds to Level III of the Russian scale of toxicity.[14] The human toxicity of the reaction mass is roughly equivalent to that of common chemicals, such as table salt (sodium chloride).

The products of detoxification are then subjected to further treatment. The second stage consists of binding the initial reaction products into a hydrophobic matrix by chemical linkage. This is done by treating the initial reaction products with a mixture of bitumen and calcium hydroxide. The most modern analytical instrumentation cannot detect even trace amounts of the CW agent. The bitumen–salt mass has a Level IV toxicity. Munitions are similarly treated. In the first stage the internal surface is chemically decontaminated, and in the second stage the munitions are thermally treated in a furnace.

Bituminization

The bituminization process is of special interest in part because of the lack of information on it in the scientific literature. The GosNIIOKhT method of using bituminization for secondary processing of CW agent detoxification products is novel. The advantages of bituminization include the fact that it meets the CWC requirement that destruction be 'essentially irreversible'.[15] During bituminization, the fluoride ions that are present in the reaction masses from G-type nerve agents (sarin and soman) are tightly bound. This occurs through the formation of calcium salts, which have the added benefit of extremely low solubility in water.[16] These features are important because of the ill effects on health of biologically active fluorine. Bituminization produces a solid material and a relatively low increase in the total quantity of waste, which is desirable in terms of safety and convenience during handling, transport and disposal. The Russian two-stage process results in approximately 3.5–6 times the volume of waste for each unit of CW agent.[17]

Disassembly

One of the most complex steps of any CW destruction technology is munition disassembly. Each method of munition disassembly has a unique set of risks

---

[14] In the Russian scale of toxicity (Russian State Standard 12.1.007-76), there are 4 levels of LD50 toxicity for reaction products: Level I, extremely dangerous (2–15 mg/kg); Level II, highly dangerous (15–150 mg/kg); Level III, moderately dangerous (150–5000 mg/kg); and Level IV, slightly dangerous (> 5 000 mg/kg).

[15] Verification Annex, Part IV(A), para. 12. The Convention on the Prohibition of the Development, Production, Stockpiling and Use of Chemical Weapons and on their Destruction (corrected version), 8 Aug. 1994, is reproduced on the SIPRI Chemical and Biological Warfare Project Internet site at URL <http://www.sipri.se/cbw/docs/cw-cwc-texts.html>.

[16] Investigations into the leachates of the bitumen–salt mass are being conducted in the scaling-up process of the 2-stage CW destruction technology.

[17] See the discussion in chapter 8 in this volume.

associated with it. The method used also determines the amount of agent which can be processed (i.e., the 'throughput' of the destruction facility). There are three main types of disassembly: opening the munition, standard reverse assembly and biological degradation.[18] Biological degradation is at an early stage of development,[19] and it is unlikely that it can be used for CW destruction.

Two disassembly methods that are widely used in the USA are reverse assembly and the punching–shearing technique. In the USA projectiles and mortars are reverse-assembled, while bombs, mines, rockets and bulk containers are opened by punching holes in the munitions. Unfortunately, these methods cannot be applied in Russia in the way that they are in the USA. First, the construction of Russian projectiles does not allow the use of reverse assembly. Second, according to the Russian requirements all disassembly operations must be conducted in protective casings with ventilation in order to prevent agent release in the air of the working area and to localize emergency situations.[20]

GosNIIOKhT has developed a multi-position carousel disassembly machine. The machine is enclosed in a ventilated metal box which has one system for collecting leaked CW agents and another for emergency decontamination. Its design fully meets the Russian requirements.

Drilling chemical munitions is complex, and, as mentioned above, Russian munitions cannot be reverse-assembled. Although it is possible to obtain access to the CW agent by unscrewing the plug to the filling hole, drilling is still necessary in order to secure the plug through clamping. In addition, it may be difficult to locate the plug and determine its orientation. Shavings are produced during drilling, and the drill is designed to ensure that the shaving action is continuous and that the shavings are pushed to the outside, where they are removed from the munition by magnets.

After drilling is complete the munition moves to the next stage, where the agent is siphoned out. The siphon is hermetically sealed against the munition body by an obturation device. In addition, negative pressure is maintained to guard against leak contamination. At the next position the internal surface of the munition is first chemically decontaminated and then heated to a temperature of at least 500°C. Monitoring is maintained to ascertain when decontamination is complete. These operations meet Russian requirements. All these operations were tested during R&D and construction of the pilot training facility at Chapaevsk. The design of the multi-position carousel disassembly machine is continually improved to reflect new technological developments and the experience obtained from testing its operation.

Although munition disassembly and CW agent detoxification form the basis of two-stage destruction technology, they constitute a relatively small portion of the overall destruction technology. Detoxification activities constitute less than 5 per cent of the entire destruction facility. The rest of the facility is used for treatment and purification of the wastes produced in CW destruction, thermal treatment of munitions, process control, monitoring of the ventilation and process air, and so on. GosNIIOKhT deals with all of these processes.

---

[18] See the discussion in chapter 6 in this volume.

[19] Varfolomeev, S.D. *et al.*, 'A new technological approach to destruction of chemical weapons: complete biological degradation of chemical munitions', *Zhurnal Vsesouznogo Khimicheskogo Obshchestva*, vol. 39, no. 4 (1995), pp. 20–24 (in Russian).

[20] Committee of the Russian Federation on Chemical and Petrochemical Industry (note 4), pp. 9–10.

Monitoring

Both Russian and other media have stated that Russia does not possess a monitoring system that is capable of reliably identifying agents at low concentrations, including the maximum allowable limit (MAL). Russia does, in fact, possess such devices, some of which were designed and developed with the participation of GosNIIOKhT. Three of them are described below.

An automatic gas alarm (ZUB-80) has been developed by GosNIIOKhT. This device is designed to detect organophosphorus agents in the air. The analytical process used in the device is based on a biochemical method and allows for the detection of organophosphorus agents (sarin, soman and VX) in the air at the MAL (see table 9.1). The ZUB-80 allows automatic monitoring of the work-zone air in the entire CW destruction facility. The detection limit for sarin, soman and VX is 1–10 MAL. The response time is 11 minutes. The ZUB-80 can operate for 24 hours without reloading.

GosNIIOKhT has also developed an automatic gas monitoring system (ZBJ-1). This system is designed for continuous and rapid automatic monitoring of the work-zone air at environmentally sensitive facilities. It allows the detection of various hazardous chemicals in the air at the MAL. The use of highly sensitive gauges and computers facilitate data transmission and rapid response in emergency situations. The monitoring system consists of the devices in separate modules. The analytical procedure used in the device is based on an integrated nuclear ionization method, and over 100 substances can be monitored. The sensitivity of the system is 1–1000 MAL, and the response time is 3–10 seconds.

In addition, an agent leak detector (JM-85) has been developed. It is designed to detect toxic agents, including CW agents, in the air and on surfaces. The device consists of a probe and a power adapter, and it can be handled by one operator. The JM-85 allows the detection of the source of agent leakage from technological equipment, pipes, flange connections and munitions. It enables control of the spread of contamination in emergency situations including control of contamination of the individual protective equipment used by facility personnel. It can detect over 100 substances. The sensitivity is 1–1000 MAL, and the response time is 3–10 seconds.

Other devices include automatic gas alarms for mustard agent and lewisite detection, fast methods for detection of different types of agents, and so on.

IV. The Russian–US joint evaluation programme

Cooperation between Russia and the United States is based on several bilateral agreements[21] and the annual plans related to US support of Russian CW destruction. This support is provided under the Cooperative Threat Reduction

---

[21] Agreement between the United States of America and the Russian Federation Concerning the Safe and Secure Transport, Storage and Destruction of Weapons and Prevention of Weapons Proliferation, 17 June 1992; and Agreement between the Department of Defense of the United States of America and the President's Committee for Conventional Problems of Chemical and Biological Weapons Concerning the Safe, Secure and Ecologically Sound Destruction of Chemical Weapons, 30 July 1992. For a detailed discussion of Russian–US joint evaluation activities see chapter 8 in this volume.

(CTR) programme, which includes the construction of a pilot CW destruction facility at Shchuchye.[22]

In January 1995 Russian technical experts participated in a meeting at the Edgewood Research, Development and Engineering Center at Aberdeen Proving Ground, in Edgewood, Maryland. The technical details of the Russian approach to the destruction of organophosphorus CW agents were shared at the meeting, and it was agreed that a joint evaluation of the Russian two-stage technology would be conducted.[23]

The first phase began when specialists from GosNIIOKhT visited the Edgewood facility on 25 May 1995. Experiments were conducted using high-purity CW agents of US origin. The agents were sarin, soman and US VX (a structural isomer of Russian VX). High-purity agents were used in order to minimize interference from impurities or other components in weapon-grade agents and to facilitate interpretation of the results of the experiments. The Russian two-stage process was used for all the experiments. After the first experiments were completed, additional ones were conducted using weapon-grade GB and US VX. Similar results were achieved, which demonstrated the efficacy of the Russian two-stage process for CW agent destruction. The second phase of the evaluation was conducted in Saratov, Russia, where Russian weapon-grade agents (sarin, soman, and Russian VX) were detoxified. The experiments were conducted under conditions similar to those at the Edgewood facility. The most modern analytical methods for the detection of CW agents were used. These methods can detect CW agents at MAL levels in the reaction and bitumen–salt mass, and they provide reliable identification of the main components.

The Russian–US joint evaluation programme has demonstrated that the Russian two-stage method can be used and is effective. The destruction efficiency was greater than 99.99999 per cent for sarin, greater than 99.9999 per cent for soman, and greater than 99.99997 per cent for VX for both Russian and US CW agents. The toxicity of the reaction and bitumen–salt masses was low and represented a significant decrease in potential hazard. The reaction mass had a Level III value on the Russian scale of toxicity, while the bitumen–salt mass had a Level IV value, the least hazardous level.

V. The Russian–US programme for optimization of two-stage technology

The next phase of Russian–US cooperation is a project to optimize the two-stage destruction process for large-scale CW destruction. Although the Joint Evaluation Programme provided valuable information about the destruction processes, additional data need to be obtained for use in the design and con-

---

[22] The CW aspects of the CTR programme are discussed in Zanders, J. P., Eckstein, S. and Hart, J., 'Chemical and biological developments and arms control', *SIPRI Yearbook 1997: Armaments, Disarmament and International Security* (Oxford University Press: Oxford, 1997), p. 448; and Zanders, J. P. and Hart, J. 'Chemical and biological weapon developments and arms control', *SIPRI Yearbook 1998: Armaments, Disarmament and International Security* (Oxford University Press: Oxford, 1998), p. 466. The CTR programme and the Shchuchye facility are also discussed in chapter 10 in this volume.

[23] Bechtel National, Inc. and US Army Program Manager for Chemical Demilitarization, Office of the Product Manager for Cooperative Threat Reduction (PM-CTR), *Joint Evaluation of the Russian Two-Stage Chemical Agent Destruction Process, Final Technical Report: Phases 1 & 2* (Bechtel National, Inc. and US Army Program Manager for Cooperative Threat Reduction, July 1996 revision).

struction of a pilot CW destruction facility. The optimization project is designed to fill data gaps and to enable the technology to be applied on a larger scale than in the laboratory.

The characteristics of reactions will be studied, and a mathematical model of the reactions will be constructed and tested. The two-stage process will focus on the following process variables: ratio or reagents, order in which the reagents are added to each other, temperature of the process, and process duration and mixing intensity. Analytical procedures (both chromatographic and biochemical methods) will also be optimized and updated. The resulting data will be applied to design a pilot CW destruction facility.

VI. Alternative technologies

The technologies which will be used to destroy the main types of chemical weapons in Russia have been chosen. Organophosphorus CW agents will be destroyed by the two-stage technology developed by GosNIIOKhT. Lewisite will be treated by alkaline hydrolysis followed by electrolysis of the reaction products; this technology was also developed by GosNIIOKhT.[24] Research continues on the development of new processes for CW destruction. Current efforts concentrate on, among other things, hydrolysis and polymerization.

The advantages of hydrolysis are its simplicity and low cost. The small size and weight of a water molecule make it possible to achieve an equimolar[25] ratio of reagent to agent with an insignificant increase in the volume of the reaction mass in comparison to the initial volume of the CW agent. Small additions of catalysts allow the reaction to be accelerated considerably. GosNIIOKhT has gained experience in the development of this process and has made significant progress in its use.[26] In 1994 the USA showed renewed interest in hydrolysis when it undertook an experimental programme to study alternative technologies for CW destruction.[27] The programme has invested substantial resources in the study of various hydrolysis techniques, particularly for the destruction of the VX that is stored at the Newport Chemical Depot in Newport, Indiana.

Polymerization results in a solid waste which can be buried or subjected to further treatment. Polymerization can be used to detoxify CW agents and the products of their detoxification. GosNIIOKhT is conducting R&D on the development of the polymerization process for the destruction of lewisite and organophosphorus CW agents. Although there has been no external financing for research into alternative technologies for CW destruction, GosNIIOKhT is proceeding with its R&D in keeping with its position as a research institute at the forefront of the latest developments.

---

[24] Russian Federation and State Scientific Institute for Organic Chemistry and Technology, *Unichtozhenie (Utilizatstiya) Luizita Metodom Shchelochnogo Gidroliza i Elektroliza Reaktsionnykh Mass s Polucheniem Metallicheskogo Myshyaka Osoboi Chistoty* [Destruction (utilization) of lewisite by alkaline hydrolysis and electrolysis of the reaction mass giving highly pure metallic arsenic] (GosNIIOKhT: Moscow, no date).

[25] Molar volume is the volume occupied by a substance per unit amount of substance.

[26] GosNIIOKhT, 1992, Patent of the Russian Federation no. 2042368.

[27] Panel on Review and Evaluation of Alternative Chemical Disposal Technologies, Board on Army Science, and Technology, Commission on Engineering and Technical Systems and National Research Council, *Review and Evaluation of Alternative Chemical Disposal Technologies* (National Research Council: Washington, DC, 1996).

10. US assistance to Russia's chemical weapon destruction programme

AMY E. SMITHSON

I. Introduction

As negotiations on the Chemical Weapons Convention were drawing to a close, policy makers around the globe could see that the collapsing Soviet Union would need assistance to destroy its chemical weapon stockpile. By its own admission the USSR possessed 40 000 agent tonnes of chemical weapons, making its stockpile the world's largest.[1] The political and economic disarray which followed the dissolution of the Soviet Union in 1991 made it extremely difficult for the new Russian Government to meet the convention's 10-year deadline to complete the destruction of its chemical weapon arsenal. Therefore, a special provision was added to the convention to enable a state party to request an extension of up to five years.[2]

Even before the convention was signed, however, a bilateral process between Moscow and Washington had been undertaken to demonstrate that the two superpowers would take the lead in eliminating this category of weapons of mass destruction. The United States, with over 30 000 tonnes, has the world's second largest declared chemical weapon stockpile. By the early 1990s the US destruction programme, initiated by a 1985 law,[3] was moving forward slowly with one destruction facility already operating and another soon to open.[4] In addition to a confidence-building measure agreement known as the Wyoming Memorandum of Understanding,[5] the USA and the USSR signed a Bilateral Destruction Agreement (BDA) in June 1990, which committed both sides to destroy all but 5000 tonnes of their chemical weapons by the end of 2002.[6]

---

[1] This declaration was made under the terms of the 1989 Wyoming Memorandum of Understanding, a confidence-building arrangement wherein the superpowers would engage in 2 phases of data exchanges and trial inspections. *Fact Sheet: U.S.–Soviet Memorandum of Understanding on Chemical Weapons* (White House: Washington, DC, 23 Sep. 1989). On 29 Dec. 1989, Washington and Moscow exchanged data on their aggregate stockpile size; the types of agents in their stockpiles; the per cent of chemical agents in munitions, devices or bulk containers; the location of storage, production and destruction facilities; and the types of agent and munitions at each storage facility. This data exchange was followed by reciprocal visits to 2 production facilities, 3 storage sites, and 2 industrial chemical facilities. Phase II of the data exchanges and trial inspections did not occur until 1994, at which time both sides voiced concern about the completeness and accuracy of the data provided.

[2] The text of the Chemical Weapons Convention is reproduced in Conference on Disarmament document CD/1170, 26 Aug. 1992. See Annex on Implementation and Verification, Part IV (A) C, paras 24–28. Depending on how the US destruction programme evolves in the next few years, the USA may also have to ask for an extension of the 10-year deadline.

[3] Public law 99-145 is discussed in US General Accounting Office (GAO), *Chemical Weapons and Materiel: Key Factors Affecting Disposal Costs and Schedule*, GAO/NSIAD-97-18 (US GAO: Washington, DC, Feb. 1997), p. 4.

[4] For an in-depth analysis of the problems confronting chemical weapon destruction in the USA, see Smithson, A. E. and Lenihan, M., *The U.S. Chemical Weapons Destruction Program: Views, Analysis, and Recommendations* (Henry L. Stimson Center: Washington, DC, Sep. 1994).

[5] For more information on the Wyoming Memorandum of Understanding see note 1.

[6] This bilateral accord provides for routine inspections of destruction-related activities, but not challenge inspections. *Fact Sheet: US–USSR Chemical Weapons Destruction Agreement* (White House: Washington, DC, 1 June 1990). Destruction was originally to have been completed by the end of 2002. Time-lines were revised to have the task finished by the end of June 2004, but the Russian Government officially backed away from implementing the bilateral agreement in mid-1996, only to indicate renewed

Despite the fact that this bilateral accord has never entered into force, a sustained effort has been mounted to provide US assistance to Russia's chemical weapon destruction programme.

This chapter provides a detailed account of the US assistance programme. Especially in Russia, expectations for a significant increase in the amount of US assistance for chemical weapon destruction are high.[7] Unfortunately, these expectations do not correlate with what Washington is likely to deliver in the years to come.

II. Assistance in increments

The 1991 Soviet Nuclear Threat Reduction Act, sponsored by Democratic Senator Sam Nunn of Georgia and Republican Senator Richard Lugar of Indiana, initiated a programme of US technical and financial assistance to prevent weapon proliferation and to facilitate the safe transport, storage, safeguarding and destruction of weapons of mass destruction in the Soviet Union, its republics and any successor states. The bulk of the more than $2.4 billion in assistance that has been provided under the Cooperative Threat Reduction (CTR) programme has gone towards the dismantlement of nuclear weapons.[8] From 1992 to 1997 over $135 million was allocated to aid Russia's chemical weapon destruction programme. The goals of CTR assistance for chemical weapon destruction are to assist in the safe, secure, timely, cost effective and environmentally sound destruction of Russia's chemical weapon stockpile, with priority given to the destruction of nerve-agent filled munitions.

On 17 June 1992 US President George Bush and Russian President Boris Yeltsin signed an agreement for the safe, secure transport, storage and destruction of weapons and prevention of weapon proliferation.[9] CTR assistance would be administered under this so-called 'umbrella agreement'. More specifically, for assistance for chemical weapon destruction, the United States and Russia signed an agreement on 30 July 1992 for the Department of Defense (DOD) to work with the Russian Ministry of Defence to enable the safe, secure and ecologically sound destruction of Russia's chemical arsenal.[10] At that time the

interest early in 1997 in revitalizing the bilateral track. For the text of the BDA see Agreement between the United States of America and the Union of Soviet Socialist Republics on Destruction and Non-Production of Chemical Weapons and on Measures to Facilitate the Multilateral Convention on Banning Chemical Weapons, *SIPRI Yearbook 1991: World Armaments and Disarmament* (Oxford University Press: Oxford, 1991), pp. 536–39.

[7] Russian legislators and officials frequently stated that Russia would not ratify chemical disarmament treaties until Moscow had been provided assurances of greater funding for CW destruction. Toups, C., 'U.S. Russia slow to destroy chemical weapons after vow', *Washington Times* (31 Jan. 1995), p. A16.

[8] Chemical weapon destruction ranked fourth in the list of CTR programme priorities, behind nuclear weapon dismantlement, material protection, control and accounting efforts, and other strategic denuclearization programmes. Ellis, J., 'Nunn–Lugar's mid-life crisis', *Survival*, vol. 39, no. 1 (spring 1997), pp. 84, 88; and Zanders, J. P., Eckstein, S. and Hart, J., 'Chemical and biological developments and arms control', *SIPRI Yearbook 1997: Armaments, Disarmament and International Security* (Oxford University Press: Oxford, 1997), p. 448.

[9] Agreement between the United States of America and the Russian Federation Concerning the Safe and Secure Transportation, Storage and Destruction of Weapons and Prevention of Weapons Proliferation (Office of the Press Secretary, White House: Washington, DC, 17 June 1992).

[10] Agreement Between the Department of Defense of the United States of America and the President's Committee on Conventional Problems of Chemical and Biological Weapons of the Russian Federation Concerning the Safe, Secure and Ecologically Sound Destruction of Chemical Weapons, signed by Under Secretary of Defense Donald Atwood and General Anatoly Kuntsevich (Pentagon: Washington, DC, 30 July 1992).

DOD earmarked $25 million in assistance for training, services and material towards that goal. The fruits of this assistance effort did not begin to materialize for some time. Both sides had to labour to put the necessary logistics in place and to conclude the detailed and technical sub-agreements that were required to deliver material and funds to Russian sites in need of assistance.[11]

The most notable early accomplishments of this effort were the June 1993 establishment in Moscow of a US programme support office; a programme at the headquarters of the US Army Chemical Stockpile Disposal Programme headquarters in Aberdeen, Maryland, to familiarize and train Russian technicians in the technology being used to destroy US chemical weapons; technical exchanges about detectors, systems of analysis and alarms; and a series of visits to stockpile storage and disposal sites in Russia and the USA.[12] Unfamiliar with the technical, political, organizational and financial hurdles that must be cleared in order to mount a destruction programme, observers in Moscow, Washington and elsewhere were critical of these rather modest results.

On 18 March 1994, the US Congress authorized $30 million for the construction of a central analytical laboratory to support the Russian destruction programme. This laboratory's mission is to develop chemical agent analytical methods and procedures, to help train destruction facility personnel, to conduct analysis of environmental samples and to serve as the quality analysis/quality control centre for the destruction programme. The laboratory is located at Building 14 of the Moscow State Scientific Research Institute for Organic Chemistry and Technology (GosNIIOKhT), which is a key facility in Russia's chemical weapon complex. After asbestos has been removed from Building 14, ConTrack International spent approximately $13 million to complete the renovation, equipping, testing and personnel training for this central laboratory. Three mobile laboratories (at a cost of $2 million) were also delivered to Russia in September 1996. One mobile laboratory was sent to GosNIIOKhT and two others went to the Saratov Military Engineering College of Chemical Defence, where the laboratory has also been refurbished to facilitate extensive testing of Russia's destruction technology.[13]

In 1995 US and Russian scientists began a joint evaluation of the technology Russia proposed to use to destroy the nerve agents that comprise 81 per cent of its stockpile—neutralization followed by bituminization. The technical data from these tests would be the basis for determining additional US assistance for the design and construction of a destruction facility. In layman's terms, neutralization is a process whereby a chemical or other material is inserted into the agent to dilute its potency significantly. Russia proposed to use monoethanolamine to neutralize sarin and soman, and potassium isobutylate to neutralize VX. Previously, Russia had successfully utilized a mobile destruction system to neutralize agent from thousands of munitions containing sarin and soman using

---

[11] Ellis (note 8).

[12] For a detailed account of the CTR programme's early efforts, see Lajoie, R. (Maj.-Gen.), 'Cooperative Threat Reduction support to the destruction of Russia's chemical weapons stockpile', *Chemical Weapons Disarmament in Russia: Problems and Prospects* (Henry L. Stimson Center: Washington, DC, Oct. 1995), pp. 35–48.

[13] Information provided to the author in a 19 Feb. 1997 briefing from the CTR Program Office in Washington, DC

monoethanolamine.[14] Bituminization further dilutes the toxicity of the resulting waste product by mixing it with asphalt and calcium oxide hydrate.[15] This two-step process produces insoluble salts, which will probably be stored indefinitely.[16]

Phase I of the bilateral testing took place at the US Army's Edgewood Research, Development and Engineering Center in Aberdeen from May to August 1995. During this time 50-gram quantities of the US agents sarin, soman and VX were destroyed using neutralization and bituminization. In Phase II agents from the Russian stockpile were neutralized and bituminized at the laboratory in Saratov. These agents were sarin, soman and Russian V-gas (a structural isomer of US VX). Unlike the tests with US agents, where high purity agents were used, the Russian agents were weapon-grade materials and therefore posed a more difficult challenge to the destruction process. This phase, which occurred in October and November 1995, coincided with analytical work at Moscow State University that examined the results of the tests. In March 1996, a Joint Evaluation Technical Report was issued.[17] Among the key findings of this report were that following neutralization and bituminization, no agent was detected in the reaction mass, the bitumen–salt mass or the distillate. In accordance with the Russian federal standard for rating the toxicity of a reaction product, the bitumen–salt mass qualified for the lowest category, Level IV ('slightly dangerous'). On the US scale, the process rated a destruction removal efficiency of five 9s, meaning it was 99.999 per cent effective. Furthermore, the Joint Evaluation Technical Report found that the testing results were scientifically credible and effective and that the process proposed used sound procedures and design. An independent peer review of this report, issued in June 1996, confirmed these results, finding the neutralization–bituminization processes feasible and effective.[18]

Building on these positive results, Russia and the USA have begun a collaborative 'optimization' of the neutralization–bituminization process. This work entails additional laboratory testing of the process against ever greater quantities of agent to ensure that it continues to perform well. Additional work includes conducting routine experiments outside the agreed scope of the work performed during the Joint Evaluation. Bench tests, an important landmark in

[14] This mobile destruction system, known as the KUASI system, first neutralizes the agent, then incinerates the resulting waste by-product. Some 4000 leaking munitions, containing approximately 200 tonnes of nerve agent, have been destroyed with the KUASI mobile system. Lajoie, (note 12), p. 37. For sarin and soman equal volumes of the chemical agent are mixed with monoethanolamine containing 15–20% water at 105°C. The reaction occurs over the next 90 minutes. For Russian VX the reaction takes place over a 30-minute period at 90°C, using a 1 : 2 volume ration of VX to anhydrous potassium isobutylate. Smithson, A. E. and Lenihan, M., 'The destruction of weapons under the Chemical Weapons Convention', *Science & Global Security*, vol. 6 (1996), p. 93. For additional information on the KUASI system, see USSR, Complex for the destruction of faulty chemical munitions (KUASI), Conference on Disarmament document CD/CW/WP.369, 8 Oct. 1991.

[15] This step of the process is conducted at a temperature of 183°C. See note 14.

[16] Current plans also call for the solvents used in the neutralization and bituminization process to be used as landfill. Neutralization and bituminization will be used to destroy the agent, but incineration will probably be used to destroy the rocket and munition casings, as well as assorted dunnage. Information provided to the author in a 19 Feb. 1997 briefing from the CTR Program Office in Washington, DC

[17] Bechtel National, Inc., *Final Joint Evaluation Technical Report, Joint Evaluation of the Two-Stage Chemical Agent Destruction Process*, contract no. DNA001-95-C-0058 (Bechtel National, Inc.: Washington, DC, 8 Mar. 1996).

[18] Bechtel National, Inc., *Final Report of the Peer Review Committee for the Russian-American Joint Evaluation Program, Joint Evaluation of the Two-Stage Chemical Agent Destruction Process*, contract no. DNA001-95-C-0058 (Bechtel National, Inc.: Washington, DC, June 1996).

this phase of the technology development, may be conducted late in 1997. Among the operational aspects of the Russian technology that will be further defined during this optimization phase are the heat parameters for the process, the optimal reactor operating conditions, cost-effectiveness and environmental standards.[19] The results of these tests will be used to develop the chemical processing systems for the first industrial-scale destruction facility.

In 1995 Congress made an additional $13 million available to the CTR programme, bringing the total to $68 million in chemical weapon destruction support. In 1996 Congress approved $78.5 million in CTR funds for the construction of a pilot chemical weapon destruction facility (CWDF).[20] The Russian Ministry of Defence selected Shchuchye, where 13.6 per cent of the Russian stockpile—artillery munitions containing the nerve agents VX, sarin and soman—is stored as the site for this pilot facility.[21] Five sites were initially considered as locations for the Shchuchye CWDF. The Russian authorities plan to construct the facility at Site 3, located 17 kilometres (km) from the storage facility.

US assistance to construct a CWDF at Shchuchye cannot truly begin until Russian Federation regulatory reports and a justification of investment are completed. This work entails topographic, engineering, geological and hydrological surveys; process feasibility and environmental support assessments; and emergency preparedness plans to thoroughly evaluate the destruction plant's impact on the Shchuchye area. In addition, the machines that will be used to drill and drain munitions need to be adapted, tested and integrated into a munition processing system. The pilot destruction facility itself must also be designed. Russia's current plan calls for the United States to build the first stage of the Shchuchye facility, which will have one line for processing 85–152-mm projectiles, and a second line for processing smaller rocket warheads. This stage 1 facility should be able to process 500 tonnes of agent per year. Russia is then supposed to build another processing facility at Shchuchye, with a line to process 85–152-mm projectiles and a second line to process 540–880-mm missile and rocket warheads. This stage 2 facility should be able to destroy 700 tonnes per year, bringing the total destruction capacity at Shchuchye to 1200 tonnes per year.[22] However, the speed with which this pilot destruction plant will be built is heavily dependent not only on the continuing success of the development and testing of Russia's technology, but also on the establishment of the legal and social infrastructure in Russia to enable destruction to begin at Shchuchye.

Given the amount of work that has already been done, many observers would presume that bulldozers have already begun preparing the site at Shchuchye. However, putting together a chemical weapon destruction programme is an

---

[19] A US contractor, Battelle, has been hired to conduct this optimization research in conjunction with the Russian firm GIPROSINTEZ. Work is being done at GosNIIOKhT, Edgewood and Saratov. Another US firm, the Ralph M. Parsons Company, will take over from Battelle and finish the scale-up activities.

[20] Other related funds included in the 1997 Defense Authorization Act were $15 million for a cooperative programme to improve border security in the former Soviet states; $15 million to improve the security of Russian weapons of mass destruction; $10 million to improve Russian control and accounting of its mass destruction weapons; and $15 million to dismantle chemical and biological weapons and facilities in Russia.

[21] Information provided to the author in a 19 Feb. 1997 briefing from the CTR Program Office in Washington, DC.

[22] See note 21.

enormously complicated endeavour. Scores of agencies and officials from Moscow and the Kurgan region, where the Shchuchye storage site is located, are involved in the planning and execution of this programme. Policy and technical concerns voiced at both a national and local level must be addressed. For example, because there are so many constituencies and contingencies to be considered the final site for the Shchuchye destruction facility will not be selected until 1998, even though the field of possibilities has already been narrowed.

A comparison with the evolution of the US destruction programme is instructive for observers trying to understand how difficult and time-consuming it can be to implement a chemical weapon destruction programme successfully. The US corollary to Shchuchye, a demonstration destruction plant built on Johnston Atoll in the Pacific Ocean south-west of Hawaii, took three years to build. Four years were required to build the first full-scale destruction facility in the continental United States at Tooele, Utah, where approximately 42 per cent of the US chemical weapon arsenal is located. Basic construction of the Tooele facility was completed in 1993. However, hot testing of the facility involving actual chemical weapon agents, as opposed to simulants, did not begin until late summer 1996. From the time that the US Army began testing destruction technologies at Tooele—a process similar to the process development efforts now under way in the Russian programme—until the first munition was processed at Tooele, a total of 17 years elapsed.[23] This 17-year time-lag for the US destruction programme is a sobering point of comparison, especially if one is inclined to believe that it would be easier to launch a complex technical endeavour in the United States than in Russia.

Crucial decisions have already been made to initiate a destruction programme in Russia, including those setting up general principals and decision-making channels.[24] However, numerous other decisions must still be taken at the national and local levels before the US assistance efforts can be fully implemented. To the extent that such decisions are not expedited, US assistance is likely to be underutilized. For example, since Congress's 1996 approval of $78.5 million for the Shchuchye pilot plant some of those funds already have been redirected towards other tasks in the CTR programme where the decision-making process has reached the point that materials and services can be pur-

---

[23] Although tests are going well, Tooele has yet to complete the rigorous environmental trial and testing stage to initiate full-time processing of munitions. Updates on the status of the Tooele destruction facility can be obtained at the US Army web site Program Manager for Chemical Demilitarization, 'Total munitions processed so far', URL <http://www-pmcd.apgea.army.mil>.

[24] For example, on 24 Mar. 1995, Presidential decree no. 314 [On preparing the Russian Federation for the implementation of its international obligations in chemical disarmament] was issued, stipulating that Russia's chemical weapons would be destroyed in the regions where they are currently stored. This decree also established the Interdepartmental Commission on Chemical Disarmament to oversee coordination of the 12 federal agencies involved in the destruction programme. On 21 Mar. 1996, Federal government edict no. 305 outlined the overall plan for Russia's destruction programme, anticipated to last 15 years. This decree also announced that a special federal programme was being established to improve the ecological conditions near Russia's CW storage sites, ensure the safety of the destruction process, protect the environment and minimize expenditures in the destruction programme. On 27 Dec. 1996, the Duma passed a national law on CW destruction by a vote of 345 to 0, with 1 abstention. This law specifies the decision-making procedures, time tables, and policies associated with Russia's destruction programme. The Federation Council has not yet approved this law, however, but negotiations are under way to reconcile differences between the upper and lower chambers of the Russian parliament. Nivikov, I., 'Duma passes law on destruction of chemical weapons', TASS News Agency, 27 Dec. 1996.

chased.[25] As with any programme that spends US taxpayer dollars, the CTR programme must obligate or spend congressionally approved funds within the designated fiscal year (FY). Congress approved an additional $35.4 million in the FY 1998 budget for the Shchuchye project.[26]

III. Expectations and political realities

Russia's fledgling chemical weapon destruction programme is clearly moving in the right direction, but the bulk of the work remains. That being the case, there are expectations in Russia and in Europe that the USA will furnish significant additional funds to help Russia eliminate its chemical weapons. Since European countries are helping with the destruction of Russia's blister agents, which are stored at two locations,[27] some observers expect the United States to pick up the entire cost of destroying all of Russia's nerve agents. Russian authorities estimate that $5–6 billion will be needed to destroy the arsenal.[28] This estimate, however, is probably several billion dollars less than what the eventual cost actually will be if the cost escalation of the US destruction programme is used as a point of reference.[29] In addition to the basic expense of five destruction facilities, it has been assumed that the USA should pay for the auxiliary costs associated with Russia's destruction programme, such as the improvement of local roads, hospitals and other infrastructure items that local communities have requested and which Moscow has promised will be delivered to enable destruction to go forward.[30] Unfortunately, political and economic realities in the USA make it highly unlikely that these expectations will be met.

Many people perceive the United States as a land of unending resources. Compared to most countries, the USA is prosperous, with a healthy economy that supports an undeniably large government budget. Those who do not follow US politics closely, however, have less of an appreciation for how difficult it has become to maintain domestic support for foreign assistance programmes, especially given the overriding emphasis in the 1990s to reduce government spending and address problems in the USA before helping others abroad. This

[25] Although there have been complications in arriving at an agreement on exactly how to dispense the funds, $2.2 million of the $78.5 million for Shchuchye has been set aside to help convert the former chemical weapon production facility at Volvograd. Another $8 million of the original $78.5 was redirected towards nuclear dismantlement and disarmament activities, leaving $68.5 million for construction of the Shchuchye pilot destruction facility.

[26] Information provided to the author in a 19 Feb. 1997 briefing from the CTR Program Office in Washington, DC

[27] Germany, the Netherlands, Sweden and other European countries are providing assistance to help destroy the mustard gas and lewisite stored at Gorny and Kambarka.

[28] Although other Russian officials have made lower cost estimates, the chairman of the presidential committee, Pavel Syutkin, gave the figure $5–6 billion on 1 Apr. 1995. 'News chronology: February–May 1995', *Chemical Weapons Convention Bulletin*, no. 28 (June 1995), p. 24.

[29] For example, Russian authorities estimate the cost of building the Shchuchye facility at $200–250 million. Bechtel, a US contractor, estimates that it will take $700–800 million to complete construction at Shchuchye.

[30] Among the social infrastructure improvements that have been requested for Shchuchye are residential housing, renovated central boiler house, new schools, children's health camp, a department store, a cafeteria, a public bath, street upgrades and a sports–health complex. The industrial infrastructure enhancements list includes natural gas and water supply, a sewage treatment facility, non-industrial waste landfill, highway upgrades, communications improvements, hospital/pharmacy upgrades, an environmental monitoring system and a civil defence control station. Information provided to the author in a 19 Feb. 1997 briefing from the CTR Program Office in Washington, DC

section of the chapter discusses why is has been difficult to keep the CTR programme on the right track in Washington.

The US Constitution created three branches of government, dividing powers between them. In the case of the budget, Congress has the 'power of the purse', approving how much money the Executive Branch can spend and for what purposes. The Executive Branch can propose a budget to Congress that contains funds to fulfil pledges made by the president or administration officials, but Congress has several opportunities to adjust or even totally cancel budgetary requests in a multi-step process whereby funds are authorized and appropriated. Budget committees in the Senate and the House of Representatives set the overall levels, in this case, for defence spending. Funds for CTR assistance are incorporated in the annual defence authorization bills prepared by the Senate Armed Services and the House National Security committees. These two committees may approve dissimilar levels of funding and then reconcile differences in conference before approving a final budget. Simultaneously, the level of CTR funding is also being set by the Senate and House Appropriations committees, and additional adjustments may be made when these two committees meet in conference. In short, even before final votes are taken on the floor of the House and the Senate, no less than six different committees, with literally hundreds of legislators, have had an opportunity to change the level of CTR funding and to propose conditions about how it can be expended. Not surprisingly, 'items of special interest' to a legislator, such as pet projects or concerns, can have a significant influence on this process.[31]

As legislators make decisions about how taxpayers' dollars should be spent, the needs and concerns of the constituents that elect them are uppermost in their minds. In recent years US taxpayers have been insisting that their elected officials deal with the US deficit problem and reduce government spending. Foreign assistance programmes are not popular with the average US citizen, who much prefers that legislators tackle domestic problems, such as reducing crime, waging the 'war' on drugs and reforming welfare and Medicare programmes. Only a small percentage of US citizens who assiduously follow foreign and defence affairs are likely to be aware of the CTR programme and appreciate why it is in the interests of the USA to help Russia destroy its weapons. Relatively few US citizens are likely to echo the following sentiment: 'Dollar for dollar, there is no better way to spend national security resources than to help eliminate a former enemy's nuclear weapons and convert its defence industry to peaceful purposes'.[32] Therefore, legislators are going to weigh their votes on the CTR programme carefully.

Given this environment, it is not surprising that some fairly stringent conditions have been put on how CTR funds can be applied. In the initial legislation Congress stipulated six conditions that indicated it would watch carefully over

[31] For more on Washington's defence budget process, see Blechman, B. M. and Ellis, W. P., *The Politics of National Security: Congress and U.S. Defense Policy* (Oxford University Press: New York, 1990); and Crabb, C. V., Jr and Holt, P. M., *Invitation to Struggle: Congress, the President and Foreign Policy* (Congressional Quarterly: Washington, DC, 1980).

[32] US Under Secretary of Defense for Policy Walter Slocombe used these words to describe the utility of the CTR programme during congressional testimony. As quoted in Ellis (note 8), p. 84. The CTR programme was also a favourite of other senior officials during the Clinton Administration's first term, including former Secretary of Defense William Perry and former National Security Adviser Anthony Lake.

how these funds were used. The president must certify that the recipient of CTR funds is committed to:

(*a*) making a substantial investment of its resources for dismantling or destroying such weapons;

(*b*) forgoing any military modernization program that exceeds legitimate defense requirements and forgoing the replacement of destroyed weapons of mass destruction;

(*c*) forgoing any use of fissionable and other components of destroyed nuclear weapons in new nuclear weapons;

(*d*) facilitating United States verification of weapons destruction carried out under section 212;

(*e*) complying with all relevant arms control agreements; and

(*f*) observing internationally recognized human rights, including the protection of minorities.[33]

Congress also mandated that CTR spending be audited to ensure that funds are used as intended and stipulated that, to the extent feasible, US technology and personnel should be used to provide the assistance.[34]

When the 1994 mid-term elections swept Republicans into the majority in both houses of Congress, legislators became more openly critical of efforts that they perceived to be above and beyond the scope of CTR, such as providing housing, converting defence facilities to civilian purposes or retraining soldiers and workers. A large number of these newly elected members of Congress were more conservative, isolationist and apparently less interested in foreign policy. In the words of Republican Representative John Linder of Georgia, 'I am not the least bit interested in the prestige of NATO', referring to the USA's principal strategic alliance with the North Atlantic Treaty Organization. Republican Mark Neumann of Wisconsin expressed a similar view: 'When I look at a $5 trillion national debt in the United States, I have a difficult time understanding how we are in a position to go in and build up someone else's country'.[35] This general attitude towards defence and foreign policy is not restricted to the CTR programme. One of the most notable trends in Congress since 1994 has been an aggressive effort to cut the US foreign policy budget and reform the State Department bureaucracy, led by Senator Jesse Helms of North Carolina.[36]

Many legislators who are interested in defence and foreign policy are inclined to build up US armed forces to confront perceived security threats, not to provide what they think of as a 'hand-out' to Russia, especially when Russia is not seen as cooperating on resolving compliance problems with its chemical and biological weapon programmes. The Duma's reluctance to ratify the 1993 Treaty on Further Reduction and Limitation of Strategic Offensive Arms (the START II nuclear arms reduction accord) also annoys many legislators. Russia, for better or worse, has inherited the Soviet Union's compliance track record,

[33] Public law 102-228, the Soviet Nuclear Threat Reduction Act of 1991. Additional information on the programme is provided in Kile, S., 'Nuclear arms control', *SIPRI Yearbook 1997* (note 8), pp. 379–82.

[34] This 'buy American' clause, which irritated and confused many recipients of CTR assistance, was not altered until the 1995 Defense Authorization Act directed that the CTR office should 'work with local contractors and expertise . . . [to] expedite more effective use of CTR funds'. Ellis (note 8), p. 94.

[35] Dewar, H., 'World of difference, GOP generations vie on global affairs', *Washington Post* (9 Apr. 1995), A1.

[36] Krebsback, K., 'The consolidation game', *Foreign Service Journal*, vol. 72, no. 49 (May 1995), pp. 37–45; and Lippman, T. W., 'Helms outlines foreign policy reorganization: prolonged hill battle expected over agency merger proposal', *Washington Post* (16 Mar. 1995), p. A19.

and, in the eyes of many in Congress, has not done nearly enough to improve on it. Until US concerns about the possible development of a new generation of nerve agents are answered,[37] for example, members of Congress are likely to be unwilling to approve large sums for money for the destruction of Russia's chemical weapon stockpile. Why, they ask, should the United States pay for a destruction programme at the same time that Russia is spending money on developing even more lethal chemical agents?[38] Some legislators are irritated by the fact that GosNIIOKhT, where the central analytical laboratory is located, allegedly was and perhaps still is deeply involved in a chemical weapon development programme.

Another factor making these representatives and senators reluctant to approve large sums for chemical weapon destruction in Russia is the high cost of the US destruction programme. Facing an expenditure of over $12 billion to destroy the US stockpile, few legislators are enthusiastic about contributing to a similar programme in Russia. Finally, another reason that it may be difficult to win congressional approval for large sums of assistance to Russia's chemical weapon destruction programme is that one of the CTR programme's chief champions, Sam Nunn, has retired from the Senate. With heroic efforts Senator Lugar has been able to keep the programme on track, but there is no guarantee that he can maintain sufficient support for the CTR programme indefinitely.

In recent years there have been signs that the CTR programme may be headed for trouble. For example, the reason that a relatively small amount was made available for the chemical weapon destruction segment of the CTR programme in 1995 was that tough conditions were put on the release of the funds. Although Congress approved $73 million in the FY 1995 Defense Authorization Act, $60 million of that amount could not be obligated or expended until the president certified that: (*a*) Russia is in compliance with its obligations under the 1972 Biological and Toxin Weapons Convention; (*b*) Russia has agreed to procedures to govern site visits under the September 1992 trilateral agreement to resolve compliance concerns about Russia's biological weapon programmes; (*c*) British and US officials have visited four declared military biological facilities in Russia; (*d*) Russia and the USA have completed the joint study of the feasibility of a chemical weapon destruction technology; (*e*) Russia is making reasonable progress towards a comprehensive plan to implement a chemical weapon destruction programme; and (*f*) substantial progress has been made towards resolution of outstanding compliance issues under the 1989 Memorandum of Understanding and the 1990 Bilateral Destruction Agreement.[39] Since few of the items on this list could be certified by the president, only $13 million of the $73 million originally authorized was released.

---

[37] For a comprehensive account of the weapon development programme, written by a 26-year veteran of the Soviet/Russian chemical weapon complex who revealed its true nature, see Mirzayanov. V., 'Dismantling the Soviet/Russian chemical weapons complex: an insider's view', *Chemical Weapons Disarmament in Russia: Problems and Prospects* (note 12), pp. 21–34.

[38] This line of thinking persists, even though Ellis points out how erroneous it is. The amount of CTR funding provided thus far is not substantial enough to finance significant force modernization or military campaigns. Ellis (note 8), p. 101.

[39] Although these conditions were incorporated in the FY 1996 Defense Authorization Act, it should be noted that a more onerous certification requirement proposed by Republican Representative Robert Dornan of California failed to gain approval. Dornan's amendment would have halted funding unless and until the president certified that Russia had shut down its offensive BW programme. Ellis (note 8), p. 97.

In 1996 Republican Representative Gerald Soloman of New York sponsored an amendment to the Defense Authorization Act that was narrowly defeated by a vote of 202 to 220 in the House. Soloman's amendment would have made the certification requirements for Russia much more rigorous, with clauses prohibiting funding until, among other things, the president certified that Russia was not modernizing its nuclear arsenal, had ceased military actions in Chechnya, was not developing offensive chemical or biological weapons and had stopped construction and operation of the underground military complex at Yemantau Mountain.[40] One can reasonably anticipate that unless US concerns about possible ongoing offensive chemical and biological weapon programmes in Russia are answered, members of Congress will probably make additional efforts to constrain the release of CTR funds for chemical weapon destruction.

IV. Conclusions

Given the circumstances outlined above, it is unrealistic to expect that the United States will provide significant additional funding for chemical weapon destruction in Russia. Congress has been told that the purpose of CTR assistance to Russia's destruction programme is to 'jump-start' that programme,[41] not to fund the entire effort. Nonetheless, once Shchuchye is successfully operating, Congress *may* authorize additional funding for another destruction facility. Russia's compliance with the Chemical Weapons Convention will influence how generous Congress will be. Finally, since Congress has been highly critical of using CTR funds for purposes other than the dismantlement and destruction of weapons, it is doubtful that any funds will be authorized for auxiliary infrastructure improvements at the Russian chemical weapon storage and destruction sites. In conclusion, the expectation that the United States will pick up the bill for destroying all of Russia's nerve agent is seriously out of line with political and economic realities in the United States.

[40] Ellis (note 8), p. 98.
[41] General Lajoie uses this term repeatedly (note 12) to describe the intent of the programme's efforts.

11. Chemical weapon destruction in Russia: prospects for increasing assistance to local communities

CYNTHIA D. MILLER

I. Introduction

Participation by the Russian Federation in the Chemical Weapons Convention was critical because Russia possesses the world's largest stockpile of chemical weapons. Russian ratification of the CWC did not occur until 5 November 1997. Russian governmental officials repeatedly cited lack of funds as the principal cause of the delay. The convention was perceived as costly because of its strict destruction requirements both in terms of time schedule and the order of destruction. The Russian Government had to balance the cost of chemical weapon destruction against internal problems such as political instability, economic difficulties, lack of adequate medical services, poverty, crime, widespread environmental contamination and the like.

Factors other than cost will affect the implementation of CW destruction activities in Russia. This issue is not the sole responsibility of one branch of government, and therefore consideration must be given to the views of national legislators, the Ministry of Defence (MOD), environmental and health-related branches of government, public interest groups, local policy makers and local communities. Broad-based policy approaches are, however, a relatively new phenomenon in Russia, and transparency, flexibility and cooperation among groups and individuals are therefore important.

In 1995, when the BICC–SIPRI project which resulted in this volume began, Russia's chemical demilitarization efforts (i.e., dismantling CW munitions, factories and storage sites), prospects for Russia's ratification of the CWC and the international political situation differed dramatically from their current status. In 1996 CW disarmament activities had stagnated in Russia and threatened to jeopardize the programmes of bilateral assistance to Russia which, at that time, were sponsored by Germany, the Netherlands, Sweden and the United States. (Ultimately, these problems were addressed to such an extent that Russia was able to ratify the CWC.) This chapter examines the prospects for continued and expanded assistance to Russia for chemical disarmament.

Within Russia there has been criticism of the foreign assistance programmes, ranging from the extent of their utility to the amounts which have been allocated to the programmes. This chapter does not evaluate the assistance programmes but rather examines them from the perspective of the local communities—as opposed to that of the Russian Government. The Russian CW destruction programme is generally perceived as a technical issue and most of the foreign assistance has been of a technical nature. On the other hand, the Russian Government has had to coordinate implementation of the CW destruction programme and take into account the interests and well-being of the people who live in the vicinity of the proposed destruction facilities. Russian national legislation contains provisions for compensation in the way of standard of living improvements both to workers at the destruction facilities and to those living in close proximity to the CW stockpiles. If the government is unable to fulfil its guarantees to the local communities, it is not unlikely that destruction activities could be obstructed by them. This chapter also discusses possible sources of assistance and the ways in which the programmes of direct aid to the local communities can be facilitated. It is only an introduction to the issue because the needs of the communities differ, and assistance probably will need to be tailored to each of them.

II. Russian chemical demilitarization efforts

By the mid- to late 1980s Russia began developing plans for the elimination of chemical weapons. The Chemical Weapons Convention made the idea of ridding the world of chemical weapons concrete, and much of the groundwork for the establishment and implementation of a Russian CW destruction programme occurred after Russia signed the convention on 13 January 1993.[1] Throughout the 1990s the international community supported the negotiations which led to the CWC, and in Russia various measures and activities, which are dealt with below, prepared the way for ratification of the convention.

National legislation on the destruction of chemical weapons

In Russia various types of legislation have been passed to establish and support the national CW destruction programme. These measures began to be introduced in 1992. The scope of the legislation and its impact on the national programme vary. The issues addressed in existing legislation include: CWC requirements, impacts of a destruction programme on workers at the CW destruction facilities and those living in the vicinity of such facilities, community approval of the location and operation of the CW destruction facilities, inter-agency coordination and supervision of the CW destruction programme, environmental monitoring, timetables and cost.

National legislation must be developed for each chemical weapon destruction site to specify how the destruction activities are to be carried out and to outline the appropriate development measures for each community. This has been done, for example, for the CW destruction facilities at Gorny in the Saratov oblast and Kambarka in Udmurtia,[2] and plans have been made and funds allocated for these facilities which are the first two of seven facilities where CW destruction is scheduled to take place under federal government edict 305.[3]

[1] As of 19 May 1998, 110 countries had ratified or acceded to the CWC. Stockholm International Peace Research Institute, SIPRI Chemical and Biological Warfare Project, 'Ratifications to the CWC', URL <http://www.sipri.se/cbw/docs/cw-cwc-rat.html>, version current on 26 June 1998.

[2] [On the organization of work for building a facility to destroy the stockpiles of poisonous agents stored on the territory of the Saratov oblast], Federal government edict no. 1470, 30 Dec. 1994, *Conversiya*, no. 3 (1995), p. 36 (in Russian); and [On the organization of work for destroying the stockpiles of lewisite stored on the territory of the Kambarka Rayon of the Udmurt Republic], Federal government edict no. 289, 22 Mar. 1995, in *Udmurtskaya Pravda*, 14 Apr. 1995 (in Russian).

[3] Federalnaya tselevaya programma [Special federal programme], Federal government edict no. 305, 21 Mar. 1996, in *Rossiyskaya Gazeta*, 2 Apr. 1996 (in Russian). However, the first operational CW destruction facility probably will be built in Shchuchye in the Kurgan oblast because US funding is available for construction of a pilot destruction facility there.

Federal government edict 305, a comprehensive federal programme for the destruction of chemical weapons in Russia, detailed the human and technical resources needed to carry out the programme and established a timetable for the required preparatory and implementation measures. The programme was necessary to enable planning and authorize destruction activities. Its presidential status ensured that the programme would be given high priority.

The Chemical Weapons Convention requires each party to take action so that appropriate legislation exists for national implementation of the convention.[4] In Russia the approval of such legislation was a lengthy process during which various objections were raised, including concern about the impact of chemical weapon destruction on the environment.[5] The Law on CW Destruction was signed by President Boris Yeltsin on 2 May 1997.[6]

The presidential plan for the CW destruction programme

In addition to legislation to allow CW destruction activities to proceed, there was a need to clarify which federal agencies were to be involved in the destruction process and their responsibilities. Presidential decree 314, On preparing the Russian Federation for the implementation of its international obligations in chemical disarmament, accomplished this task.[7] The roles of 12 executive branch ministries and committees with responsibilities related to CW disarmament were defined, and an Interdepartmental Commission on Chemical Disarmament, headed by former National Security Advisor Yuri Baturin, was established to coordinate these efforts and administer funding.[8]

Presidential decree 314 included a provision which specified that approximately $21 million should be earmarked for CW destruction activities in the federal budget. The creation of a separate budgetary item was intended to ensure that funds allocated specifically for the destruction of chemical weapons would not be diverted to other programmes.[9]

[4] The Convention on the Prohibition of the Development, Production, Stockpiling and Use of Chemical Weapons and on their Destruction (corrected version), 8 Aug. 1994, is reproduced on the SIPRI Chemical and Biological Warfare Project Internet site at URL <http://www.sipri.se/cbw/docs/cw-cwc-texts.html>. 'Each State Party shall inform the Organization of the legislative and administrative measures taken to implement this Convention'. Article VII, para. 5.

[5] The draft law was introduced several times before it was approved. A detailed discussion of the legislative process which resulted in the Law on CW Destruction is presented in chapter 3 in this volume.

[6] Interfax (Moscow), 3 May 1997 (in English), in 'Russia: law details how chemical weapons to be destroyed', Foreign Broadcast Information Service, *Daily Report–Central Eurasia (FBIS-SOV)*, FBIS-SOV-97-123, 6 May 1997.

[7] [On preparing the Russian Federation for the implementation of its international obligations in chemical disarmament], Presidential decree no. 314, 24 Mar. 1995, in *Yaderny Kontrol,* no. 8 (Aug. 1995) (in Russian).

[8] LaJoie, R. (Maj.-Gen.), 'US support to the Russian CW destruction program', Paper presented at the Conference on Dismantlement and Destruction of Nuclear, Chemical and Conventional Weapons, Bonn, Germany, 19–21 May 1996.

[9] United States General Accounting Office, *Weapons of Mass Destruction, Reducing the Threat from the Former Soviet Union: An Update*, GAO/NSIAD-95-165 (US General Accounting Office: Washington, DC, June 1995).

Cooperation between the Ministry of Defence and the local communities

There is a history of mistrust between the citizens of communities near the CW stockpiles and the Ministry of Defence. The local residents see themselves as victims of environmental abuse that has resulted from past military training and operations in nearby areas. Related to this is the fact that the CW stockpiles were situated near their homes for many years without their knowledge. The MOD and the Committee on Problems of Chemical and Biological Weapon Conventions are the governmental bodies which are primarily responsible for overseeing CW destruction activities. The MOD participated in open discussion forums with the residents of Gorny in October 1995, Kambarka in May 1996 and Shchuchye in July 1997.

Development and testing of CW destruction technologies

Separate technologies are being examined for the destruction of blister and organophosphorus agents. In 1994 Russia declared that a two-step method (neutralization followed by bituminization) had been chosen as the 'national CW destruction technology'.[10] In January 1996 a joint experiment by Russian and US experts to evaluate the two-step technology was concluded. It showed that the method is safe and effective.[11] For the destruction of lewisite, Russia has chosen a technology which uses hydrolysis and electrolysis followed by remediation (i.e., soil detoxification) techniques.[12]

Bilateral governmental cooperation on CW demilitarization

Russia and the United States share a special relationship as regards CW disarmament in part because until recently they were the only two countries that had officially declared that they possess CW stockpiles.[13] The USA also views granting assistance to disarmament in Russia as a way to further its own national security interests. On 23 September 1989, the United States and the former Soviet Union signed a Memorandum of Understanding (MOU) which was designed to build confidence that a CW disarmament treaty could be successfully realized.[14] Data exchanges on stockpiles and reciprocal inspections of production, storage and destruction facilities took place following the signing of the MOU. Further cooperation was achieved with the 1 June 1990 Bilateral

---

[10] United States General Accounting Office (note 9).

[11] Petrunin, V., [Technological approaches to the destruction of chemical weapons], *Khimicheskoe Oruzhie I Problemy Ego Unichtozheniya* [Chemical weapons and problems of their destruction], no. 1 (spring 1996), p. 19 (in Russian); see also chapter 8 in this volume.

[12] 'West to help in safe but costly disposal of Russia's CW stocks', *Jane's Defence Weekly*, vol. 26, no. 6 (7 Aug. 1996), p. 15.

[13] Declarations of CW possession and programmes are discussed in Zanders, J. P. and Hart, J., 'Chemical and biological weapon developments and arms control', *SIPRI Yearbook 1998: Armaments, Disarmament and International Security* (Oxford University Press: Oxford, 1998), pp. 460–61.

[14] The Memorandum of Understanding Between the Government of the Union of Soviet Socialist Republics and the Government of the United States of America Regarding a Bilateral Verification Experiment and Data Exchange Related to Prohibition of Chemical Weapons is discussed in Lundin, S. J., 'Multilateral and bilateral talks on chemical and biological weapons', *SIPRI Yearbook 1990: World Armaments and Disarmament* (Oxford University Press: Oxford, 1990), pp. 521, 531–32.

Destruction Agreement (BDA)[15] and a special programme of assistance to Russia for CW destruction as part of the Cooperative Threat Reduction (CTR) programme.[16] In addition to eliminating the existing CW stockpiles, under the BDA both countries pledged to work together to explore various destruction technologies and to cooperate in developing, testing and implementing appropriate inspection procedures.

However, a change in relations occurred, and on 22 July 1996 the Russian delegation to the Organisation for the Prohibition of Chemical Weapons stated that the BDA, which provides a mechanism for Russian–US mutual data declarations and inspections,[17] had 'lapsed' and was 'by no means useful for the global Convention'.[18] The argument was made that the Russian Federation preferred to work towards global CW disarmament by using a multilateral rather than a bilateral approach. This is not inconsistent with the general purpose of the bilateral agreement.

The CTR chemical weapon destruction support programme began with the Agreement between the Department of Defense of the United States of America and the President's Committee on Conventional Problems of Chemical and Biological Weapons of the Russian Federation Concerning the Safe, Secure and Ecologically Sound Destruction of Chemical Weapons.[19] By 1998 a total of $138.7 million had been allocated under the CTR programme.[20] Of the $55.4 million authorized by the USA in 1997, $35.4 million was set aside to support planning and design of a chemical demilitarization facility at Shchuchye in the Kurgan oblast. The other $20 million is for the dismantlement and conversion of a chemical weapon production facility at Volgograd. Other aspects of the assistance programme include: Russian–US joint evaluation of destruction technologies, an analytical laboratory to ensure quality control of the destruction activities and environmental monitoring at the sites, laboratory equipment and training activities, and three mobile laboratories for monitoring at the destruction and storage sites.

Germany, the Netherlands, Sweden and Finland are also providing assistance to Russia. Between 1993 and 1996 Germany contributed 25 million Deutschmarks for the destruction site at Gorny. In May 1996 the Netherlands announced that it would provide assistance worth 25 million guilders over a

---

[15] For the text of the BDA see Agreement between the United States of America and the Union of Soviet Socialist Republics on Destruction and Non-Production of Chemical Weapons and on Measures to Facilitate the Multilateral Convention on Banning Chemical Weapons, *SIPRI Yearbook 1991: World Armaments and Disarmament* (Oxford University Press: Oxford, 1991), pp. 536–39.

[16] The CTR programme is discussed in Zanders, J. P., Eckstein, S. and Hart, J., 'Chemical and biological developments and arms control', *SIPRI Yearbook 1997: Armaments, Disarmament and International Security* (Oxford University Press: Oxford, 1997), p. 448; Zanders and Hart (note 13), p. 466; and chapter 10 in this volume.

[17] Article IV, para. 13 of the CWC allows for a reduction of OPCW verification measures if they are determined to be complementary to other bilateral or multilateral agreements.

[18] Statement by the delegation of the Russian Federation at the XIV session of the Preparatory Commission for the Organisation for the Prohibition of Chemical Weapons, 22 July 1996.

[19] *Agreement between the Department of Defense of the United States of America and the President's Committee on Conventional Problems of Chemical and Biological Weapons of the Russian Federation Concerning the Safe, Secure and Ecologically Sound Destruction of Chemical Weapons*, signed by Under Secretary of Defense Donald Atwood and General Anatoly Kuntsevish (Pentagon: Washington, DC, 30 July 1992).

[20] The initial CTR funding limit in July 1992 was $25 million and increased to $55 million in Mar. 1994. By spring 1996, the total was increased to $68 million and in 1998 an additional $55.4 million was authorized. Later in 1998, a special amendment of $2.2 million was issued to start the remodelling of the former CW production facility in Volgograd.

five-year period to the Kambarka facility for the destruction of lewisite and for environmental and medical protection measures. Sweden provided $500 000 in 1993–96 in two phases. The first phase was devoted primarily to risk analysis at Kambarka. The second phase, which includes a comprehensive package of social projects such as improvements to hospitals and the installation of early-warning systems in the surrounding area, has been delayed for bureaucratic reasons. Finland has allocated 2 million Finnish marks to the programme.[21]

III. Significant events

The discussions and negotiations which preceded the achievements outlined above were time-consuming and often difficult. Passing a federal law on CW destruction and ratification of the CWC took longer than expected because of various domestic and international events. In 1996 there were presidential elections and more attention was focused on domestic concerns such as the war in Chechnya and the continued decline of socio-economic conditions. The US delay in ratifying the CWC may also have influenced events in Russia. Other developments in Russia, such as decreased funding, slowed ratification of the CWC and implementation of the chemical weapon destruction programme.

Decrease in available funding

In 1994, 32.2 per cent of the requested budget for CW destruction was allocated.[22] By 1995 the allocation had declined to less than 10 per cent of what was requested, and in September 1996 only 1 per cent of the required funding for 1996 had been disbursed.[23] In addition, the various sites were not receiving the funds which have been allocated to them. Udmurtia received no funds to initiate CW destruction in 1993 or 1994.[24] Funding has not been authorized for programmes that complement CW destruction, such as medical services and environmental monitoring, and the 1996 programme allocated nothing for these aims.[25] The allocation for CW destruction for 1997 was 120 billion roubles,[26] and 500 billion roubles will reportedly be allocated for destruction in 1998.[27]

Slow-down of technical developments

Federal government edict 305 lists six technical components of the Russian CW destruction programme: (a) selection and approval of the sites for the CW

[21] *The CBW Conventions Bulletin*, no. 36 (June 1997), p. 21.

[22] *Moscow News,* 21–28 Jan. 1996, p. 11.

[23] *Chemical Weapons Convention Bulletin*, no. 30 (Dec. 1995), p. 11; and Smolyakova, T., 'Oruzhie, kotorie ne strelyayet, no tselitsya . . . v svoikh' [Weapons not fired, but which are targeted . . . at their own [people]], *Rossiyskaya Gazeta*, 6 Sep. 1996, p. 6.

[24] Khripunov, I., 'The human element in Russia's chemical weapons disposal efforts, *Arms Control Today*, July/Aug. 1995, p. 20.

[25] Bakina, A., ITAR-TASS (Moscow), 7 May 1996, in 'Russia: Moscow to build facilities for destroying chemical weapons', Foreign Broadcast Information Service, *Daily Report–Central Eurasia: Military Affairs (FBIS-UMA)*, FBIS-UMA-96-100-S, 23 May 1996.

[26] Averre, D. and Khripunov, I., 'Russian chemdemil coaxing communities', *Jane's Intelligence Review*, vol. 9, no. 6 (June 1997), pp. 257–59.

[27] 'Russia: law on Chemical Weapons Convention ratification detailed', FBIS-SOV-97-310, 6 Nov. 1997.

destruction facilities; (*b*) choice of destruction technologies that are environmentally sound, safe and cost-effective; (*c*) design and construction of the pilot plants to test destruction technologies and obtain data for the design of the industrial-scale facilities; (*d*) development of an industrial base to produce the equipment needed for the industrial-scale facilities; (*e*) design and construction of the destruction facilities; and (f) establishment of a system of comprehensive testing at the CW destruction sites.[28] However, thus far only some of the technologies to be employed have been chosen, and the site selection at Gorny and Kambarka has not been completed despite lengthy efforts to do so. Deadlines have not been determined for the next step, design and construction of facilities, and work has not begun.

IV. Concerns prior to ratification

The difficulties mentioned above and the delay in ratification of the convention were balanced by statements at The Hague which affirmed Russia's commitment to ratify the CWC and by proposals made during hearings in the Duma which called for rapid adoption of laws on CW destruction and compensation to those affected by CW production and destruction activities.[29] Russian officials stressed that the delay in ratification of the CWC was linked to the financing of destruction activities. There was opposition in the Russian Federation to ratification because implementation of the CWC was felt to be a cost which the country could not afford. However, Russian officials agreed that the chemical weapons had to be destroyed. In the spring of 1996 General Yuri Tarasevich, Deputy Commander of the Radiation, Chemical and Biological Protection Forces of the Russian Ministry of Defence, stated that although Russia might not ratify the convention a programme for destruction had been accepted and work had begun. Realization of the programme was not dependent on ratification of the CWC.[30]

Although the assumption was made that Russia would proceed with a national programme to dispose of its chemical weapons, two critical and interdependent issues were at stake: ratification of the CWC and continued foreign assistance. Russia had expressed its inability to pay for its CW destruction programme and had stated that it needed foreign assistance to finance 35–50 per cent of the programme.[31] Russia requested $1.75–$2.5 billion of the estimated total cost of $5 billion, but the aid offered amounted to just over $100 million. At a May 1996 NATO conference on CW disposal in Bonn, Germany, representatives from several countries reaffirmed their support for the Russian programme and urged Russia to ratify the CWC.[32] It appeared that if Russia ratified the convention but was unable to comply with the CWC's destruction timetable, that the countries which had supported Russia would continue to do so, provided that Russia demonstrated the political will to eliminate its CW

[28] Note 3.

[29] Parrish, S., 'Duma passes law on chemical weapons destruction', Open Media Research Institute (OMRI), *OMRI Daily Digest*, no. 99, part I (22 May 1996).

[30] Tarasevich, Yu., 'Today Russia is preparing for chemical weapon destruction', *Khimicheskoe Oruzhie I Problemy Ego Unichtozheniya* (note 11), p. 5.

[31] United States General Accounting Office (note 9).

[32] Conference on Dismantlement and Destruction of Nuclear, Chemical and Conventional Weapons, Bonn, Germany, 19–21 May 1996.

stockpile. Foreign assistance has been considered necessary to launch the CW destruction programme. Assistance alone, however, is not enough, and Russia will need to demonstrate the political will, cooperation and transparency that are required to proceed in working with partners on a disposal programme.

Financial assistance from one or more countries would have been jeopardized if Russia had not ratified the convention—thereby increasing the time needed for CW disposal and its cost. Modest estimates indicate that the cost of the Russian CW destruction programme would increase by 25 per cent if the 10-year time-limit for the destruction of chemical weapons were extended to 15 years, and by 50 per cent if it were extended to 20 years.[33] If Russia had not ratified the CWC the local communities might have further scrutinized the safety of the CW destruction operations and their adherence to environmental protection regulations.[34]

Two of the four programmes of bilateral assistance include environmental monitoring or health and medical provisions, while the other two programmes focus on the development of laboratories, destruction facilities and destruction technologies. The budget for CW destruction covers not only technical materials and projects, but also programmes of 'social compensation' to provide access to special health care programmes for the workers at the former CW production facilities and the CW destruction facilities. In the affected communities there are expected to be improvements to medical services, the local infrastructure, telecommunication systems and the standard of living.

The decline in funding from the federal budget for CW destruction will probably mean that technology will be given higher priority than improvement of the local infrastructure. However, various legislative acts and numerous statements by officials have emphasized the necessity of community development, and the establishment of health, environmental and safety standards to limit risk are seen as integral components of the programme. The citizens of the affected communities expect that these objectives will be met, and if they are not, credibility and trust in the government will erode. If communities protest against the start-up of destruction activities, the scientific and financial investments in technological developments and future projects could be at risk. In 1989, for example, protests from the residents prevented the destruction facility at Chapayevsk from beginning operation. Seven communities in the Russian Federation will be affected by the measures to be taken for destruction of the Russian CW stockpile. Each site will require development, but the prospects for this may be bleak given that no funding was provided in the 1996 programme for environmental monitoring projects or medical services.

The timing of health care measures and infrastructure projects is critical. If these developments do not occur simultaneously with the construction of CW destruction facilities, the starting date for disposal activities could be postponed or cancelled. Federal government edicts 289 and 1470 stated that medical programmes and other projects would be available both during CW destruction activities and afterwards.[35] Concerns about the ability to fund these projects were expressed in a report presented to the OPCW in the spring of 1998 by the Rus-

[33] Gorbovsky, A., 'Chemical weapons under a ban at turn of the 21st century', *Khimicheskoe Oruzhie I Problemy Ego Unichtozheniya* (note 11), p. 9.
[34] Gorbovsky (note 33).
[35] Note 2.

sian Government. It was noted that additional assistance will be required for both technical and non-technical projects linked to the chemical demilitarization programme; the report invited potential donors to give special attention to 'infrastructure components'.[36] Efforts should be made by the Russian Government to ensure that these measures are instituted before the start of destruction at Gorny, which was originally scheduled to begin in 1998, and at other sites.

V. Defining need

On 13–17 May 1996 Green Cross Russia sponsored local hearings at Izhevsk, near Kambarka. Representatives were present from the Duma, the Ministry of Defence, the Ministry of Public Health, the Committee on Problems of Chemical and Biological Weapon Conventions, the State Scientific Research Institute for Organic Chemistry and Technology (GosNIIOKhtT), Udmurt State University and various local governmental and non-governmental organizations (NGOs). One day of the hearings was held in Kambarka so that local citizens could express their concerns to local and national authorities and ask questions about the plans for CW destruction. Some citizens strongly emphasized the need to prioritize improvements to local living conditions more than the destruction of chemical weapons in light of the fact that the region is underdeveloped. Concern was also expressed that CW destruction activities should not jeopardize the lives or health of the people in the community or the workers at the destruction facility. It did not appear that the community would try to prevent the start-up of CW destruction activities. The guarantees of social compensation were seen as being made in exchange for allowing destruction to take place, and these claims will not be forgotten.

The Federal Programme for chemical weapon destruction calls for the development of several projects which fall into four categories: construction of CW destruction facilities and technology development; the environment; medical and health-related services; and local infrastructure. Federal legislation established objectives, schedules and costs for such projects for Gorny and Kambarka, two of the seven destruction sites (see tables 11.1 and 11.2) The initial budgets for the destruction sites are 84.5 billion roubles or $8 million (in 1994 prices) for Gorny, and 15.6 billion roubles ($43 million) for Kambarka.

The funding allocated to Gorny is significantly higher than that allocated to Kambarka. More than one-half of the funds will be spent on construction of the destruction facility and on a pilot facility. Nearly 40 per cent will be spent on development of infrastructure, and the remainder will be allocated to environmental measures such as continuous monitoring and evaluation of the storage area and the proposed destruction site. The first phase is supposed to develop the social infrastructure, housing and telecommunications. The second phase consists of start-up activities for the destruction facility, designation of industrial zones and waste burial.

At Kambarka slightly more than one-half of the available funds will be used for design and construction of the industrial base at the CW destruction site. Approximately 40 per cent of the funds will be used to develop infrastructure projects, including construction of a gas pipeline, improvement of the water

---

[36] *The CBW Conventions Bulletin*, no. 40 (June 1998), p. 37.

Table 11.1. Chemical weapon destruction at Gorny, Saratov oblast

Description of work	Volume of financing[a]	Cost (US $)[b]
Evaluation of environmental conditions at the storage area and future chemical weapon destruction site	2 340	1 190 000
Environmental monitoring of the storage area and future chemical weapon destruction site	864	440 000
Construction of pilot industrial facility and development of related infrastructure for future work	6 739	3 420 000
Development of the infrastructure at Gorny	36 052	18 290 000
Design and construction of the chemical weapon destruction facility	38 500	19 530 000

[a] Figures are in million roubles at June 1994 prices.

[b] The dollar figure is calculated at the June 1994 rate of exchange of 1 dollar = 1971 roubles. *Obzor Ekonomiki Rossii* [Russian economic survey], issue 3 (Progress Academia: Moscow, 1994), pp. 200–208.

Source: [On the organization of work for building a facility to destroy the stockpiles of poisonous agents stored on the territory of the Saratov oblast], Federal government edict no. 1470, 30 Dec. 1994, *Conversiya*, no. 3 (1995), p. 36 (in Russian).

purification system, feasibility studies for detoxification of a pond and construction of a modern sewage treatment system. The remaining amount has been allocated for the creation of an emergency preparedness system, individual protection for the local citizens in the event of an accident and medical measures. Future work has been divided into two phases. Phase one, preparation for chemical demilitarization activities, will focus on the social infrastructure and telecommunications and on implementation of health and environmental protection measures. In phase two work will be concluded on the test pilot facility and the design and construction of the destruction facility.

While federal legislation indicates the amount to be spent on the various aspects of the CW demilitarization programmes at Gorny and Kambarka, it does not establish a timetable for the two phases, set priorities, indicate how the projects are to be conducted or specify their length. The Federal Programme states that the social infrastructure projects and the schedules for their construction and start-up are to be determined by feasibility studies which are to be conducted for each site. It is not known if such studies have been done. It is known, however, that infrastructure projects at Gorny and Kambarka will cost approximately $18 million and $3 million, respectively. The total cost of the CW destruction programme is approximately $5 billion, and the provision of developmental assistance to local communities to complement the programme and safeguard its implementation seems a worthwhile investment.

VI. Possible sources of foreign assistance

There are various sources of international assistance. The donors differ based on the type of assistance they lend, the amount of money they commit, their organizational status (governmental, NGO, international), their motivation, the

Table 11.2. Chemical weapon destruction at Kambarka, Udmurtia

Description of work	Volume of financing[a]	Cost (US $)[b]
Design and construction of an industrial base at the chemical weapon (lewisite) destruction facility	8 970	4 550 000
Creation of emergency preparedness system and early-warning measures for the local citizens	310	160 000
Emergency response and protective equipment for the local citizens in case of accident	213	120 000
Stores of antidotes in case of contamination by lewisite	20	10 000
Special medical equipment and pharmaceuticals	49	20 000
Construction of a gas pipeline	4 197	2 130 000
Development of water purification and sewage treatment systems	915	460 000
Estimates for detoxification of the pond at Kambarka	177	90 000
Construction of a water supply network	720	370 000

[a] Figures are in million roubles at June 1994 prices.

[b] The dollar figure is calculated at the June 1994 rate of exchange of 1 dollar = 1971 roubles. *Obzor Ekonomiki Rossii* [Russian economic survey], issue 3 (Progress Academia: Moscow, 1994), pp. 200–208.

Source: [On the organization of work for destroying the stockpiles of lewisite stored on the territory of the Kambarka Rayon of the Udmurt Republic], Federal government edict no. 289, 22 Mar. 1995, in *Udmurtskaya Pravda*, 14 Apr. 1995 (in Russian).

size of their bureaucracy and their decision-making procedures. The following sections discuss the types of available assistance.

Bilateral governmental assistance

Bilateral government assistance is a traditional form of support which is characterized by bureaucracy and a long decision-making process. It is subject to delays in negotiations, fund allocation and project implementation. In order to be more effective, assistance programmes could be expanded and coordinated by governmental agencies other than the defence departments of the countries which currently provide assistance. If such activities were carried out at the national level the input and preferences of the affected communities would be limited and control over the assistance granted would be exercised in large part by the donor.

Multilateral organizations

Multilateral organizations are another traditional source of developmental assistance and are characterized by bureaucracy and slow decision-making processes. The support which may be obtained from these sources is limited and certain stipulations may apply (e.g., ratification of the CWC). Developmental assistance that is targeted at local communities is consistent with the expressed goals of international security and equitable social conditions of organizations such as the European Union (EU) and Tacis (Technical Assistance for the Commonwealth of Independent States). The EU and Tacis currently sponsor several projects in Eastern Europe and Russia.

Table 11.3. Tacis funds committed to Russia for the national CW destruction programme, 1991–96

Figures are in m. ECU.

Sector	Funds
Restructuring state enterprises and private sector development	226.76
Public administration reform, social services and education	220.66
Agriculture	128.74
Energy	127.60
Transport	95.67
Nuclear safety and the environment	13.84
Policy advice	18.95
Telecommunications	22.53
Other sectors	42.59

Source: European Union, 'EU–Russia Relations', URL <http://www.eurunion.org/legislat/extrel/russia.htm>, version current on 19 Aug. 1998.

The Tacis programme is a European Union initiative which was established in 1990 to strengthen democracy in the CIS countries and to help them make a successful transition to a market economy. The Tacis environmental and demilitarization subcommittees are possible sources of assistance. Tacis sponsors infrastructure and social service programmes such as restructuring the energy sector, telecommunications and transport networks. These are also some of the areas addressed by the Russian CW demilitarization programme's plans for improvement of the community infrastructure. Tacis provides funding for social service projects related to the provision of health care. Tacis does not carry out the programmes but rather facilitates them by providing policy advice, conducting feasibility studies and pairing countries and regions with donors that specialize in a particular type of assistance. Such donors often require that a feasibility study be conducted by an independent or designated expert group prior to granting assistance.

The Russian federal government has determined that evaluations of environmental conditions should be carried out in the regions where CW destruction is to take place prior to, during and after such activities. Tacis and several other NGOs have the capability to conduct environmental impact analyses and could assist in developing a policy to ensure compliance with established regulations. Tacis possesses the expertise to sponsor a variety of projects, and in 1991–96 the Russian Federation received 1200 million European Currency Units (ECU) for Tacis-funded programmes, which is approximately 55–60 per cent of the total Tacis budget (see table 11.3).

In the autumn of 1996 the European Commission, the executive body of the European Union, met to discuss issues pertaining to its international security and non-proliferation agenda. An initiative known as the Tacis Indicative Programme was established for the period 1996–99. During these four years, a total of approximately ECU 600 million will be provided to Russia in the way of assistance (excluding the nuclear safety and inter-states programmes to be addressed separately). Support for Russian CW demilitarization is envisioned as part of the initiative for enhanced EU–Russian political cooperation. There are several other multilateral agencies that sponsor programmes of assistance, such as the International Monetary Fund (IMF), the World Bank, the European Bank for Reconstruction and Development (EBRD) and the EU member states. The European Union is the largest source of grants for technical assistance.

Non-governmental organizations

Although the presence of independent non-governmental organizations is a relatively new phenomenon in Russia, NGOs have been well established in other parts of the world for decades. NGOs can often provide limited direct developmental or technical assistance. The development of relationships between Western NGOs and local communities, universities and NGOs in Russia could be useful for several reasons. First, there is a gap between donors in the West and Russia. A wide range of assistance is available from foundations, organizations and governmental agencies for different types of technical and developmental projects, but in Russia there is a lack of knowledge about how to approach these potential donors. Second, a degree of risk is involved in projects which require significant financing. From the point of view of the donor, the success of such a programme would be more likely if an established, reputable NGO which is experienced in supervising assistance projects were to participate.

International foundations

There are many international foundations which actively seek to promote development, health, environmental or scientific programmes; international security; disarmament; and the like. The issue of CW destruction and the challenges it poses to local communities correspond with the interests and objectives of these organizations. Numerous projects currently exist in Russia which are funded by international foundations such as the Soros, W. Alton Jones and the Ford foundations. These types of organizations, which often focus their assistance on helping former communist countries through a period of economic and political transition, are able to provide funds for a range of training, educational, technical and community-based projects.

Community-to-community assistance

Some bilateral programmes of assistance pair communities from different parts of the world in order to promote cultural understanding and improvements in health or education systems through exchange visits and training. Countries such as Germany and the United States currently sponsor such programmes, and it may be possible to pair some or all of the seven communities where CW destruction is scheduled to take place with seven other communities. This type of support functions on a small scale but has the advantage of less bureaucratic decision-making processes. Assistance may therefore be facilitated more rapidly and easily, and the Russian communities could more directly affect the desired relation to and assistance from their 'partner' communities. Such city partnerships are usually based on mutual economic, industrial, demographic, cultural, historical or social factors.

In the early 1990s German cities increased their community-level assistance to cities in Eastern European with the aim of transferring know-how for developing local governmental administration. However, recent budget restrictions have caused the volume of financing to decline to one-third of its earlier level.[37] The city of Frankfurt, for example, has partner relationships with 13 foreign cities, but it is currently unable to properly manage all of them. German communities have historically preferred developing partnerships with other European communities because of the similarity of their areas of concern. There are also some German city partnerships with Eastern European and Russian cities (e.g., there are 140 such partnerships with cities in Poland).[38] The trend, however, is towards seeking partners in Asia, and the rationale for fostering relations is increasingly based on mutual economic considerations rather than on development of the economy of only one of the partners.

The Sister Cities International (SCI) programme was established in the United States in 1967. It is intended to develop 'people-to-people' relations that transcend international boundaries and is based on an idea which was presented at a White House conference in 1956.[39] Since 1986 the number of partnerships has grown from 6 to 152 between the USA and the former Soviet Union alone. Sister city programmes are usually initiated at the grass-roots level. Approximately 80 per cent of the existing partnerships sponsor small-scale projects such as programmes for the exchange of personnel for training and education, cultural exchanges and assistance to schools and hospitals. Partnerships are becoming increasingly popular for their economic utility (e.g., a company in one city may be interested in linking with another city in order to locate an industrial plant in the latter). It may be possible to connect the seven communities in Russia where chemical weapons are stored with seven of the US communities which host or will host CW destruction facilities. Both groups of communities share similar environmental, health, education and safety concerns.

In order to find a sister city for a Russian city the following are needed: (a) a letter from the mayor or administrative head of a Russian city expressing interest in establishing an official partnership with a US city and requesting the assistance of SCI to develop the affiliation; (b) a list of the people in the Russian city who will be responsible for the programme and who can be contacted by SCI or the US city representative; and (c) a city profile including descriptive material about the city, information on the population, economy, educational and cultural institutions, sports and mass media and the priority of each in the future sister city exchanges. Naturally, it will take time to establish the partnership programmes.

Individual actors

Assistance may be available from particular hospitals, universities or individuals in the West, but identifying these actors is a difficult task. If contact is made with a hospital or university it is possible that assistance will be provided at

---

[37] Klemm, T., 'Wenig chancen für neue städtpartnerschaften' [Little chance for new city partnerships], *Frankfurter Allgemeine Zeitung*, no. 253 (30 Oct. 1996), p. 16.

[38] Klemm (note 37).

[39] Sister Cities International, 'Sister Cities International: history and mission', URL <http://www.sister-cities.org/membership/his_mis.html>, version current on 2 Feb. 1998.

little or no cost and that there will be a high level of flexibility. However, the extent of the funding may be limited.

Corporate groups

Corporate groups generally are most interested in long-term, large-scale projects and are motivated by profit. They may be able to provide more assistance to local communities where chemical weapon destruction sites are located than can the small- or medium-sized development programmes which are funded by the groups discussed above. However, some projects such as the construction of a gas pipeline or the installation of a new sewage treatment system will require large investments which are beyond the means of multilateral organizations, individual actors or corporate groups.

VII. Coordinating federal assistance programmes

Project design and planning

Programmes of federal assistance to the communities where CW destruction will be conducted were established by government edicts 289 and 1470,[40] but questions remain about the planning and implementation of specific projects. More detailed information is needed on questions such as the following:

1. On what basis are projects prioritized, and who makes these decisions?
2. Should projects receive local or federal supervision?
3. What are the projected timetables and 'milestones' for each project?
4. Which agencies are to become involved in each project?

Clear and precise project planning is critical to any development programme. While the federal government is responsible for ensuring that funds are provided for these projects, the local communities must also set priorities and prepare for their implementation.

Relations with Western partners

Western organizations and governments are willing to offer assistance but will proceed with a plan only if it is carefully designed. In many cases local communities may lack the competence to prepare the project proposals. International organizations can provide this service and help to facilitate the process of obtaining assistance because of their expertise. In some cases a multilateral organization or corporate sponsor will only work with a partner in the former Soviet Union if solid ties have been established with a Western intermediary organization which can oversee the disbursement of funds and assist with programme management. A relationship with a Western partner is mutually beneficial. A potential foreign donor can benefit from having a local partner (e.g., an office of the mayor, an NGO or a special government agency) who can serve as a bridge between the donor and the local community and whose ideas and input are considered when plans are made for future development activities.

[40] Note 2.

Transparency, flexibility and cooperation

Owing to the fact that various Russian and non-Russian groups will be involved in planning assistance programmes, all parties must recognize the need for active participation by local and national authorities in determining which programmes to pursue and the manner in which this should be done. This will be a precondition for foreign assistance to Russia. Similarly, the Russian authorities must acknowledge that the donors have significant expertise which could be of use to Russian institutions. In addition, there must be a continuous and open exchange of information on political, social and financial matters. Currently, such information is scarce and difficult to acquire for Western researchers and technical experts. There may be hesitation on the part of donors to assist with development measures in local communities if public finance records, in particular, are not open to scrutiny.

Coordination of donor programmes

Currently, bilateral assistance programmes are not well coordinated. If there were increased involvement by companies, multilateral organizations and NGOs in the programme to assist Russia with CW destruction the exchange of information could help to improve the way such aid is utilized. In addition, increased transparency would facilitate the exchange of information, division of labour and distribution of funds. All such discussions ought to include input from the local and national authorities, which should also be encouraged to strengthen their coordination efforts.

Some donors may hesitate to become involved because of the current lack of a recognized and credible institutional counterpart with which to plan and negotiate. This problem could be addressed if the Russian Government were to set up a project steering committee composed of Russians and non-Russians. Its members might include citizens of local communities, one or two local governmental representatives, one representative each from a Russian NGO, the national government and an international NGO, and one additional international consultant. Such a combination would allow for effective decision making, information exchange and transparency and could address local, national and international concerns about community development in conjunction with the Russian CW dismantlement and destruction programme. The responsibilities of the project steering committee might include monitoring that assistance efforts are coordinated and soliciting possible continued and expanded foreign assistance for communities where chemical weapons are currently stored. The 'networking' and project coordination experience of such a committee could be applied to other areas of regional development in Russia.

Involvement of local citizens

This chapter focuses largely on establishing and defining the need for developmental assistance to areas where chemical weapons are to be destroyed. When financial and other assistance is solicited from foreign sources there should be a high probability that the projects which result will successfully meet the needs of the citizens of the local communities. Not only should their views be taken into account during project planning, but international donors should also attempt to use local labour, skills and expertise in the development programmes.

VIII. Conclusions

Efforts to support the development and implementation of a workable CW destruction programme in Russia had reached a critical point when, on 31 October 1996, Hungary became the 65th state to deposit its instrument of ratification of the CWC. This triggered the entry into force of the convention six months later on 29 April 1997.

The main argument which delayed Russian ratification of the CWC until November 1997 was cost. There was agreement in Russia that the 40 000 tonne stockpile of Russian chemical weapons had to be destroyed regardless of whether or not it was done under the aegis of an international convention. Had Russia not become a party to the CWC, programmes of bilateral assistance might not have been cancelled, but the probability of their continuation increased with Russian ratification. Foreign assistance may have strengthened Russian resolve to destroy its CW stockpile. In the end, however, the government of the Russian Federation itself remains responsible for the destruction of its chemical weapons.

Five countries currently provide technical assistance to aid Russia in initiating its CW destruction programme. Current and potential donors may want to consider expanding the scope of their assistance to target developmental projects in the communities where destruction is scheduled to take place. Federal legislation has been passed in Russia which addresses the need to improve the standard of living and ensures that destruction will be carried out with due respect for the environment and the safety of people living near destruction facilities. However, if such measures are not taken at the Gorny and Kambarka facilities, the first two to begin destruction activities, the credibility of the federal government will be seriously damaged. The mistake of not taking the views of local citizens into account was made once and ought not to be repeated. The chemical weapon destruction programme must address the needs of seven different communities, and the national government must accept the challenge of working with each of them so that their individual needs are not ignored.

There are numerous possible sources of foreign assistance to support community development and establish a framework that is designed to help guarantee safety during CW destruction activities. Potential projects will benefit from proper planning, transparency and flexibility when dealing with potential donors. In addition, the donors should be experienced in this type of assistance, and efforts should be coordinated so that the maximum benefit to the local community is achieved. There should also be public involvement in planning and implementation. The cost of financing community projects is small compared to the total investment for CW destruction. Meeting the needs and concerns of the local citizens is a key component of the plan to destroy the CW stockpile in Russia.

Annexe A. CWC definitions and terms

JOHN HART

The following are some of the key definitions and terms in the Chemical Weapons Convention as defined in the text of the convention.[1] Their location in the CWC is indicated in parentheses.

Abandoned Chemical Weapons (Article II, para. 6)

'Abandoned Chemical Weapons' means:
   Chemical weapons, including old chemical weapons, abandoned by a State after 1 January 1925 on the territory of another State without the consent of the latter.

Approved Equipment (Part I of the Verification Annex, para. 1)

'Approved Equipment' means the devices and instruments necessary for the performance of the inspection team's duties that have been certified by the Technical Secretariat in accordance with regulations prepared by the Technical Secretariat pursuant to Part II, paragraph 27 of this Annex. Such equipment may also refer to the administrative supplies or recording materials that would be used by the inspection team.

Building (Part I of the Verification Annex, para. 2)

'Building' as referred to in the definition of chemical weapons production facility in Article II comprises specialized buildings and standard buildings.
   (a) 'Specialized Building' means:
   (i) Any building, including underground structures, containing specialized equipment in a production or filling configuration;
   (ii) Any building, including underground structures, which has distinctive features which distinguish it from buildings normally used for chemical production or filling activities not prohibited under this Convention.
   (b) 'Standard Building' means any building, including underground structures, constructed to prevailing industry standards for facilities not producing any chemical specified in Article II, paragraph 8 (a) (i), or corrosive chemicals.

Challenge Inspection (Part I of the Verification Annex, para. 3)

'Challenge Inspection' means the inspection of any facility or location in the territory or in any other place under the jurisdiction or control of a State Party requested by another State Party pursuant to Article IX, paragraphs 8 to 25.[2]

Chemical Weapons (Article II, para. 1)

'Chemical Weapons' means the following, together or separately:
   a) Toxic chemicals and their precursors, except where intended for purposes not prohibited under this Convention, as long as the types and quantities are consistent with such purposes;

---

[1] The Convention on the Prohibition of the Development, Production, Stockpiling and Use of Chemical Weapons and on their Destruction (corrected version), 8 Aug. 1994, is reproduced on the SIPRI Chemical and Biological Warfare Project Internet site at URL <http://www.sipri.se/cbw/docs/cw-cwc-texts.html>.
   [2] These paragraphs describe the procedures for challenge inspections.

(b) Munitions and devices, specifically designed to cause death or other harm through the toxic properties of those toxic chemicals specified in subparagraph (a), which would be released as a result of the employment of such munitions and devices;

(c) Any equipment specifically designed for use directly in connection with the employment of munitions and devices specified in subparagraph (b).

Chemical Weapons Production Facility (Article II, para. 8)

'Chemical Weapons Production Facility':

(a) Means any equipment, as well as any building housing such equipment, that was designed, constructed or used at any time since 1 January 1946:

(i) As part of the stage in the production of chemicals ('final technological stage') where the material flows would contain, when the equipment is in operation:

(1) Any chemical listed in Schedule 1 in the Annex on Chemicals; or

(2) Any other chemical that has no use, above 1 tonne per year on the territory of a State Party or in any other place under the jurisdiction or control of a State Party, for purposes not prohibited under this Convention, but can be used for chemical weapons purposes; or

(ii) For filling chemical weapons, including, *inter alia*, the filling of chemicals listed in Schedule 1 into munitions, devices or bulk storage containers; the filling of chemicals into containers that form part of assembled binary munitions and devices or into chemical submunitions that form part of assembled unitary munitions and devices, and the loading of the containers and chemical submunitions into the respective munitions and devices;

(b) Does not mean:

(i) Any facility having a production capacity for synthesis of chemicals specified in subparagraph (a) (i) that is less than 1 tonne;

(ii) Any facility in which a chemical specified in subparagraph (a) (i) is or was produced as an unavoidable by-product of activities for purposes not prohibited under this Convention, provided that the chemical does not exceed 3 per cent of the total product and that the facility is subject to declaration and inspection under the Annex on Implementation and Verification (hereinafter referred to as 'Verification Annex'); or

(iii) The single small-scale facility for production of chemicals listed in Schedule 1 for purposes not prohibited under this Convention as referred to in Part VI of the Verification Annex.

Consumption (Article II, para. 12)

'Consumption' of a chemical means its conversion into another chemical via a chemical reaction.

Conversion (Part V of the Verification Annex, para. 19)[3]

Chemical weapons production facilities converted into chemical weapons destruction facilities before entry into force of this Convention shall be declared under the category of chemical weapons production facilities.

They shall be subject to an initial visit by inspectors, who shall confirm the correctness of the information about these facilities. Verification that the conversion of these facilities was *performed in such a manner as to render them inoperable as chemical weapons production facilities* shall also be required, and shall fall within the frame-

---

[3] The convention does not provide a definition of the term 'conversion'. The italicized section (added by the present author) of para. 19 of Part V of the Verification Annex appears to provide the clearest indication of what is meant.

work of measures provided for the facilities that are to be rendered inoperable not later than 90 days after entry into force of this Convention.[4]

Discrete Organic Chemical (Part I of the Verification Annex, para. 4)

'Discrete Organic Chemical' means any chemical belonging to the class of chemical compounds consisting of all compounds of carbon except for its oxides, sulfides and metal carbonates, identifiable by chemical name, by structural formula, if known, and by Chemical Abstract Service registry number, if assigned.

Equipment (Part I of the Verification Annex, para. 5)

'Equipment' as referred to in the definition of chemical weapons production facility in Article II comprises specialized equipment and standard equipment.

(a) 'Specialized Equipment' means:

(i) The main production train, including any reactor or equipment for product synthesis, separation or purification, any equipment used directly for heat transfer in the final technological stage, such as in reactors or in product separation, as well as any other equipment which has been in contact with any chemical specified in Article II, paragraph 8 (a) (i),[5] or would be in contact with such a chemical if the facility were operated;

(ii) Any chemical weapon filling machines;

(iii) Any other equipment specially designed, built or installed for the operation of the facility as a chemical weapons production facility, as distinct from a facility constructed according to prevailing commercial industry standards for facilities not producing any chemical specified in Article II, paragraph 8 (a) (i),[6] or corrosive chemicals, such as: equipment made of high-nickel alloys or other special corrosion-resistant material; special equipment for waste control, waste treatment, air filtering, or solvent recovery; special containment enclosures and safety shields; non-standard laboratory equipment used to analyse toxic chemicals for chemical weapons purposes; custom-designed process control panels; or dedicated spares for specialized equipment.

(b) 'Standard Equipment' means:

(i) Production equipment which is generally used in the chemical industry and is not included in the types of specialized equipment;

(ii) Other equipment commonly used in the chemical industry, such as: fire-fighting equipment; guard and security/safety surveillance equipment; medical facilities, laboratory facilities; or communications equipment.

Facility (Part I of the Verification Annex, para. 6)

'Facility' in the context of Article VI[7] means any of the industrial sites as defined below ('plant site', 'plant' and 'unit').

(a) 'Plant Site' (Works, Factory) means the local integration of one or more plants, with any intermediate administrative levels, which are under one operational control, and includes common infrastructure, such as:

(i) Administration and other offices;

(ii) Repair and maintenance shops;

(iii) Medical centre;

(iv) Utilities;

(v) Central analytical laboratory;

---

[4] Emphasis added.

[5] The paragraph includes part of the definition of a chemical weapons production facility.

[6] Note 5.

[7] That article describes activities not prohibited under the provisions of the convention.

(vi) Research and development laboratories;

(vii) Central effluent and waste treatment area; and

(viii) Warehouse storage.

(b) 'Plant' (Production facility, Workshop) means a relatively self-contained area, structure or building containing one or more units with auxiliary and associated infrastructure, such as;

(i) Small administrative section;

(ii) Storage/handling areas for feedstock and products;

(iii) Effluent/waste handling/treatment area;

(iv) Control/analytical laboratory;

(v) First aid service/related medical section; and

(vi) Records associated with the movement into, around and from the site, of declared chemicals and their feedstock or product chemicals formed from them, as appropriate.

(c) 'Unit' (Production unit, Process unit) means the combination of those items of equipment, including vessels and vessel set up, necessary for the production, processing or consumption of a chemical.

Facility Agreement (Part I of the Verification Annex, para. 7)

'Facility Agreement' means an agreement or arrangement between a State Party and the Organization relating to a specific facility subject to on-site verification pursuant to Articles IV, V and VI.[8]

Host State (Part I of the Verification Annex, para. 8)

'Host State' means the State on whose territory lie facilities or areas of another State, Party to this Convention, which are subject to inspection under this Convention.

In-Country Escort (Part I of the Verification Annex, para. 9)

'In-Country Escort' means individuals specified by the inspected State Party and, if appropriate, by the Host State, if they so wish, to accompany and assist the inspection team during the in-country period.

In-Country Period (Part I of the Verification Annex, para. 10)

'In-Country Period' means the period from the arrival of the inspection team at a point of entry until its departure from the State at a point of entry.

Initial Inspection (Part I of the Verification Annex, para. 11)

'Initial Inspection' means the first on-site inspection of facilities to verify declarations submitted pursuant to Articles III, IV, V and VI and this Annex.[9]

Inspected State Party (Part I of the Verification Annex, para. 12)

'Inspected State Party' means the State Party on whose territory or in any other place under its jurisdiction or control an inspection pursuant to this Convention takes place, or the State Party whose facility or area on the territory of a Host State is subject to such an inspection; it does not, however, include the State Party specified in Part II, paragraph 21 of this Annex.[10]

---

[8] Article IV addresses chemical weapons; Article V deals with chemical weapons production facilities; and Article VI covers activities not prohibited under the convention.

[9] Article III covers declarations. Note 8 lists the areas addressed by Articles IV, V and VI.

[10] Part II of the Verification Annex, para. 21 states: 'In cases where the facilities or areas sought to be inspected are located on the territory of a State Party, but in a place under the jurisdiction or control of a

Inspection Assistant (Part I of the Verification Annex, para. 13)

'Inspection Assistant' means an individual designated by the Technical Secretariat as set forth in Part II, Section A, of this Annex[11] to assist inspectors in an inspection or visit, such as medical, security and administrative personnel and interpreters.

Inspection Mandate (Part I of the Verification Annex, para. 14)

'Inspection Mandate' means the instructions issued by the Director-General to the inspection team for the conduct of a particular inspection.

Inspection Manual (Part I of the Verification Annex, para. 15)

'Inspection Manual' means the compilation of additional procedures for the conduct of inspections developed by the Technical Secretariat.

Inspection Site (Part I of the Verification Annex, para. 16)

'Inspection Site' means any facility or area at which an inspection is carried out and which is specifically defined in the respective facility agreement or inspection request or mandate or inspection request as expanded by the alternative or final perimeter.

Inspection Team (Part I of the Verification Annex, para. 17)

'Inspection Team' means the group of inspectors and inspection assistants assigned by the Director-General to conduct a particular inspection.

Inspector (Part I of the Verification Annex, para. 18)

'Inspector' means an individual designated by the Technical Secretariat according to the procedures as set forth in Part II, Section A, of this Annex,[12] to carry out an inspection or visit in accordance with this Convention.

Key Component (Article II, para. 4)

'Key Component of Binary or Multicomponent Chemical Systems' (hereinafter referred to as 'key component') means:

The precursor which plays the most important role in determining the toxic properties of the final product and reacts rapidly with other chemicals in the binary or multicomponent system.

Model Agreement (Part I of the Verification Annex, para. 19)

'Model Agreement' means a document specifying the general form and content for an agreement concluded between a State Party and the Organization for fulfilling the verification provisions specified in this Annex.[13]

State not Party to this Convention, the State Party shall take all necessary measures as would be required of an inspected State Party and a Host State Party to ensure that inspections of such facilities or areas can be carried out in accordance with the provisions of this Annex. If the State Party is unable to ensure access to those facilities or areas, it shall demonstrate that it took all necessary measures to ensure access. This paragraph shall not apply where the facilities or areas sought to be inspected are those of the State Party'.

[11] The reference is to the Verification Annex.

[12] Part II, describes the general rules of verification and the designation of inspectors and inspection assistants.

[13] The reference is to the Verification Annex.

Observer (Part I of the Verification Annex, para. 20)

'Observer' means a representative of a requesting State Party or a third State Party to observe a challenge inspection.

Old Chemical Weapons (Article II, para. 5)

'Old Chemical Weapons means:

(a) Chemical weapons which were produced before 1925; or

(b) Chemical weapons produced in the period between 1925 and 1946 that have deteriorated to such an extent that they can no longer be used as chemical weapons.

Organization (Article II, para. 11)

'Organization' means the Organization for the Prohibition of Chemical Weapons established pursuant to Article VIII of this Convention.

Perimeter (Part I of the Verification Annex, para. 21)

'Perimeter' in case of challenge inspection means the external boundary of the inspection site, defined by either geographic coordinates or description on a map.

(a) 'Requested Perimeter' means the inspection site perimeter as specified in conformity with Part X, paragraph 8, of this Annex;[14]

(b) 'Alternative Perimeter' means the inspection site perimeter as specified, alternatively to the requested perimeter, by the inspected State Party; it shall conform to the requirements specified in Part X, paragraph 17 of this Annex;[15]

(c) 'Final Perimeter' means the final inspection site perimeter as agreed in negotiations between the inspection team and the inspected State Party, in accordance with Part X, paragraphs 16 to 21, of this Annex;[16]

(d) 'Declared Perimeter' means the external boundary of the facility declared pursuant to Articles III, IV, V and VI.[17]

Period of Inspection (Part I of the Verification Annex, para. 22)

'Period of Inspection', for the purposes of Article IX,[18] means the period of time from provision of access to the inspection team to the inspection site until its departure from the inspection site, exclusive of time spent on briefings before and after the verification activities.

[14] It states: 'The requested perimeter shall: (a) Run at least a 10 metre distance outside any buildings or structures; (b) Not cut through existing security enclosures; and (c) Run at least a 10 metre distance outside any existing security enclosures that the requesting State Party intends to include within the requested perimeter'.

[15] It states: 'The alternative perimeter should be designated as specifically as possible in accordance with paragraph 8 [of Part X of the Verification Annex]. It shall include the whole of the requested perimeter and should, as a rule, bear a close relationship to the latter, taking into account natural terrain features and man-made boundaries. It should normally run close to the surrounding security barrier if such a barrier exists. The inspected State Party should seek to establish such a relationship between the perimeters by a combination of at least two of the following means: (a) An alternative perimeter that does not extend to an area significantly greater than that of the requested perimeter; (b) An alternative perimeter that is a short, uniform distance from the requested perimeter; (c) At least part of the requested perimeter is visible from the alternative perimeter'.

[16] The annexe includes guidelines for alternative determination of final perimeter.

[17] Notes 8 and 9.

[18] These paragraphs describe consultations, cooperation and fact-finding.

Period of Inspection (Part I of the Verification Annex, para. 23)

'Period of Inspection', for the purposes of Articles IV, V and VI,[19] means the period of time from arrival of the inspection team at the inspection site until its departure from the inspection site, exclusive of time spent on briefings before and after the verification activities.

Plant (Part I of the Verification Annex, para. 6 (b))

'Plant' (Production facility, Workshop) means a relatively self-contained area, structure or building containing one or more units with auxiliary and associated infrastructure, such as;
    (i) Small administrative section;
    (ii) Storage/handling areas for feedstock and products;
    (iii) Effluent/waste handling/treatment area;
    (iv) Control/analytical laboratory;
    (v) First aid service/related medical section; and
    (vi) Records associated with the movement into, around and from the site, of declared chemicals and their feedstock or product chemicals formed from them, as appropriate.

Plant Site (Part I of the Verification Annex, para. 6 (a))

'Plant Site' (Works, Factory) means the local integration of one or more plants, with any intermediate administrative levels, which are under one operational control, and includes common infrastructure, such as:
    (i) Administration and other offices;
    (ii) Repair and maintenance shops;
    (iii) Medical centre;
    (iv) Utilities;
    (v) Central analytical laboratory;
    (vi) Research and development laboratories;
    (vii) Central effluent and waste treatment area; and
    (viii) Warehouse storage.

Point of Entry/Point of Exit (Part I of the Verification Annex, para. 24)

'Point of Entry'/'Point of Exit' means a location designated for the in-country arrival of inspection teams for inspections pursuant to this Convention or for their departure after completion of their mission.

Precursor (Article II, para. 3)

'Precursor' means:
  Any chemical reactant which takes part at any stage in the production by whatever method of a toxic chemical. This includes any key component of a binary or multi-component chemical system.

(For the purpose of implementing this Convention, precursors which have been identified for the application of verification measures are listed in Schedules contained in the Annex on Chemicals.)

Processing (Article II, para. 12)

'Processing' of a chemical means a physical process, such as formulation, extraction and purification, in which a chemical is not converted into another chemical.

---

[19] Note 8.

Production (Article II, para. 12)

'Production' of a chemical means its formation through chemical reaction.

Production Capacity (Article II, para. 10)

'Production Capacity' means:

The annual quantitative potential for manufacturing a specific chemical based on the technological process actually used or, if the process is not yet operational, planned to be used at the relevant facility. It shall be deemed to be equal to the nameplate capacity or, if the nameplate capacity is not available, to the design capacity. The nameplate capacity is the product output under conditions optimized for maximum quantity for the production facility, as demonstrated by one or more test-runs. The design capacity is the corresponding theoretically calculated product output.

Purposes Not Prohibited Under this Convention (Article II, para. 9)

'Purposes Not Prohibited Under this Convention' means:

(a) Industrial, agricultural, research, medical, pharmaceutical or other peaceful purposes;

(b) Protective purposes, namely those purposes directly related to protection against toxic chemicals and to protection against chemical weapons;

(c) Military purposes not connected with the use of chemical weapons and not dependent on the use of the toxic properties of chemicals as a method of warfare;

(d) Law enforcement including domestic riot control purposes.

Requesting State Party (Part I of the Verification Annex, para. 25)

'Requesting State Party' means a State Party which has requested a challenge inspection pursuant to Article IX.[20]

Riot Control Agent (Article II, para. 7)

'Riot Control Agent' means:

Any chemical not listed in a Schedule, which can produce rapidly in humans sensory irritation or disabling physical effects which disappear within a short time following termination of exposure.

Specialized Building (Part I of the Verification Annex, para. 2 (a))

'Specialized Building' means:

(i) Any building, including underground structures, containing specialized equipment in a production or filling configuration;

(ii) Any building, including underground structures, which has distinctive features which distinguish it from buildings normally used for chemical production or filling activities not prohibited under this Convention.

Standard Building (Part I of the Verification Annex, para. 2 (b))

'Standard Building' means any building, including underground structures, constructed to prevailing industry standards for facilities not producing any chemical specified in Article II, paragraph 8 (a) (i),[21] or corrosive chemicals.

[20] Note 18.
[21] See the definition of chemical weapons production facility.

Specialized Equipment (Part I of the Verification Annex, para. 5 (a))

'Specialized Equipment' means:

(i) The main production train, including any reactor or equipment for product synthesis, separation or purification, any equipment used directly for heat transfer in the final technological stage, such as in reactors or in product separation, as well as any other equipment which has been in contact with any chemical specified in Article II, paragraph 8 (a) (i),[22] or would be in contact with such a chemical if the facility were operated;

(ii) Any chemical weapon filling machines;

(iii) Any other equipment specially designed, built or installed for the operation of the facility as a chemical weapons production facility, as distinct from a facility constructed according to prevailing commercial industry standards for facilities not producing any chemical specified in Article II, paragraph 8 (a) (i),[23] or corrosive chemicals, such as: equipment made of high-nickel alloys or other special corrosion-resistant material; special equipment for waste control, waste treatment, air filtering, or solvent recovery; special containment enclosures and safety shields; non-standard laboratory equipment used to analyse toxic chemicals for chemical weapons purposes; custom-designed process control panels; or dedicated spares for specialized equipment.

Standard Equipment (Part I of the Verification Annex, para. 5 (b))

'Standard Equipment' means:

(i) Production equipment which is generally used in the chemical industry and is not included in the types of specialized equipment;

(ii) Other equipment commonly used in the chemical industry, such as: fire-fighting equipment; guard and security/safety surveillance equipment; medical facilities, laboratory facilities; or communications equipment.

Tonne (Part I of the Verification Annex, para. 26)

'Tonne' means metric ton, i.e. 1,000 kg.

Toxic Chemical (Article II, para. 2)

'Toxic Chemical' means:

Any chemical which through its chemical action on life processes can cause death, temporary incapacitation or permanent harm to humans or animals. This includes all such chemicals, regardless of their origin or of their method of production, and regardless of whether they are produced in facilities, in munitions or elsewhere.

(For the purpose of implementing this Convention, toxic chemicals which have been identified for the application of verification measures are listed in Schedules contained in the Annex on Chemicals.)

Unit (Part I of the Verification Annex, para. 6 (c)

'Unit' (Production unit, Process unit) means the combination of those items of equipment, including vessels and vessel set up, necessary for the production, processing or consumption of a chemical.

---

[22] Note 5.
[23] Note 5.

SIPRI publications on CBW

- The Problem of Chemical and Biological Warfare, 6 volumes

  1. The Rise of CB Weapons. 1971. ISBN 91–85114–10–3.
  2. CB Weapons Today. 1973. 91–85114–16–2.
  3. CBW and the Law of War. 1974. 91–85114–17–0.
  4. CB Disarmament Negotiations, 1920–1970. 1971. 91–85114–11–1.
  5. The Prevention of CBW. 1971. 91–85114–13–8.
  6. Technical Aspects of Early Warning and Verification. 1975. 91–85114–18–9.

- Chapters in the SIPRI Yearbooks

  SIPRI Yearbook of World Armaments and Disarmament, 1968/69. 1969. 91–85114–03–0.
  pp. 112–34. Development in chemical and biological warfare.

  SIPRI Yearbook of World Armaments and Disarmament, 1969/70. 1970. 91–85114–07–3.
  pp. 185–206. The CBW debate and other disarmament measures.

  World Armaments and Disarmament: SIPRI Yearbook 1972. 1972. 91–85114–12–X.
  pp. 501–22. Chemical and biological disarmament.

  World Armaments and Disarmament: SIPRI Yearbook 1973. 1973. 91–85114–19–7.
  pp. 383–91. Chemical disarmament.

  World Armaments and Disarmament: SIPRI Yearbook 1974. 1974. 0–262–19129–6.
  pp. 370–84. Chemical disarmament.

  World Armaments and Disarmament: SIPRI Yearbook 1975. 1975. 0–262–19140–7.
  pp. 426–32. Chemical disarmament.

  World Armaments and Disarmament: SIPRI Yearbook 1977. 1977. 91–22–00116–6.
  pp. 86–102. Dioxin: a potential chemical-warfare agent; and
  pp. 364–67. Prohibition of biological and chemical weapons.

  World Armaments and Disarmament: SIPRI Yearbook 1978. 1978. 0–85066–134–X.
  pp. 360–76. The destruction of chemical warfare agents.

  World Armaments and Disarmament: SIPRI Yearbook 1979. 1979. 0–85066–181–1.
  pp. 470–89. Stockpiles of chemical weapons and their destruction.

  World Armaments and Disarmament: SIPRI Yearbook 1980. 1980. 0–85066–201–X.
  pp. 365–79. Chemical disarmament.

  World Armaments and Disarmament: SIPRI Yearbook 1982. 1982. 0–85066–230–3.
  pp. 317–61. The changing status of chemical and biological warfare: recent technical,
  military and political developments; and
  pp. 456–57. Chemical weapons.

  World Armaments and Disarmament: SIPRI Yearbook 1983. 1983. 0–85066–247–8.
  pp. 391–426. Chemical and biological warfare: developments in 1982; and
  pp. 563–67. Chemical disarmament.

  World Armaments and Disarmament: SIPRI Yearbook 1984. 1984. 0–85066–263–X.
  pp. 319–49. Chemical and biological warfare: developments in 1983; and
  pp. 421–54. Implications of genetic engineering for chemical and biological warfare.

  World Armaments and Disarmament: SIPRI Yearbook 1985. 1985. 0–85066–297–4.
  pp. 159–205. Chemical and biological warfare: developments in 1984; and
  pp. 206–19. An analysis of the reports of Iraqi chemical warfare against Iran, 1980–84.

  World Armaments and Disarmament: SIPRI Yearbook 1986. 1986. 0–19–829100–0.
  pp. 159–79. Chemical and biological warfare: developments in 1985.

  SIPRI Yearbook 1987: World Armaments and Disarmament. 1987. 0–19–829114–0.
  pp. 97–115. Chemical and biological warfare: developments in 1986.

  SIPRI Yearbook 1988: World Armaments and Disarmament. 1988. 0–19–829126–4.
  pp. 101–25. Chemical and biological warfare: developments in 1987.

SIPRI Yearbook 1989: World Armaments and Disarmament. 1989. 0–19–827751–2.
  pp. 99–130. Chemical and biological warfare: developments in 1988.
SIPRI Yearbook 1990: World Armaments and Disarmament. 1990. 0–19–827862–4.
  pp. 107–40. Chemical and biological warfare: developments in 1989; and
  pp. 521–44. Multilateral and bilateral talks on chemical and biological weapons.
SIPRI Yearbook 1991: World Armaments and Disarmament. 1991. 0–19–829145–0.
  pp. 85–112. Chemical and biological warfare: developments in 1990; and
  pp. 513–39. Multilateral and bilateral talks on chemical and biological weapons.
SIPRI Yearbook 1992: World Armaments and Disarmament. 1992. 0–19–829159–0.
  pp. 147–86. Chemical and biological warfare and arms control developments in 1991; and
  pp. 509–30. The United Nations Special Commission on Iraq.
SIPRI Yearbook 1993: World Armaments and Disarmament. 1993. 0–19–829166–3.
  pp. 259–92. Chemical and biological weapons: developments and proliferation;
  pp. 293–305. Benefits and threats of developments in biotechnology and genetic
  engineering;
  pp. 691–703. The United Nations Special Commission on Iraq: activities in 1992;
  pp. 705–34. The Chemical Weapons Convention: the success of chemical disarmament
  negotiations; and
  pp. 735–56. The Convention on the Prohibition of the Development, Production,
  Stockpiling and Use of Chemical Weapons and on their Destruction.
SIPRI Yearbook 1994. 1994. 0–19–829182–5.
  pp. 315–42. Chemical weapon developments;
  pp. 685–711. The Chemical Weapons Convention: institutionalization and preparation for
  entry into force;
  pp. 713–38. Biological weapon and arms control developments; and
  pp. 739–58. UNSCOM: activities in 1993.
SIPRI Yearbook 1995: Armaments, Disarmament and International Security. 1995.
0–19–829193–0.
  pp. 337–57. Chemical and biological weapons: developments and destruction;
  pp. 597–633. Multilateral weapon-related export control measures; and
  pp. 725–60. Chemical and biological arms control.
SIPRI Yearbook 1996: Armaments, Disarmament and International Security. 1996.
0–19–829202–3.
  pp. 537–59. Multilateral military-related export control measures; and
  pp. 661–708. Chemical and biological weapon developments and arms control.
SIPRI Yearbook 1997: Armaments, Disarmament and International Security. 1997.
0–19–829312–7.
  pp. 345–63. Multilateral military-related export control measures; and
  pp. 437–68. Chemical and biological weapon developments and arms control.
SIPRI Yearbook 1998: Armaments, Disarmament and International Security. 1998.
0–19–829454–9.
  pp. 373–402. Multilateral security-related export controls;
  pp. 457–489. Chemical and biological weapon developments and arms control; and
  pp. 490–500. Entry into force of the Chemical Weapons Convention.

• Other SIPRI publications

Chemical Disarmament: Some Problems of Verification. 1973. 91–85114–20–0.
The Effects of Developments in the Biological and Chemical Sciences on
  CW Disarmament Negotiations. SIPRI research report 13, SIPRI, 1974.
Delayed Toxic Effects of Chemical Warfare Agents. 1975. 91–85114–29–4.
Chemical Disarmament: New Weapons for Old. 1975. 91–85114–27–8.
Medical Protection against Chemical-Warfare Agents. 1976. 91–22000–44–5.
Ecological Consequences of the Second Indochina War. 1976. 91–22000–62–3, pp. 24–45,
  53–55.
Weapons of Mass Destruction and the Environment. 1977. 0–85066–132–3, pp. 31–48.

The Fight against Infectious Diseases: A Role for Applied Microbiology in Military
 Redeployment. SIPRI, 1979, mimeo. 91–85114–26–X.
Chemical Weapons: Destruction and Conversion. 1980. 0–85066–199–4.
Herbicides in War. 1984. 0–85066–265–6.
Biological and Toxin Weapons Today. 1986. 0–19–829108–6.

SIPRI publications may be obtained through all main bookshops. In case of difficulty,
please contact the publishers or SIPRI.